I FOUGHT AT DUNKIRK

Also by Mike Rossiter

Ark Royal
Sink the *Belgrano*
Target Basra
Bomber Flight Berlin
We Fought at Arnhem

with Lieutenant Commander John Moffat
I Sank the *Bismarck*

I FOUGHT AT DUNKIRK

MIKE ROSSITER

BANTAM PRESS

LONDON • TORONTO • SYDNEY • AUCKLAND • JOHANNESBURG

TRANSWORLD PUBLISHERS
61–63 Uxbridge Road, London W5 5SA
A Random House Group Company
www.transworldbooks.co.uk

First published in Great Britain
in 2012 by Bantam Press
an imprint of Transworld Publishers

A CIP catalogue record for this book
is available from the British Library.

ISBNs 9780593065938 (cased)
9780593065945 (tpb)

Addresses for Random House Group Ltd companies outside the UK
can be found at: www.randomhouse.co.uk
The Random House Group Ltd Reg. No. 954009

The Random House Group Limited supports the Forest Stewardship Council (FSC®),
the leading international forest-certification organization. Our books carrying the FSC
label are printed on FSC®-certified paper. FSC is the only forest-certification scheme
endorsed by the leading environmental organizations, including Greenpeace.
Our paper procurement policy can be found at
www.randomhouse.co.uk/environment.

Typeset in 12/16pt Times New Roman by
Falcon Oast Graphic Art Ltd.
Printed and bound in Great Britain by
Clays Ltd, Bungay, Suffolk

2 4 6 8 10 9 7 5 3 1

MIX
Paper from
responsible sources
FSC® C016897

CONTENTS

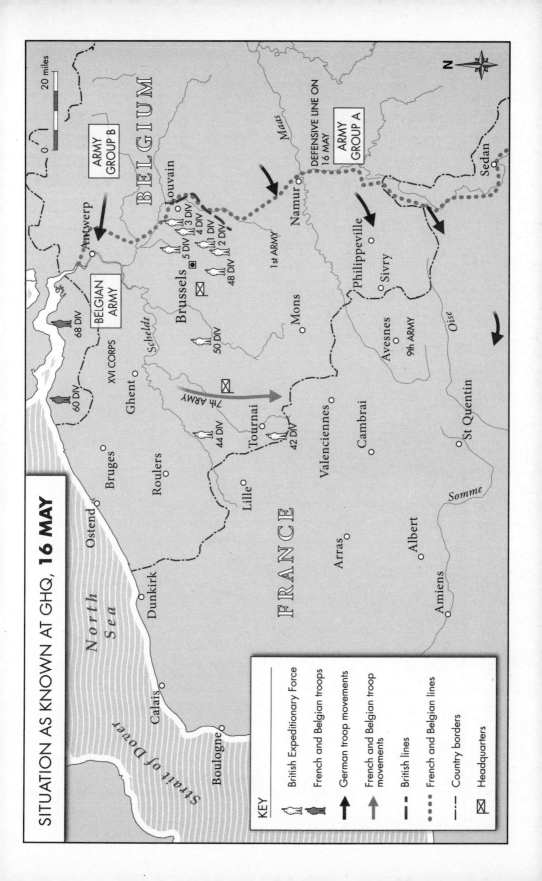

SITUATION AS KNOWN AT GHQ, **16 MAY**

KEY

	British Expeditionary Force
	French and Belgian troops
	German troop movements
	French and Belgian troop movements
	British lines
	French and Belgian lines
	Country borders
	Headquarters

North Sea

Strait of Dover

20 miles

N

BELGIUM

FRANCE

ARMY GROUP B

ARMY GROUP A

BELGIAN ARMY

Antwerp

Louvain

Namur

Sedan

DEFENSIVE LINE ON 16 MAY

Maas

68 DIV

60 DIV

XVI CORPS

Ghent

Bruges

Roulers

Ostend

Dunkirk

Calais

Boulogne

Scheldt

Brussels

3 DIV
4 DIV
2 DIV
5 DIV
48 DIV

1st ARMY

Mons

Philippeville

Sivry

Avesnes

9th ARMY

Oise

50 DIV

7th ARMY

44 DIV

42 DIV

Tournai

Lille

Valenciennes

Cambrai

Arras

Albert

Amiens

St Quentin

Somme

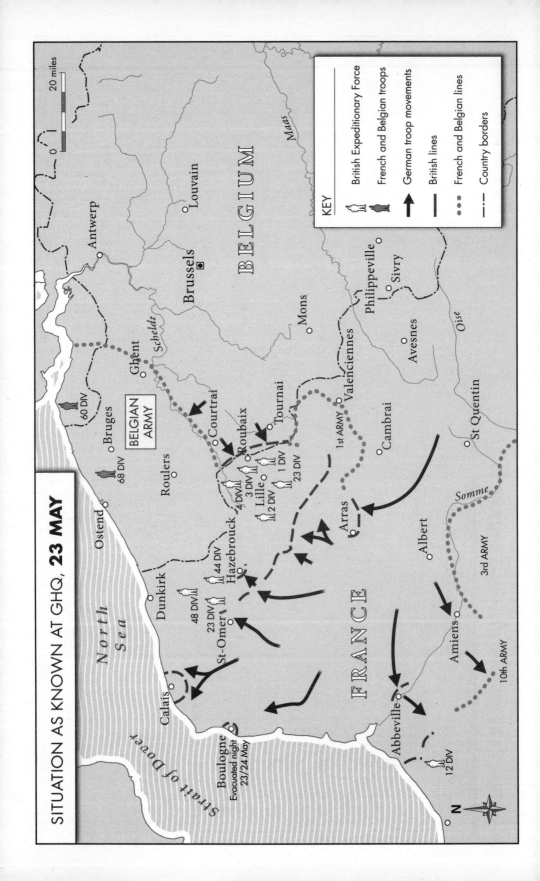

SITUATION AS KNOWN AT GHQ, **23 MAY**

KEY

	British Expeditionary Force
	French and Belgian troops
↑	German troop movements
—	British lines
····	French and Belgian lines
—·—·	Country borders

20 miles

North Sea

Strait of Dover

Calais

Boulogne
Evacuated night
23/24 May

Dunkirk

Ostend

St-Omer

48 DIV
23 DIV

44 DIV
Hazebrouck

60 DIV

Bruges

68 DIV

Roulers

Ghent

Scheldt

BELGIAN
ARMY

Courtrai

Roubaix
4 DIV
3 DIV
Lille
2 DIV
1 DIV
23 DIV

Tournai

Antwerp

Louvain

Brussels

BELGIUM

Maas

Mons

Valenciennes

1st ARMY

Cambrai

Philippeville

Sivry

Avesnes

Oise

St Quentin

Arras

FRANCE

Albert

Somme

3rd ARMY

Amiens

10th ARMY

Abbeville

12 DIV

N

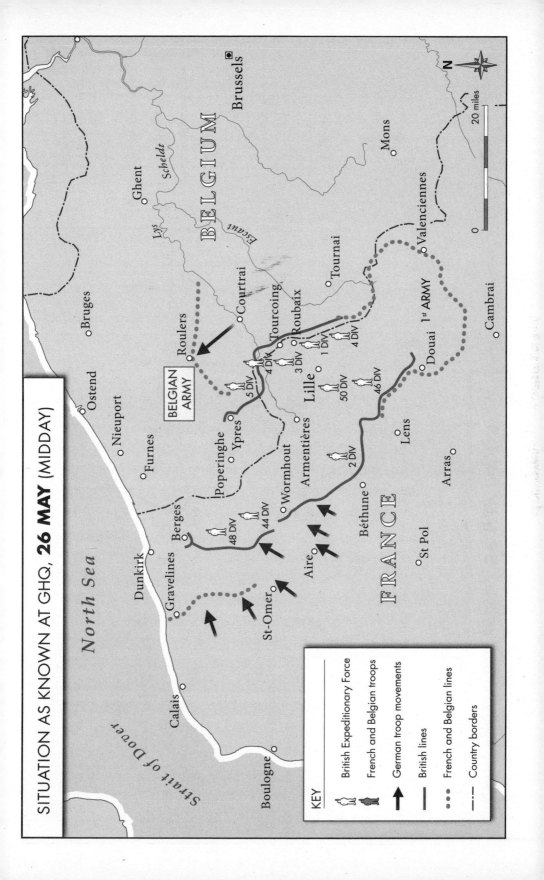

SITUATION AS KNOWN AT GHQ, **26 MAY** (MIDDAY)

KEY

British Expeditionary Force
French and Belgian troops
German troop movements
British lines
French and Belgian lines
Country borders

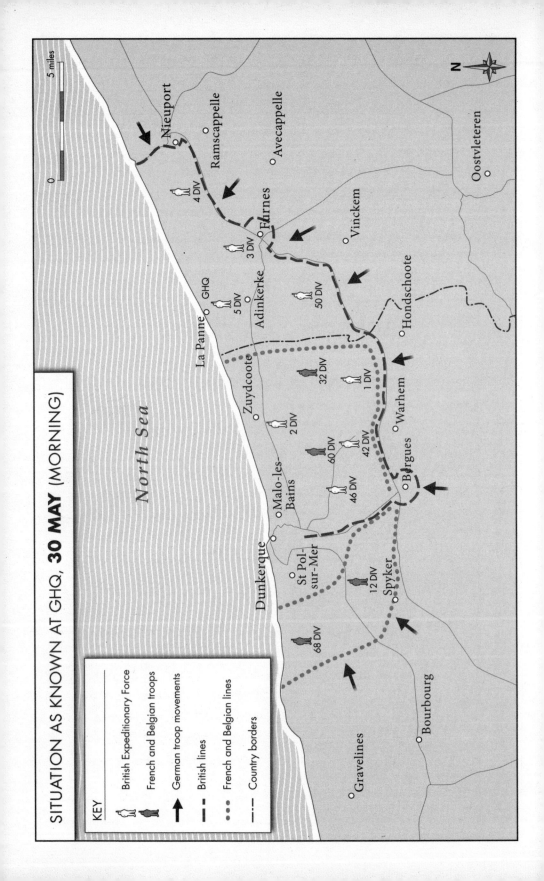

SITUATION AS KNOWN AT GHQ, **30 MAY** (MORNING)

KEY

British Expeditionary Force
French and Belgian troops
German troop movements
British lines
French and Belgian lines
Country borders

North Sea

5 miles

N

Gravelines

Bourbourg

Spyker

68 DIV

12 DIV

St Pol-sur-Mer

Dunkerque

Malo-les-Bains

Bergues

Warhem

Hondschoote

46 DIV

42 DIV

60 DIV

2 DIV

1 DIV

32 DIV

Zuydcoote

La Panne

GHQ

5 DIV

Adinkerke

50 DIV

3 DIV

4 DIV

Nieuport

Ramscappelle

Furnes

Vinckem

Avecappelle

Oostvleteren

ACKNOWLEDGEMENTS

First of all, I would like to thank Sydney Whiteside for the effort he put into helping me make the initial contacts with members of the Cornwall Dunkirk Veterans' Association, and to the members themselves who welcomed me into their homes and told me their stories. All of them, Larry Urens, Stanley Chappell, Les Clarke, Reg Beeston and Sydney himself put up with several visits and long telephone calls as I tried to reconcile their memories with an often sparse and partial historical record. I would also like to thank Adam Harcourt-Webster and the Hospital Sargeant Major of the Royal Hospital Chelsea, Bob Appleby, for their assistance in talking to Sid Lewis and Jack Haskett.

The advice of my editor at Transworld, Simon Thorogood, and copy editor, Brenda Updegraff, was intelligent and invaluable. The book has also benefited greatly from the efforts of Sheila Lee who researched the illustrations, and from the work of Philip Lord who designed the layout. I also need to thank the photographer Rod Shone for the portraits, and Tom Coulson at Encompass Graphics who created the maps.

Finally, I would like to acknowledge the help of my agent, Luigi Bonomi, and pay thanks to the patience of my wife, Anne, and two children Max and Alex.

INTRODUCTION

As a small child I remember one of my primary-school teachers telling our class about 'the miracle' of Dunkirk. She was an old-fashioned schoolmistress, very strict, and we children were both frightened and in awe of her. But that day, as she told us the story of Dunkirk, she was forced to stop her account by a wave of what was extremely strong emotion. I saw tears in her eyes. Whatever the personal meaning Dunkirk had for my teacher I naturally never discovered, but that moment has stayed with me and it has always coloured my view of those events. Only now, by talking to the men who were there, has it changed.

Very few of the men who were snatched to safety off the beaches are still alive. I made efforts to contact various Dunkirk veterans' associations, but the only one that responded was in Cornwall. A small group of men met regularly, and there was a convenor who was able to provide me with names and addresses. I subsequently met two other men via personal contacts. But no national organization seemed now to exist.

So I travelled down to Cornwall and started talking to the men whose stories are told in this book, and I discovered that for most of them the events on the beach or in the port of Dunkirk were only a part of what they remember. Their first impressions of France were extremely vivid. At the time these were boys of just nineteen or twenty, some of whom had never travelled very far from the village or town where they were born before finding themselves in an exotic foreign country, with strange food and even stranger mores. Most of them spent some time in France and it was, as one of them said to me, 'like a very long holiday' before the fighting started. Only one, Sid Lewis, met the German Army before they invaded Belgium and Holland, and that encounter scarred him for months afterwards. The other men were also deeply affected by what they did and saw when the fighting finally started.

What surprised me was that in the three weeks between the start of the German offensive and the height of the evacuation from Dunkirk these young soldiers were engaged in more than one intense battle and at times seemed to be permanently under fire. Naturally, sometimes they were hazy about dates and locations of the events that they remembered. It was a very long while ago, none of them could afford watches, and their officers never told them anything about where they were going or what their objective was. Anyway, as Larry Uren said, 'I've been bombed so many times, Mike, that it's hard to remember the specifics.'

I was sure that I would be able to clarify things by looking at the brigade or battalion war diaries and the Official History – *The War in France and Flanders 1939–1940: Official*

Campaign History, edited by Major L. F. Ellis. I was surprised to discover, however, that the war diaries for the units concerned were produced some time after the events, back in the United Kingdom. Because of this they are written from a very partial point of view, from the perspective of the author, who was usually from the headquarters company, with the result that, for example, a minor accident to a commanding officer is reported in detail, while the loss of the equivalent of a company is never mentioned. Communication was erratic and the movements of battalions and regiments so confused at times that even when the diaries are contemporaneous they do not mention the separate movements of companies or gun batteries. Out of all the unit diaries that I looked at, only one, the 2nd Regiment Royal Horse Artillery, records the names of men killed, wounded or missing.

The Official History takes a much broader overview of the campaign, concerned with the strategic decisions faced by General Lord Gort in his negotiations with the French generals, attempting to give some shape to an enormously complicated campaign in which the Allies were always on the back foot. Written shortly after the war, the Official History tries to deal with two of the most urgent political questions raised by the retreat to Dunkirk. The first was the allegation by French generals and the Vichy government that essentially France was betrayed, and that the withdrawal of British forces gave the French no option but to capitulate. The second issue was the claim by German generals that the British Army had escaped because of wrongheaded orders from Hitler. Major Ellis deals with both claims, demonstrating that the French were overwhelmingly responsible for their own collapse, and that the German Army was not the sleekly efficient war machine that its generals, and some modern historians, seek to portray. I can't believe that these questions have such pressing importance any more, but the Official History is still the template for the majority of books about Dunkirk.

It took several visits, and lengthy telephone calls, to build up eyewitness stories that were somehow compatible with battalion, brigade or divisional narratives. At times they will always be in conflict, but what I want to do is describe how ordinary soldiers saw the campaign in France and Belgium that led to the evacuation. There are, of course, as many stories as there were people in the British Expeditionary Force (BEF), but the seven veterans whose stories I tell in this book saw a fair number of the events of the campaign, even if from widely separated viewpoints. Everybody who was a member of the BEF shared one thing, however, and that was a rapid and brutal introduction to the horrors of total war. Whatever their own fears, and whatever the fate of their comrades, all the men that I spoke to talked about the horrible impact of the sight of dead civilians, the destruction of towns and villages and the huge columns of fleeing refugees, and that must have been an almost universal experience.

One of the men in this book, Jack Haskett, saw little in the way of action and his unit was never part of the fighting in Belgium and Flanders. He was a member of a battalion of the Queen's Regiment that was newly recruited and untrained, arriving late in France, destined for support work in the rear. The story of his sudden encounter with the German Army is testament to the great speed of the enemy advance and shows how quickly it cut thousands of men off from the haven of the Dunkirk beaches.

By the time the rest of the men in this book had managed to make their way to the beaches at La Panne or Bray Dunes, or to the port of Dunkirk itself, they had been through a very intense baptism of fire. This is what made Dunkirk so important. The nearly quarter of a million men of the BEF who were rescued and carried back to England were now far more experienced and battle-hardened than they had been just a month previously. That experience counted for a lot when they moved on to North Africa and elsewhere.

The war in Flanders was important for other reasons. It exposed just how inadequate some of the equipment with which the men had to fight was. The British Army was not as old fashioned as some like to make out. Unlike the German Army, it no longer relied on horses for much of its transport. The infantry battalions were equipped with lorries and tracked vehicles, the ubiquitous Bren-gun carrier. But its tanks were inadequate and its anti-tank weapons completely useless. Communication depended mainly on telephone land lines or on runners. There were very few radios, and those that did exist were not very effective, being unreliable and with poor range. The army was also to some extent affected by the class prejudices of its officers. Some of the men I interviewed described incidents where they were treated with contempt by their officers, and this of course was reciprocated. Everyone was kept in the dark about what they were doing and why. The army started to change after Dunkirk. Some problems with equipment were never solved, but there was greater communication between the ranks. Those who served in North Africa remarked on the briefings that Montgomery gave to the troops. And the road to becoming an officer, of necessity, was opened up. Larry Uren refused the offer of a commission because it meant he would have to leave his battalion, but Stanley Chappell left the army as a lieutenant.

One aspect of the evacuation from Dunkirk that struck me was the effect it had on the morale of the troops in the BEF. Everyone described to me a time during the retreat when they felt close to despair. Sometimes it was on the beach, at the sight of thousands of men, the wreckage of an army, lined up in endless queues. For others it was when they had to destroy their weapons or transport. Yet by the time they got to England this despair had lifted – and of course it did so partly because the threat of immediate death or captivity had gone, but two other things were also important. One was the greeting that the men received on the dockside from women volunteers who gave them tea and sandwiches and welcomed them home. Apart from Les Clarke, no one was made to feel that they had cut and run, or that they had been defeated. The second, and perhaps the most important element, was the fact that they had not been abandoned. An enormous national effort went into providing the ships to get them home. Stanley Chappell pointed out that the difference between the BEF in 1940 and the German Afrika Korp in 1943 was that the German soldiers were trapped. There was no German Navy to get them off the beaches of North Africa. They had to surrender. But the BEF was not alone, and every soldier lifted from the Dunkirk perimeter knew that.

So Dunkirk was important in many ways, although I never discovered why its memory had such a powerful emotional charge for my strict schoolmistress. She was unmarried. Perhaps a boyfriend had never returned. I hope that isn't the case. Many did return. These are the stories of seven of them.

Prologue

RESCUE

Sydney Whiteside fell in with the men of the 145 Field Ambulance Unit and the rest of the medical officers from the casualty clearing station. They were evacuating La Panne. The wounded men had already been taken away to the port of Dunkirk in a convoy of field ambulances.

They had gone, but the smell of dried blood, stale sweat, the sickly sweet odour of gas gangrene in some doomed soldier's wound seemed to cling to everything, even Sydney's dirty and crumpled uniform. Sydney felt that he hadn't slept for days. He was so tired that sometimes his mind appeared just to shut down, although he didn't physically stop what he was doing. He looked around. They were some of the last to leave. Those who were left of General Gort's headquarters staff in the big house by the sea were burning piles of documents. The Belgian Army had capitulated three days ago and the Germans would be arriving very soon; the first shells had already exploded in the town. Sydney and the group of medical staff – they numbered about sixty – started loosely marching along the sand, keeping to the margins of the beach where the going was reasonably firm. Sydney was amazed to see that the beach was almost empty. There were a few men in the beach parties, organizing the small boats that came in from the larger ships in the bay, and scattered groups of soldiers were waiting to be told where to form up. It was a strange sight, in marked contrast to the thousands that had thronged there the day before.

They made their way towards Dunkirk, the town and port covered in thick, oily smoke, great columns of it rising into the sky, so broad that they dwarfed the enemy dive-bombers circling around the mole that stretched into the sea. Sydney trudged along. They had walked along on the edge of the dunes for about two miles when the sound of aircraft engines behind them made the whole group scatter to their left where the dunes offered some shelter. Sydney lay pressed into the sand, his guts tensing for the siren scream of an attacking Stuka, but the roaring sound of the engines passed low over-head and faded away. The enemy planes were more intent on attacking another target further along the beach. He heard the rattle of gunfire and the thud of the exploding bombs, but Sydney and his group were left alone.

They resumed their march after the attacking aircraft had run out of bombs and ammunition and flown away, and in another twenty minutes they reached the small resort town of Bray Dunes. Most of the grand houses that once faced the sea were now lying in ruins. Rubble littered the front. Sydney walked on and came to a row of wrecked vehicles stretching out for almost half a mile across the flat beach into the sea. Jammed nose to tail, the now sea-stained and already rusting army lorries supported a walkway of rough planks, old doors and ladders that had been laid out on the roofs of the vehicles.

Sydney and the rest of his party climbed up and walked out along the planks. They were shaky in places, but everybody got out to the end and formed an orderly line. Waiting for them, gently rocking in the slight swell, was a Royal Navy cutter. The sailors did what they could to keep the boat steady and Sydney found it easy to step down and wedge himself in. It took just a few minutes before the boat was full, then the seamen pushed the cutter away and took them out to a destroyer that was waiting another mile or so out at sea. The warship had scrambling nets hanging down the side of its hull and Sydney was surprised at how easy it was to grasp the rope mesh and climb on board. He didn't even get his feet wet.

He made his way down into the ship and sat on the floor in the crew's mess deck with his back to a bulkhead. Looking at his watch, he saw that it was nine o'clock. A little later, he looked at his watch again: twenty minutes past five. Sydney was wholly taken aback, and for a few moments felt completely disorientated. But he was still leaning against the bulkhead, and some of the men from the field ambulance unit were still sitting next to him. He wondered if something had happened to his watch, or if he had misread the time, before it occurred to him that in his exhaustion he had plunged straight into a deep sleep, and that it must now be almost 5.30 the next morning.

The destroyer wasn't moving, so Sydney assumed that the ship had docked somewhere in England and that he could start to get off. He put on his webbing and his backpack and climbed back up the companionway to the forward deck. He reached the passageway that led out on to the deck, but it was blocked solid with soldiers packed so close together it was impossible to squeeze between them. Sydney was quite tall and he could see forward above the heads of those nearest to him – the whole of the forward deck of the destroyer was crammed with men.

He tapped one of those closest to him on the shoulder. 'Where are we?' he asked. The man looked at him strangely and just said, 'Dunkirk.'

Sydney now understood what had happened. The destroyer hadn't reached England; it had merely travelled two miles along the coast from Bray Dunes to the harbour at Dunkirk, where it had taken on board hundreds of other men. They must have been loading all these extra soldiers from the mole in the harbour while he slept. He had no chance to say anything more, because above the noise of machinery he heard the sound of nearby gunfire, then of aircraft. The next instant an immensely bright flash filled his eyes, and a wave of heat and a very loud explosion hit him, punching him to the core. Then it was immediately repeated. The two giant detonations were separated by less than a second, a gap as long as the blink of an eyelid. Two bombs had exploded on the packed deck of the destroyer, just yards away from Sydney.

1

WAR BUT NO WAR

September 1939

Sydney Whiteside was just nineteen years old on 3 September 1939. He sat in his small living room with his mother and listened to the BBC as Prime Minister Neville Chamberlain made a short speech, declaring in his dry, clipped manner that 'this country is at war with Germany.' Hearing those simple but dreadful words, Sydney felt glad that he had made the right decision. He was an intelligent boy, born in Birmingham, whose father had died when Sydney was just ten years old. His mother struggled to bring him up well. Money was tight, but he won a county scholarship to a grammar school at the age of eleven. However, the financial assistance wasn't extended past the age of sixteen, so he had had to leave school and abandon a dream of going to university, despite the fact that he had passed all his exams with flying colours. This arbitrary and unjust decision rankles with Sydney to this day and is one of the few things capable of sending a cloud across his finely drawn, equable features. Instead, he started work as a clerical officer in the Civil Service.

While continuing with his job, Sydney signed up for the Territorial Army in March 1939. He became a part-time soldier and volunteered for the Royal Army Medical Corps. His reasoning was simple. It was obvious to him that there would soon be war and he believed that joining the Territorials before the fighting started would give him some control over what he did when he was finally called up into the regular army.

The approach to war between Britain, with her ally France, and Germany was slow and delayed. It was just twenty years since an Armistice agreement between these three countries had been signed, and that last war, from 1914 to 1918, had caused the deaths of millions of men, women and children across the whole of Europe. The horrors of total war in Europe were still very much a living memory, and there was hardly a family in Britain from which someone hadn't fought or been killed in that slaughter. It's hard to criticize any politician who sought to avoid a repetition of such carnage, but the new war with Germany was not a surprise; in hindsight, it approached with horrible inevitability. Even young men like Sydney knew at the time that it was not a question of if, but of when. It's also hard to believe that men more powerful and important than Sydney Whiteside ignored the question for as long as they did.

The new Germany that brought about a new war had been in the making long before 1933 when Adolf Hitler and the Nazi Party took power. A year later, in a purge that became known as 'the Night of the Long Knives', Hitler and his SS –

the *Schutzstaffel*, or Defence Corps, the black-uniformed, armed wing of the party – murdered, in just twenty-four hours, thousands of fellow Fascists who were members of the SA – the *Sturmabteilung*, or stormtroopers. Meanwhile tens of thousands of other political opponents, communists, trade unionists, pacifists and 'social deviants' were imprisoned in concentration camps.

Hitler was equally ruthless when it came to dealing with the victorious Allies of the First World War – Britain and France. In 1936, German troops marched into the Rhineland, a part of Germany that had been demilitarized under the treaties following the end of the war. In March 1938, in collaboration with Austrian Nazis, the German Army marched into Austria and forced a referendum for unity with Germany. Simultaneously, Hitler started a political campaign to absorb the German-speaking population of Czechoslovakia, a country that had been created by the Allies after the First World War from the remnants of the Austro-Hungarian empire. The Allies refused to contemplate going to war to defend Czechoslovakia, which was described by Prime Minister Chamberlain as 'a country far away about which we know nothing'. In September 1938, in Munich, Chamberlain and French Prime Minister Edouard Daladier agreed with Hitler and the Italian dictator Benito Mussolini that the Czech government should give in to Hitler's demands or fight a war on their own. At that same meeting, Chamberlain got Hitler to sign a piece of paper stating that the parties agreed to pursue peace in Europe. This allowed Chamberlain to return to London, where he made his now infamous speech claiming that he had achieved 'peace in our time'. Six months later, in March 1939, Hitler had broken up Czechoslovakia and was making claims on various provinces in Poland. The Nazis had made no effort to hide either their aggressive ambitions or their ruthless nature. By 1939 they had extended their control over every part of the German state and the SS had grown to include its own regiments, the Waffen-SS, which were put under the command of the regular army. Part of their initiation ceremony was to swear an oath never to surrender or to take prisoners.

Sydney was more alert to the threat from Germany than the governments of France and Britain, because it was only after German troops marched into Prague on 15 March 1939 that the General Staffs of the British and French armies started to have regular meetings to discuss what to do in the event of war. Up until that time, the policy had been that British support of France against a German enemy would amount to attacks by the Royal Air Force against German targets and a blockade of Germany by the Royal Navy. This now changed to accepting that Britain would send around 250,000 troops to help in the defence of France, although it would take several months to reach this number. When German forces invaded Poland on 1 September and Britain declared war on the 3rd, there were no British troops in France. However, the armed forces had prepared some contingency plans and the effort to get troops into France quickly swung into action. Advance parties sailed from Portsmouth on 4 September and the first troopships sailed on the 9th.

Within a few weeks over 150,000 soldiers, their vehicles, ammunition, petrol and food had been transported across the Channel. The very first men to go were meant to be full-time soldiers, not men like Sydney from the Territorials, but their experience and training varied a great deal. Sid Lewis was one of those who went almost immediately, sailing from Southampton on 23 September, just twenty days after the declaration of war. His unit, the 2nd Battalion Royal Warwickshire Regiment, had started to mobilize on 2 September, but had to call in an extra 116 reservists – men who had once been members of the regiment – to bring it up to its official strength of 786 men. The battalion HQ found it hard to get the extra equipment they needed, and the battalion had started its journey from Aldershot barracks early on the morning of the 23rd with a trail of unfinished paperwork and missing equipment that the adjutant and his staff hoped would be sorted out in France. Their troopships left Southampton at 5.30 in the evening and headed straight into a storm in the Channel. Sid and most of the other soldiers on board were violently seasick. Sid believed that the ship was in grave danger of sinking and, as it tossed and heaved, almost motionless on the huge waves, it was circled by two Royal Navy destroyers prepared for a catastrophe. Sid and his comrades finally disembarked at Cherbourg the next morning. It was 9.30 – the crossing had taken fourteen hours, and they were dehydrated, exhausted and reeking of vomit.

Cherbourg had been chosen as a main port for the British soldiers landing in France because it was a good distance from German Luftwaffe bases, and safer from attack, but this meant that Sid's journey to his unit's planned positions on the French border took several days.

His first billet was at Château de Varennes, then, a few days later, to his excitement, they stopped close to the motor-racing circuit at Le Mans, where the army had established a large depot for equipment and supplies. From there Sid and his battalion went by troop train to Arras, the headquarters of the British Expeditionary Force, then by lorry to their first positions along the French border with Belgium. By 6 October he was bedding down in a cow shed at a small town called Rumegies, with one half of the shed given over to soldiers, the other half left to the cows.

Sid had been a soldier for barely six months and before that his life had been hard and unforgiving, untouched by much show of love or affection. He had been born in Martley in Worcestershire and never knew his father. His mother was unable or unwilling to look after him, so he was taken into the care of the local authority, ending up in an orphanage at the age of seven. He finished elementary education and was then sent to the workhouse, where he was trained to be a porter and doorkeeper. A dispute with the head warden of the workhouse resulted in a charge of theft, which Sid claims was completely trumped up, and he was hauled up in front of the local magistrates, from where he was ordered on probation to the Salvation Army hostel in Bow. Here he was found work at a tailor's in Whitechapel, for which he was paid a shilling a day by the Salvation Army. He had to stay in the hostel for two years. At the end of his probation, he returned to Worcester and eked out a living from casual unskilled work. He was, he says, desperately poor, so, with the example of an elder brother in the army, he decided that he would join up and find food, clothing and some regular pay.

He trained for six months and proved to be a good marksman with the standard-issue Lee-Enfield .303in rifle. He also volunteered to be a stretcher-bearer, a member of a unit that can dress wounds. This didn't amount to much more than applying a tourniquet or some splints, pouring antiseptic powder on the wound and slapping a dressing over it, then carrying the wounded away from the front line to an ambulance or regimental aid post. It did, however, mean a bit of extra pay.

Sid had almost no expectations in life, so had no complaints about where he slept, despite its being a cow shed. It was warm, with regular meals and mobile laundry and bathhouse facilities every week. The pay had risen from 11s 3d [56p] a week when he joined to 35 shillings [£1.75] now that he was on active service, but he knew that in his six months' training he had learned little except how to fire his rifle and keep his boots polished. Compared to some of the experienced men in his battalion he was still just a raw recruit, but he was now part of the British Expeditionary Force, a visible and growing commitment by Britain to the defence of France.

Another regular soldier to be part of these first contingents was Stanley Chappell. He was just nineteen years old, slim, intelligent and quiet, with a suppressed desire for adventure. There was no question in his or anybody else's mind about his training and professionalism. Stan was a lance bombardier in the 2nd Regiment Royal Horse Artillery. He had come from a large family of eight children, in Shirehampton just outside Bristol. He was a quick-witted and independent lad who had shown real promise at school but left at fourteen years old unable to afford any more schooling. He worked at various jobs, delivering groceries at first, but soon became a deck-hand on a tug working out of Avonmouth docks. It was sometimes dangerous work, but for a young lad it paid well. Coming home from a stormy crossing of the Irish Sea, a recruiting poster for the Royal Navy caught his eye. He could see the world, it said, and he knew, immediately, that was what he wanted to do. The following Monday he cycled to the navy recruiting office in Bristol. Sadly, there was a problem. Stan was still only sixteen years old and the recruiting officer pointed out that he would need his father to sign all the papers. His father, who had fought in the First World War, refused outright to see his youngest son go into the forces. Stanley was a stubborn lad, however, and the next day went again to Bristol, but this time to the army recruiting office. He lied about his age, signed the papers himself and joined the Royal Horse Artillery. It was March 1937 and he was just sixteen years and four months old.

The Royal Horse Artillery was established to give mobile firepower to the cavalry and they have always thought of themselves as a cut above the rest of the artillery regiments. They took great pride in their appearance, and in the barracks Stan and his fellow gunners would spend long hours polishing their riding boots and pressing their uniforms. Stan enjoyed galloping and leading the teams of horses that pulled the gun limbers on manoeuvres on Salisbury Plain for the annual summer exercises. Within a few months of joining, he had become an excellent rider and could set his mount at jumps sitting on just a saddle blanket. On finishing his training he was assigned to L (Néry) Battery, in the 2nd Regiment, based at Bulford Camp in Wiltshire.

L (Néry) Battery had its peculiar name because of a famous action it had fought in the First World War. The mess at Bulford had a huge mural depicting this scene and Stan gazed upon it at every meal. The men in L Battery had woken one morning in their billet at the French town of Néry. There was a thick mist in the valley and they discovered that under its cover a battery of German guns had moved closer, on to nearby higher ground, from where they started firing at the village at close range. L Battery rushed into action and returned the fire, but at first the German guns prevailed. Finally, just one gun of L Battery survived. Only three men were left alive to keep it in action – Captain Bradbury, Battery Sergeant Major George Dorrell and Sergeant David Nelson. The captain had his leg shot away, but continued to fire the gun until he died. The other two men then kept the gun going, and one by one they knocked out the German artillery, so that the enemy gun crews lay slumped, dead or dying around their weapons. All three men were awarded the Victoria Cross for bravery under fire, and the battery used the name of the village in its title from then on. The mural on the mess wall showed the three men in action at their gun, bloodied, surrounded by their dead comrades – a picture rendered with a lurid realism. This scene, and the story of the battery's finest hour, fascinated Stan. Rather than finding it disturbing – a reminder of the death and mutilation that might lie in wait for him – he was deeply inspired by it and, like most of the men in the battery, admired the courage of the three gunners.

After many hours learning how to look after the gun team's horses and developing a love of horse riding, Stan was sad to discover that their splendid mounts were either to be sold off or destroyed. The regiment was becoming mechanized, and within a few weeks petrol-driven quad tractors to haul the 2-pounder guns and their limbers were introduced, along with 15cwt and 30cwt lorries (approximately 0.75 and 1.5 metric tons) and tracked carriers. Modernization, however, didn't dent the gunners' self-regard. Stan remembers that within a few weeks everybody was as adept at maintaining their vehicles and their engines as they had been in looking after their horses, and that they were expected to appear gleaming and immaculate on parade.

Despite many claims that the British Army was out of date and poorly equipped, it had been completely mechanized. The artillery were adopting the new 25lb howitzers, with gun tractors to pull them, and infantry battalions were now provided with lorries to transport troops and the mobile kitchens and washing facilities that accompanied them. The Universal carrier, a tracked armoured vehicle that became known as a Bren-gun carrier, also came into service and every infantry battalion had a section of ten of them. Each could mount a Bren gun or mortar and they provided a mobile firing position, as well as carrying ammunition or stores to the front line.

Stan had a good grasp of maths, and his role was to help the gun-position officer in his troop. The guns were set up in various patterns, depending on the terrain and the field of fire the battery commander had been ordered to cover. A small plotting table would be set up and a blank map with grid squares marked up with the gun positions. The bearing and range of geographical points such as woods or crossroads were then worked out, so that fire could be directed at them quickly and accurately whenever it was called for by the units they were supporting.

Stanley loved firing the guns on the practice ranges, particularly when the guns were being registered – aiming at a target whose range was precisely known so that the sights and controls of the gun could be properly calibrated. The cartridge would explode, the recoil forcing the gun back against its firing platform, and it was possible to see the shell leaving the barrel; then a few seconds later the shell would explode at the end of its flight. It never failed to lift Stan's spirits and provide a sense of power and accomplishment.

Disembarking at Cherbourg, Stan felt no apprehension at the approach of battle. He thought of himself as a professional soldier and he had no doubts that L (Néry) Battery would do its job and that he would do his. After the long, four-day journey across northern France they reached their first post, near the town of La Bassée. They found their billets and next morning started placing their guns and digging them into defensive positions. Officers from the regiment went out to reconnoitre the field of fire and aiming points given to them from brigade HQ. Autumn had passed and the weather was cold. Their journey from Cherbourg had been in the teeth of a snowstorm that had made driving slow and difficult on the narrow, poorly maintained roads. The general opinion of Stan's troop was that they were in for a very tough winter.

2

THE TERRITORIALS

September 1939–January 1940

The plan was to build up the British Expeditionary Force by sending out regular army divisions and then to supplement this by other units made up of conscripts from the Territorial Army. Some Territorials found themselves arriving in France fairly quickly, though.

Larry Uren of the 1/7th Battalion Queen's Royal Regiment and Les Clarke of the 6th Battalion Durham Light Infantry were both in the advance parties of their units, and both were former Territorial Army members, although their units were not part of the Territorial contingent.

Larry Uren travelled to France in December 1939 as part of the advance party of just fifteen men and officers from the 131st Brigade. They were responsible for finding billets for the battalions that were due to arrive later. Larry was a Cornishman, a big lad, open and direct with a sense of humour. He had joined the Militia, an organization set up after the Munich Crisis to boost the army reservists in 1938, and had been attached to the Devon and Cornwall Light Infantry. The Militia was a strange organization, uncomfortably placed between the regular forces and the Territorial Army, but Larry had been given some basic training and was then sent off on various guard duties. The Irish Republican Army had recently become active again on the British mainland and Larry was part of a detachment that carried out guard duties at Plymouth docks and at the Marconi Station where the Atlantic telephone cable came ashore at Land's End.

He was drafted into the 1/7th Queen's in October and became a driver for Major Snowden, the battalion's commanding officer, who was part of the advance party which was based in the area of Béthune, a town in the Pas-de-Calais close to the Belgian border that had been heavily shelled by German artillery in the First World War. Larry's military skills were of the most basic kind but, as a nineteen-year-old who had barely left Cornwall before arriving in France, he felt that he had fallen into the most exciting adventure.

Les Clarke, another young lad of nineteen, crossed the Channel in October, in the forward reconnaissance party for his battalion, the 6th Durham Light Infantry. He had trained as the driver of a Bren-gun carrier, which was steered by using levers to disengage one or other of its tracks, but in his role in the advance party he was also given the task of driving 30cwt lorries or a 500cc BSA motorbike as a despatch rider.

Les's father had been an officer in the British Army, but Les cannot remember ever meeting him as he had died when Les was very young. Les had not done well at school, and at fourteen left to work in a foundry in Bishop Auckland, doing a menial and dirty job as a 'fettler', knocking the tangs off the edges of iron castings. He joined the Territorial Army as a boy in 1935, for the same reason as thousands of other working-class boys – it provided some outdoor activity, it got him away from home and he got paid for it. Les enjoyed the life, learned to drive, and his limited education improved no end. After four years in the Territorials he was, in his own eyes, a proficient soldier. Called up three weeks before the outbreak of war, he was a trusted rifleman in the battalion and on his journey to France he wore the flash of the British Expeditionary Force with pride.

He accompanied his commanding officer, Major Michael Ferens, the scion of a milling family in Sunderland. The advance party was responsible for planning the route from the disembarkation port in France to the final positions of the battalion along the Franco-Belgian border. Each stage of the journey had to be researched and physically inspected by the reconnaissance team to make sure that it could take the long columns of lorries and carriers, and to secure proper accommodation for over eight hundred men and their equipment at each resting point along the way. Les confesses that he had no idea at first what to do, but quickly picked up the tricks of the trade from the CO. A key skill was how to assess a building to work out how many men could bed down in it. 'If you saw a likely barn you had to persuade the local French owner to let you borrow it. We did it in a nice way, but whether they liked it or not we were going to do it.'

Les had left for France from Southampton, where they marched to the quayside on a Sunday with a local band playing all the popular songs, like 'Run Rabbit Run' and 'We're

Going to Hang Out the Washing on the Siegfried Line'. Then he travelled, as most of the British soldiers did, via Le Mans, through Lille and a host of small villages. The idea, he says, was to try to avoid large towns and cities because of the disruption that the convoys caused. As they drove through the small towns and villages the air of celebration remained with them, local girls waving and blowing kisses, gifts of bread and wine thrust at them. It was, he thought, as though they were going on a two-week holiday.

He was in northern France for eight weeks, then returned to join his battalion at Chipping Norton. As well as Major Ferens, other officers in the regiment had County Durham connections, including Les's immediate officer, Lieutenant Lockhart, who came from a local Sunderland brewing family. On the whole Les liked them, and thought that they were decent men and good officers. He had had a good time in France as part of the forward party, as had everyone else, and their mood on their return had infected the whole of the battalion.

And so over a few months the British Expeditionary Force gradually moved into France. The process of transporting a division from its various bases in the UK across the Channel and then to its positions along the French border took considerable preparation and enormous resources. The basic fighting units to which Sid Lewis and Stanley Chappell belonged were either infantry battalions or artillery regiments. An infantry battalion had a normal strength of around 780 men, and these were organized in battalion HQ staff and an HQ company, with another four rifle companies. In addition to the basic Lee-Enfield rifles carried by the men, there would in the battalion be fifty Bren guns, two 3in mortars, twelve 2in mortars and twenty-two anti-tank rifles. There would also be the usual section of ten Bren-gun carriers. The mortar section and the Bren-gun carriers would normally be under the direct control of the battalion HQ.

Higher up the chain of command would be a brigade, which would usually be made up of three battalions. The brigade would have its own HQ and its own attached anti-tank artillery company. Two or three brigades would be under the direction of a division, which again would have its own HQ staff and field artillery attached to it, bringing the head-count up to around seventeen thousand men of all ranks. These were just the fighting men and those directly involved in supporting them, with considerable numbers of vehicles such as the carriers, gun tractors, troop-carrying lorries, despatch riders' motorcycles, command vehicles, and ammunition and stores vehicles. Accompanying these were the armourers and mechanics, with their equipment, and vehicles that carried fuel, food and water, as well as mobile field kitchens to prepare food for the troops in the front line or on manoeuvres. Many of the vehicles were the responsibility of the Royal Army Service Corps, and there were the ambulances and field hospitals of the Royal Army Medical Corps and the specialized vehicles of the Royal Engineers. Every fighting man needed a huge train of men and equipment, stores, fuel and ammunition to keep him alive and able to fight.

Shifting a division was an enormously complex task. Transport had to be organized to carry the men from each brigade or regimental HQ. The route to the docks had to be marked out in advance, and the journey times well planned so that the ships to take the men across the Channel were ready to embark them. They boarded with just their haversacks and overnight rations, their kitbags and weapons loaded in bulk into the ships' holds. The sea crossing was made at night under an escort of destroyers to avoid attacks from U-boats, but a minefield laid across the Straits of Dover had effectively sealed off the Channel.

The vehicles and heavy equipment went by separate boat. Once driven on to the dockside their petrol tanks were drained and the ignition keys were tied to the steering wheel. Then large printed numbers were stuck on the windscreens, indicating where in the ships' holds the vehicles were to be loaded. The largest and heaviest were loaded first, and it was the responsibility of the brigade staff to know in which order the vehicles were loaded in the ship and when they would appear out of the hold and become available at Cherbourg. From there it was another long journey to their final areas on the front line.

The British Expeditionary Force was responsible for the defence of the Franco-Belgian border along a front that ran from the town of Maulde in the south, where the River Scheldt crossed the frontier, to the town of Armentières in the north, a distance of about forty miles. Two French armies were defending the front on both of the BEF's flanks. The French First Army was to their right, on the southern flank, and the French Seventh Army was on their left flank to the north.

The British Army established a general headquarters headed by General the Viscount Gort in the town of Arras. John Gort was a First World War veteran, a Guards officer who had seen considerable action. He had been wounded four times, mentioned in despatches nine times, and been awarded the Military Cross, the Distinguished Service Order and two Bars, and the Victoria Cross, the ultimate award for bravery in the face of the enemy. Gort was not a popular officer in the senior ranks of the army, partly because they felt that he had been promoted to Chief of the Imperial General Staff above others with more seniority. He had no experience of a large command, but he was now in overall charge of the British Army in France. He was responsible to the Imperial Staff and the War Cabinet, but had also been given orders that put him under the command of General Georges, the French commander-in-chief of the North-East Theatre of Operations. Georges was himself under the command of the French commander-in-chief, General Maurice Gamelin. This subordinate role was understandable given that the British Expeditionary Force, barely 160,000 men at the end of September, was small compared to the French mobilization of an army of two million. Lord Gort was, however, granted the right to appeal to the British government if he thought that any order given to him might imperil the British Field Force. It was a potentially confusing chain of command, but Gort accepted it without complaint.

Despite the size of the French Army, French military doctrine was defensive. Since the First World War vast sums of money had been spent on the Maginot Line, a ten-kilometre-deep line of border posts, anti-tank obstacles and reinforced concrete forts, some of which could accommodate up to a thousand soldiers. Stretching along the length of the frontier between France and Germany, from the Swiss border to Luxembourg, the eighty-seven miles completed by 1935 had cost seven billion francs. The array of large forts, each armed with 5.7in guns, were connected to a string of smaller casemates (emplacements) with anti-tank guns and machine guns. Together with the deep anti-tank traps and obstacles and the fifty-metre-thick coils of barbed wire it was a formidable obstacle. The line of concrete and steel stopped abruptly at the Belgian border, however. When the massive forts were built, Belgium was an ally of France, so extending the Maginot Line would have been undiplomatic, raising difficult questions about the nature of the alliance between the two countries. In 1936 the Belgian government once more decided to declare strict neutrality, but now to extend the French line of defences along the 250-mile border would have been cripplingly expensive and would have cut through one of the most heavily industrialized areas in Europe centred around the cities of Lille and Valenciennes.

On the other hand, if the Germans chose to ignore Belgian neutrality, as they had in the First World War, then it would clearly be necessary to have some defences in place and so the construction of lines of trenches and pillboxes was begun by the French. The British Army, whose troops were now responsible for defending part of this border, did not think that these lines were up to their standards, and General Gort and his staff wanted them improved. In November 1939 twelve field companies of Royal Engineers arrived in France to start building anti-tank ditches, concrete pillboxes and lines of trenches along the border with Belgium. These engineer units were supplemented in the new year by more sappers, who arrived with the 48th Division, one of the Territorial units.

Reg Beeston, in the 224 Field Company Royal Engineers, was one of those men. He had joined the Territorials in the middle of 1939, at the age of nineteen, because he wanted to be in the army. His father had been a regular soldier in the Royal Horse Artillery who had fought in the First World War and remained in the army afterwards, taking his family to Gibraltar and the West Indies. Soldiering was in the blood. As a Territorial, Reg went to his first annual camp and was then called up in August. He carried out his basic training on the downs near Marlborough, digging tank traps and trenches, learning rifle drill and taking part in exercises, then landed in France in January 1940, ending up in billets in Lille. The field regiments had a constant need for skilled craftsmen, in trades that changed as the process of construction went on – from excavator drivers, to carpenters building shuttering, to welders for the reinforcing bars in the concrete pillboxes. The pillboxes had been scheduled to be completed by March 1940 but were taking a long while to build. They were the main responsibility of the sappers like Reg, but in between them men from the infantry regiments were set to work to dig anti-tank ditches six feet deep and sixteen feet wide, with sides sloping steeply down to the floor.

Also in the 48th Division was Sydney Whiteside, who had, as he expected, been called up in September. Trained as a medical orderly, he was attached to the 144th Brigade as the 144 Field Ambulance Unit, with billets in a barracks that had been built for Polish migrant workers in the town of Thumeries, near Douai. It was a coalmining area, poor and economically depressed. He worked in a large first aid post that had been set up in the village hall. Despite the lack of hostilities, there was a steady stream of casualties, from men going down with the flu to the large number of injuries from the construction work on the border defences. They were, he recalls, kept very busy.

Over forty miles of anti-tank obstacles and ditches were being built, with four hundred concrete pillboxes covering them. Around eight hundred construction vehicles, bulldozers, excavators, concrete mixers and so on, had to be transported across the Channel for this enormous project. As well as this work, the General Staff in Arras knew that a regular training programme was urgently needed to help bridge the gap between the professional soldiers like Bombardier Stanley Chappell and the raw recruits like Sid Lewis. Britain was at war with Germany once again, and troops were being sent to France to defend the country. That there was time to begin the construction of major defences, as well as to train up the troops, was remarkable. In some people's minds it was shameful. Major General Bernard Montgomery, in command of the 3rd Division under Lieutenant General Alan Brooke's II Corps at that time, wrote later that 'my soul revolted at what was happening. France and Britain stood still while Germany swallowed Poland; we stood still while the German armies moved over to the west, obviously to attack us later on; we waited patiently to be attacked; and all this time we occasionally bombed Germany with leaflets. If this was war I did not understand it.'

The German armed forces were preoccupied with the annexation of Poland, and only after that country had been defeated did Hitler's attention turn to the western front. He initially wanted to make an assault in November, but the German High Command persuaded him that the approaching winter weather would create too many obstacles to a rapid Blitzkrieg. Anyway, just where the German thrust should be focused was beginning to be the subject of intense argument.

The French Army, as we have seen, was defensive. It was incapable of mounting an attack across the Maginot Line into Germany, and the Allies were determined to respect Belgian neutrality.

There was also a more profound split between the Allies. Various aggressive initiatives were put forward in the War Cabinet. Winston Churchill, then the First Lord of the Admiralty, wanted the Rhine, that great commercial waterway that fed German industry, to be sown with aerial mines. He also proposed that troops capture Swedish iron ore in order to deny it to the Germans. Other proposals were made to bomb German industry and airfields. All these operations were vetoed by the French government on the grounds that they would invite retaliation, and that France was powerless against attack from the German Luftwaffe. It wasn't only Montgomery who didn't understand it. Churchill, and some other members of the War Cabinet, failed to appreciate the logic of their ally's position but could do nothing to change it. Few of the ordinary soldiers on the ground understood it either, but their attitude was different. In Sid Lewis's words, 'There was war, but there was no war. And thank God for that!'

3

A WINTER WONDERLAND

January–early May 1940

So for eight months the British Expeditionary Force established itself in northern France without any significant
conflict with the German Army or Air Force. The greater
enemy during this period was, in fact, the weather – the winter of 1939/40 was one of the hardest in living memory.
Stanley Chappell's 2nd Regiment Royal Horse Artillery had
started their journey through northern France to their final
billets in a snowstorm, and the weather had clamped in from
then on. The roads were so icy that movement along them
was severely limited. Nevertheless, II Corps, under
Lieutenant General Alan Brooke, to which the 2nd Regiment
was attached, continued a series of training manoeuvres that
focused on rapid movements in a fluid battlefield. They were
sent on long night moves to set up battery positions in the
dark and, without any previous reconnaissance of the area, to
be prepared and fully deployed, with target positions and

ranges plotted, by first light the following morning. Other exercises tested their ability to limber up and withdraw rapidly, then be ready to give covering fire to rearguard infantry.

The manoeuvres were hard and extremely challenging, but Stanley enjoyed them on the whole. He was young and fit and found everything a great adventure. The weather was bright and extremely crisp, and the cold posed no problems as long as the proper precautions were taken. It became standard practice for the radiators of every vehicle to be drained before nightfall because of the damage that could be caused by the freezing temperatures. On one exercise that called for Stan's battery to charge around in the dark over ploughed fields, where the furrows had frozen into giant iron corduroy, they were away from their base for three or four days. One evening they took refuge in a small hamlet, bedding down in an unheated drill hall. A bombardier in the battery, Jim Nicholls, had a full set of false teeth. When he woke the next morning he found that they had been frozen solid in a tin cup full of water. Stan found it hilarious, but they all stopped laughing at him when they went outside to discover that one of them had forgotten to drain a Bren-gun carrier's radiator. The cylinder head had cracked in two and the engine was a write-off. It was an expensive mistake and a serious disciplinary offence. By the middle of January the roads were so badly affected by the freezing conditions that all vehicle movements were stopped for several days.

The weather slowed everything. Reg Beeston's field company found the going extremely hard in the snow. They needed more mechanical excavators to dig the foundations for the pillboxes, and concrete would be ruined if it were poured in freezing conditions. Some of the anti-tank trenches were completed quickly, however, as Les Clarke found out quite suddenly. With the 6th Battalion Durham Light Infantry now in France, he had been appointed as a despatch rider, taking signals and reports from the battalion HQ to the various companies. It was a job that gave him a great deal of freedom, as well as advance knowledge of information that affected the men. 'Once you delivered the report, whatever it was, you waited there to see if you had to take a reply. So you heard a lot of the discussions going on in the battalion HQ. But I was under strict orders not to discuss anything, or contribute in any way to the spreading of information or rumours. If I did I would be in serious trouble.'

Les was delivering a report from B Company HQ to the battalion HQ, using a route that he had often taken in the past. It was a narrow country lane connecting two metalled roads and it cut the journey time considerably. He swung the 500cc BSA motorbike round a corner to find that an anti-tank ditch had been dug right across his path. He had the quick wits to let go of the bike, but he went flying and landed by the side of the wide trench, while the big BSA ended up in the bottom of it. Neither Les nor the bike was seriously damaged, but it took a couple of hours to recover the machine and get it started again.

When Les finally reached the battalion HQ, he got no sympathy. 'The snotty-faced adjutant, who was a nasty piece of work, said he had heard the excuse about trenches so many times before that if it happened again I would be on a charge. I was black and blue all over, and covered in dirt from getting the bike out of the trench. "Don't come into the battalion looking like that again," was all he said. I could have landed him one.' The offhand treatment still rankles with Les even today as he sits in his chair, his now sightless eyes staring into the past. His Labrador jerks his head up as he hears the venom in Les's voice.

But Les's background had not promised him much and he took most things as they came. He balanced the sometimes brutal hardships of army life with the enjoyment he got from speeding through the French countryside on his powerful motorbike. France was another country, and an exotic one at that. He enjoyed his leave in the cafés and bars of Lille, and his pay went a long way. One experience that he did not enjoy, though, was when he was invited with a pal into a farmhouse for a meal. The only person in the family who could speak English was the young daughter of around fourteen, and her knowledge was basic. They all sat down to a very tasty stew, with lots of strong red wine, but the conversation was stilted. Les guessed that the invitation had been at the suggestion of the daughter who wanted to practise her English. They left, the daughter passing on their thanks to her parents, and once in the yard, in the open air, they realized how much they had drunk. Before finally leaving they asked the daughter the name of the food that they had eaten. She laughed, smacked her thigh and pointed to a carthorse in the stable. Les and his friend walked quickly away and could hardly wait until they were out of sight before throwing up in the hedge.

In February Les received a letter from a neighbour telling him that his mother had died. He had last seen her on a visit he had made before his journey to France. The date of her funeral had already passed, so he was told there was no need for any compassionate leave. It was a heartless decision, but Les accepted it and, strangely, he felt that the only family he now had was the army, more particularly the men in his battalion.

As the winter progressed, sudden thaws left the roads like quagmires, to be followed by sudden snowfalls, but eventually the weather improved enough for exercises and manoeuvres to start again. The strange, peaceful war dragged on. The Germans had a strong air force – the Luftwaffe – which had been used to good effect in the invasion of Poland, and were also known to have developed a new type of fighting unit that used parachutes to drop behind the front line from aircraft. British infantry units were ordered to take measures to deal with both. Detailed instructions were issued for precautions to be taken against enemy aircraft on manoeuvres or while units were moving from location to location. The orders said that small arms were not to be fired at aircraft flying above two thousand feet, and that soldiers were on no account to look upwards, because their white faces were easier to spot. During a march or relocation one NCO of each platoon was detailed to be on air raid alert and on spotting any enemy aircraft he was to give a series of short sharp blasts on a whistle. During any halt each platoon would have one light machine gun manned at instant readiness for anti-aircraft fire, and companies were to disperse away from their vehicles during stops.

Other orders emphasized the need for instant aggressive response against airborne troops before they had time to collect themselves into a coherent fighting force. Each battalion was to create a special mobile reserve made up of a section of Bren-gun carriers with three Bren guns and three anti-tank rifles – the Boys .5in calibre – one box of Mills hand grenades and three signal pistols. Two trucks carrying a

2in mortar, a section of riflemen and a Bren gun, plus one section of riflemen on bicycles, were also part of the initial response unit. These were to be backed up with quick support from a carrier platoon or rifle company. Just how effective these measures would be no one knew. Airborne troops had yet to be encountered, and, although there were regular air raid warnings, the Luftwaffe was also an unknown quantity. Les noticed that no one took the orders seriously. Men didn't think of trying to distinguish between enemy or friendly aircraft, and no one could resist the temptation to look upwards as the roar of aero-engines passed overhead.

Stan Chappell's battery remained at their position in the large village of Ancoisne, south-west of Lille. He was having a very pleasant time. Like every other soldier on leave in Lille or Béthune on a twenty-four-hour pass, he had been to the dance halls, the estaminets (small cafés) and brothels. Despite his time as a deckhand on tugs and coasters sailing out of Avonmouth, Stan was a thoughtful, quiet lad. It took him a while to realize that the young ladies clustered by the bars in these places were prostitutes. The fact that the British soldiers were paid much better than their French counterparts, and could easily afford not only the women but also to drink themselves under the table on every spirit and liquor lined up behind the bar, was more obvious. He realized the folly of this when one member of their battery was hospitalized with alcohol poisoning after a weekend in Lille. It was fun to have a trip to town every now and then, but what improved Stan's life immeasurably was the decision to find some digs in Ancoisne and move out of the communal billets in the local school hall. The idea was really that of his mate Bert. After walking around the centre and talking to some local shopkeepers they found a double room in the house of a prosperous family, where they were treated as part of the family and quickly introduced to the life of the village. The home cooking was excellent, and every morning they were given a large cup of freshly brewed coffee with a good shot of cognac in it. What better way to prepare for parade in the freezing winter morning? So Stanley settled extremely happily into a life of French bourgeois comfort.

In March 1940 three more Territorial Divisions arrived in France. They were not fully up to strength, but they were sent to France to help provide the labour needed to improve railways and roads in the rear areas. They were also meant to continue a rigorous training programme, because everybody realized that they were not in any fit state to perform in the front line. Jack Haskett, who was in the 12th Division, 2/6th Queen's Own Royal Regiment, was very well aware of this and he was very unhappy with his lot.

Jack had been born in 1918, and his father, who had died when Jack was ten, had served in the Royal Navy for twenty-one years. Jack lived with his mother and two older brothers in a flat above stables in a mews in Notting Hill. He left school at fourteen and ended up working as a sign-maker for a firm of shopfitters. In need of some extra money and recreation, he joined the Territorials when he was sixteen, signing up for the Royal Artillery. His first day in uniform was an unhappy one. He had put his spurs on with the buckles facing inward and the bus conductor, a First World War veteran, loudly pointed this out to all and sundry when he got on the bus. Young Jack, scarlet with embarrassment, had to endure the laughter of all the other passengers. But he was a smart, lively lad and he didn't make many other mistakes. He learned quickly, did well in the artillery and enjoyed the Territorials for the four years that he had signed up for. This time came to an end in June 1939, and he delayed signing up again, wanting instead to spend more time in the local Hammersmith dance halls with his girlfriends.

It was a bad move, because when he was called up in December 1939 he was drafted into the 2/6th Battalion Queen's Royal Regiment, an infantry unit, and his four years' experience in the artillery counted for nothing.

Jack wasn't happy either with the work that he was ordered to do in France, excavating gravel from a quarry and then shovelling it out as ballast on to railway lines. In between this navvying work there was training, route march after route march. The only pleasant part of his posting was the weekly leave in the nearby town of Amiens. 'We wanted entertainment today, because who knew what was going to happen tomorrow? So we drank, and went to the dance halls, and met the women and had a good time. Everything was foreign, even the air once you got across the Channel. It smelled different, exciting.'

He was not impressed with the quality of his fellow recruits, nor of his non-commissioned officers, whom he thought were incompetent. The junior officers seemed younger and less experienced than he was. 'It was embarrassing,' he recalls. On their first parade, before they went into Amiens they were lined up for a talk about the dangers of prostitutes and the need for hygiene. 'The lieutenant, he couldn't have been more than twenty, stood there for ages smacking his stick against his leg. You could see the sergeant thinking, "Say something, for chrissake," then he just said, "Just remember you're going to put your old man where I wouldn't put my umbrella." Then he wandered off. That was our sex education!'

Weapons training was also a source of irritation to Jack. 'The training was nothing like as thorough as what I had been through in the artillery. We had rifle practice every now and then, and it was difficult with a fixed bayonet, which is heavy. Then we had to have firing practice wearing a gas mask. Try firing a rifle with a gas mask. The bullets went everywhere, of course. But it was as though we had to just get experience of it, not improve in any way.'

Worst of all for Jack were the route marches. 'I'm certain they hadn't got the faintest idea what to do with us – it was just doing something to keep us occupied. There were two chaps who had a mouth organ and we used to sing a song about Hore-Belisha, the War Minister:

> *We had to join Belisha's army,*
> *Ten bob a week, nothing to eat, bloody great blisters on*
>   *your feet,*
> *We had to join, we had to join, we had to join Belisha's army!*

Every day I wondered why I hadn't signed up again for the artillery.'

So the men of the BEF lived through the winter and spring of the peace-in-war, working, training and taking what pleasure they could find. Nothing, however, could compare with the life that Larry Uren was leading. Most advance reconnaissance units spent two weeks investigating their routes and billets before returning to HQ, but the arrival of Larry's battalion was constantly postponed. The foreign ministers of Germany and the Soviet Union, Joachim von

Ribbentrop and Vyacheslav Molotov, had signed a non-aggression pact in August 1939 and the Soviet Union had made claims on the territory of various Baltic states, as well as occupying the eastern part of Poland. The Finnish government had rejected the Soviet claim on Karelia and gone to war. The British government was thinking of sending military assistance to Finland in its fight against Hitler's ally, and the 1/7th Battalion Queen's Regiment, potentially part of that assistance, was being held in readiness in England. Larry remained in Lille, set adrift on an open-ended assignment, also waiting for a decision to be made. He was overjoyed at the situation. He is a big man, with a warm, open character, full of life. The French liaison officer to whom he and his major had been assigned was none other than Pierre Dubonnet, heir to the giant French drinks company, and he and Larry quickly hit it off. Dubonnet was an exceptional host and at weekends Larry was soon a constant guest of the family at their chateau, or else was driven in a very fast and enormous limousine to Paris to see the sights, the restaurants and the night life. Larry was particularly intrigued by the fact that several of the dancing girls in the Folies Bergère were from England. They got on like a house on fire and he met them regularly throughout that long winter.

Larry could never get over the way that his life had been transformed, and his ready acceptance by a member of the moneyed class was a constant source of surprise. Being a house guest of Pierre Dubonnet was like entering another universe. 'There were flunkeys everywhere – it was impossible to finish a glass of wine without it being topped up. And there was a different wine for every course. I sometimes had no idea what I was eating, but it was delicious. And I had my own valet to help me undress when I went to bed. Can you imagine? Me, a young lad from a Cornish mining village, living in the lap of luxury like that.'

The 1/7th Queen's Regiment did finally arrive in France, disembarking at Cherbourg on the morning of 3 April. Larry and the others in the advance party had no choice but to tear themselves away from their comfortable billets, their girl-friends and their servants to meet the battalion at the docks. By late afternoon the convoy was on the road and heading for the Franco-Belgian border. Larry was now a driver and in the cab of a 15cwt lorry with Captain Dickenson, his command-ing officer, leading a group of four lorries in the convoy of twenty troop-carrying vehicles. His life of hot baths in hotels and a valet at Pierre Dubonnet's chateau was over. At their first stop in Fresnay-sur-Sarthe, and then at Nieppe, where they relieved the Gordon Highlanders, weekly baths were provided by a mobile shower and laundry. The men would strip off, be inspected for venereal disease or lice, then walk through the hot showers that had been erected in the village squares or a local street. As they left they would receive freshly laundered underwear and battledress. It was efficient and hygienic, but it meant that hundreds of naked young men were lined up every week in full view of the local residents. The weather, fortunately, was getting warmer.

Les Clarke would have given his eyeteeth for the oppor-tunity to experience the life of luxury enjoyed by Larry, even for a very brief time. In March of 1940 his division organized a boxing match. It was, as Les says drily, 'a knockout competition'. Les was told that he had volunteered, though he knew nothing about boxing. He was about five foot eight and eleven stone, and was put in the welterweight category.

There were, unfortunately, some very good boxers in the battalion. Corporal Harry Allen, the captain of the boxing team, had been a boxer in a fairground boxing booth and was a big lad, a light heavyweight. Les's first fight in the preliminary bouts was his last. That morning he had been to the dentist and had five teeth removed. It was a rough business visiting an army dentist. He was given one injection to kill the pain, then 'it was a knee in the chest, the pliers in the mouth and yank, yank, yank, and that was it.' When he climbed into the ring that evening he knew what he was going to do. He took three or four heavy blows, fell down and stayed there to be counted out.

His reward was a meal, which he could barely eat because of his still bleeding gums, and a packet of five Woodbine cigarettes. From then on his only involvement in the boxing tournament was to help set out the chairs in the large hall in Lille for the final. That was on 9 May and, although Les and the others in the boxing tournament were not yet aware of it, the long days of war without fighting were already over.

4

ON THE BORDER

October 1939–April 1940

Sid Lewis had been stationed close to the Franco-Belgian border since his arrival in France. The days were hard, digging tank traps and machine-gun posts along the border, extending the barbed-wire barriers and draining trenches, because everyone on the front line – not just the sappers like Reg Beeston – had to work on improving the defences. Reveille was at 6.50 in the morning and they were at work by 8.30. Dinner was from 12.30 for an hour and work finished at 16.30.

Working details were interspersed with periods on the border, manning the existing French pillboxes that were placed every two hundred yards along the frontier with Belgium. The battalion HQ was in the small town of Rumegies, with companies billeted in the surrounding countryside. If they were on border duty, a platoon was billeted in a nearby farm and each eight-man section of the platoon would occupy a pillbox for twenty-four hours. When every section had carried out its twenty-four-hour stint, another platoon would replace it in the farmhouse.

Because they were on the border, and were in one of the first divisions to form part of the BEF, Sid's brigade saw a series of visits from VIPs. General Montgomery, commander of the 3rd Division, paid a visit in October; His Majesty King George made an inspection a month later; General Gort went round the battalion's positions on 14 November; and in the new year, on 3 January, Clement Attlee, leader of the Labour opposition in Parliament, made a tour of the front. Sid was unmoved by all of them. He remembers that during the king's visit everybody was issued with a bottle of beer to drink to his health, with strict instructions that it was not to be drunk beforehand. His Majesty visited the pillbox next to Sid's and after he had left the beer was taken away again.

Aside from work on the defences, the battalion ran patrols to assist the French border guards in checking the credentials of travellers and stopping unauthorized foreigners from entering the country. It was a strange detail. The border crossed farms and villages in an arbitrary manner, and the normal daily movement of people and vehicles to and fro across it was suddenly interrupted by the fact that France was a country at war and Belgium was not. There was also a regular traffic in smuggled goods, mainly cigarettes and other luxury items, to which the border guards turned a blind eye. The widely held opinion was that they took bribes. After two Belgians were arrested for trying to bring black-market cigarettes into France, instructions came down from the division that the patrols were to make more effort to form good relations with the local people.

The border was closed completely on 14 January, when the battalion was placed on alert and told to concentrate at Rumegies in preparation for forward mobilization. A general alert had been announced all along the front, because intelligence had been received that the German Army was planning an attack. On 10 January a German aircraft had made a forced landing in a field in Belgium. The pilot, Major Erich Hoenmanns, an officer in the Luftwaffe, had got lost in poor weather and the engine of the plane had cut out. He believed that he was landing in Germany. The passenger in the aircraft was a major in the planning staff of the German airborne forces and he had with him details of German plans to invade Holland and Belgium – 'Plan Yellow'. A Belgian border unit captured the two men and, despite the Germans' attempts to destroy the documents, they were seized by the border guards and taken to be examined by the Belgian General HQ Staff. Details of the plans were sent quickly to the French and the Dutch. The French Army went to a state of high alert and moved forwards to the Belgian frontier. They went no further, however, because King Leopold of the Belgians wasn't prepared to provide any excuse for the Germans to invade, even though it was clear that plans already existed for them to do exactly that. The plans could have been a plant, but after questioning the two hapless Germans the Belgians decided that they were genuine. So too did the French. These documents were to have a far-reaching impact, because the information in them provided General Gamelin with enough evidence to change his own plans, committing more French units to the defence of Belgium when the fighting started.

Sid's battalion stood down after this alert and the next few weeks passed without any incident. And so the routine continued throughout the harsh winter. The battalion suffered some casualties, but these were self-inflicted. Two men died of carbon monoxide poisoning from a faulty stove in one of the billets at Le Forest, and Private Locke opened fire with his rifle in his billet, killing one of the men he shared with and wounding another. He was arrested and charged with murder. Sid carried out his duties as a stretcher-bearer just once when a lorry carrying men back from their weekly trip to the brothels of Lille spun off the road and crashed into a ditch. The accident was caused by severe ice on the roads – at least that was the official reason, but Sid thinks that the driver was drunk. Anyway, he was not put on a charge, despite the fact that three men were badly injured in the accident.

In March a sudden announcement changed the monotonous routine of life in France. The CO told the assembled men of the battalion that they were on orders to move to different positions further south, where France had a common border with Germany. Sid had no reason to think that this would be any different from life on the Belgian border, although he remembers that one man fainted when he heard what the CO had to say. In fact there had already been many clashes with the enemy along this border, and the General HQ of the British Expeditionary Force had decided to send every division here for a period to get them acclimatized to combat.

On 21 March Sid climbed on board a goods wagon and the trainload of troops steamed slowly away from Rumegies and the flat farmlands of Belgium where they had now lived for six months and which they had started to think of as home.

The journey was broken by a stop for breakfast, with petrol-fuelled cookers set up by the side of the line to brew up tea, served with bread and jam and tinned fish. The landscape became more wooded and hilly, and the sun shone all day. The rail journey ended in the town of Metz in the evening, and the battalion marched to temporary sleeping quarters in French army barracks. From there they went by lorry to a village that had been evacuated by its civilian population some time ago, where the buildings were now used as billets for troops in transit to the front line, a few miles further east. Next morning Sid and the battalion resumed their journey, arriving at Waldweisstroff, another evacuated village that would be their base when they were not on duty on the front line. This was another mile or so further east, and the huge fortifications of the Maginot Line lay some miles to the west of them. There was a forbidding atmosphere about the area. The deserted villages were depressing, and unlike the Belgian border area there was no civilian life to be seen anywhere.

The region they were in was to the south of the border with Luxembourg, part of the province of Alsace-Lorraine, which had been contested by Germany and France for many years. On the other side of the present border was the German Saarland; further south were the Vosges mountains. The area was a farming district, producing Moselle wine, but none of that was in evidence now.

The following morning the battalion moved forward to replace the 5th Battalion Northamptonshire Regiment, who were directly on the front line, or, as the French called it, the *ligne de contact*. If the Germans realized that a new unit was moving forward and the current one was withdrawing, there was a chance that they would mount a sudden raid to take advantage of the new men's inexperience and to exploit any break in the chain of command. The replacement was therefore carried out as covertly as possible, with the 2nd Warwickshires moving slowly up to the line in small groups of two or three towards the observation posts, machine-gun emplacements and slit trenches and the same numbers of Northamptonshires moving back. This dribbling in of the replacements took almost the whole day and was not completed until 17.50. As Sid moved up to the front he heard for the first time the sound of guns fired in anger. French artillery opened up a barrage from behind him and he heard the whistle of the 75mm shells like an express train passing over him. There had been no warning that the battery would open fire and at first he thought that they were under attack. He nearly jumped out of his skin.

The battalion HQ was set up in a village called Bizing and the front line went through the next village, Grindorff, barely a mile to the east. This was really a small hamlet which had a few houses down one main street, with a church, whose bell tower was used as an observation post, at one end. At the other end of the main street was the frontier, marked by thick coils of barbed wire and signs warning of the presence of land mines. Beyond was a vague no man's land. Then the enemy barbed wire started and beyond that was Germany itself.

This line between the two combatant armies was not deeply entrenched. The front was very fluid, with patrols from both sides penetrating several miles into enemy territory, but men would be stationed in Grindorff for up to twenty-four hours at a time.

The battalion started their patrols on their first night on

the front line. They left the abandoned village as darkness fell, crouching low, crawling along the zigzag path through the barbed wire and making their way quietly through wooded areas that stretched north and south along the sloping valley of a narrow river. They went out in search of enemy patrols, and as they made their way along the side of the valley they looked for signs that the Germans were preparing new positions or observation posts, or for anything – like fresh scratches on stone bridges, or damaged undergrowth – that would reveal that the enemy had recently been operating in the area.

There were two types of patrol. The first was a fighting patrol, where the men made as much noise as possible, hoping to attract a German patrol and engage them in a firefight. Sometimes they would shout out, 'Hey, Jerry, come to me then – I'm over here.' These patrols were large, heavily armed and would often divide, one section trying to set a trap while a smaller section created the disturbance, acting as the bait. The other type was a reconnaissance patrol, and on these it was important to remain silent, gathering information about the enemy's movements in the hope of setting up a later raid along a known enemy route. A lot of information was gathered from the observation post in the church tower. It offered a view about three miles into Germany and Sid, when he was on duty here during the day, could see the movements of German army lorries, patrols and work details. If he saw any new concentration of vehicles or men, their position would be marked and a patrol would be sent out that night to investigate.

Sid's first patrol was with the company CO, Major Cecil Chichester-Constable, a man who had already won the

Military Cross in the First World War. They had been in Grindorff for just two days when Chichester-Constable led his party of fourteen men, moving through the deserted houses down to the end of the village, where they lay up in an empty barn until it was dark. Then they left the village and followed a stream to a ford across the river. Here the patrol split up, one section to go and investigate an abandoned French mill to make sure that the enemy had not tried to use the building as a forward base or observation post. Sid was part of this one. They approached their target slowly, listening for any hint of an enemy presence. Finally two of them burst into the building, but the mill was still derelict, filled with rubbish and open to the sky. Chichester-Constable remarked that Jerry could find something better than this if he wanted.

The battalion found that life on the front line was completely different from that on the Belgian border. Death was much closer and might strike out of the blue. On the first day, when they had slowly moved into Grindorff and the French had fired their barrage, Sid had realized that no exercises could prepare you for the first momentary confusion caused by the outbreak of deadly fire. After a while, however, he became accustomed to gunfire, though he was never happy on patrol. The most dreadful times were when he was bringing up the rear, keeping a watchful eye out that the patrol was not being followed. He felt particularly vulnerable then, expecting a bullet to hit him at any moment. He knew how easy it was to walk into an ambush. A week after they had been in place a reconnaissance patrol had left the village and made its way into the wood nearby. After crossing the stream as they normally did they had split up, one party heading along the bank to the west, the other going through the wood. Sid was in the first party. They could hear a dog barking. The German patrols were sometimes accompanied by Alsatians, which they used as tracker dogs. The officer in charge of Sid's patrol, Captain Fisher, decided to move up the side of a hill and wait, so he told the men to split up and cover both sides of a path that straggled up the hill. They waited, silently. Hearing the sound of voices, Sid tensed, straining his eyes against the darkness. A German patrol was moving up the track that they had previously taken. There was the sound of boots on stones and the clink of metal, then silhouettes appeared against a line of trees. Captain Fisher fired at the leader, who fell. The second man in the German troop pulled the trigger on his machine gun, the flashes splitting the darkness, but with shots now coming at them from both sides of the track the Germans realized they were in a deadly trap and retreated, spraying machine-gun bullets into the trees. The night was filled with a cacophony of gunfire. Sid fired wildly, deafened and blinded by the muzzle-flash of his own gun. It seemed to take a long time before his night vision returned.

The battalion suffered no casualties that night, but they had killed the leading German. He was a lieutenant, a big man whose body was far too heavy for the men to carry back. They took all the papers and identification tags off the body, emptying his pack and his pockets before making their way back to Grindorff.

It was clear to Sid that the border was a dangerous place, where death lurked unseen. The patrols were nerve-racking and Sid's instinct, which he could barely control, was just to blast away at anything that moved rather than waiting to see what it was.

The most frightening moment for Sid, however, came when he was in a forward listening post. These were shallow pits in the ground covered by shrubs; they were dug in the no man's land contested by the nightly patrols. As far as Sid knew, every sector of the front had similar positions. The hole in the ground, which was little more than a foxhole three or four feet deep, was meant to conceal a man for several hours so that he could observe any enemy movements.

On this particular night, Sid went out with a patrol at the normal time, but took water and some iron rations with him. The patrol passed by the observation post in the nearby wood and Sid got into it via a short tunnel. Once inside he tried to make himself comfortable and settle down until a patrol returned to recover him. A field telephone connected him to the signallers at company HQ in Grindorff.

It was a lonely night. At first Sid struggled to keep awake. He wanted to phone the signallers to talk to someone, not to feel so lonely, but he knew that would see him put on a charge straight away. Strange noises in the wood, from the wind or wild animals, startled him, sending a jolt of fear through him. Then suddenly he heard noises that he knew were human! Within just a few yards from his concealed pit was a German patrol. They were moving cautiously, talking in whispers to each other. Sid's hand started shaking. He should have picked up the handset and spoken to the company HQ so that a patrol could be sent out to have a crack at the enemy, but he was too scared even to pick up the phone, let alone speak into the mouthpiece.

The Germans were stopping. They had come to a halt in front of him. He could barely breathe for fear of discovery. The enemy patrol waited probably for half an hour, but it felt like an age to Sid, whose nerves were at screaming point. Were they waiting for his patrol to return for him? Did they know there was something suspicious in the area? How could he warn people without making a noise? He felt doomed.

Then the Germans left. As Sid heard them slowly moving away he wanted to laugh and cry simultaneously. He was covered in a cold sweat and shaking. His patrol finally returned to recover him and reported the presence of the German patrol back to HQ. A Bren-gun carrier section was mobilized in case an enemy attack was in the offing, but the night ended without any incident.

The effect on Sid of this close encounter with the enemy was so obvious that nothing was said about his failure to use the field telephone, although his mates in the section ribbed him unmercifully about it. Sid never told anybody, but he started to have nightmares about being trapped.

German activity in the area increased considerably in the month of April. There were constant skirmishes along the battalion's positions and attempts by some German patrols to infiltrate behind them. The enemy also started to establish mortar posts on the edge of the woods and mortar shells began to hit the battalion's rear areas. There was heavy artillery fire across the border almost every day, with the French 75mm guns targeting working parties, followed by return fire from German batteries. Sid remembers that the Germans used a frightening tactic to 'sanitize' areas of no man's land by firing a barrage of shells on a small area, following this up with a line of up to forty men who would march across the blasted area, shooting anyone who was left alive. It was a very effective way of destroying any forward listening posts.

The Germans were becoming markedly more aggressive, and on 10 April they mounted an ambush inside Grindorff itself. It was an incident that increased the men's respect for their CO, Chichester-Constable, whom they already regarded as a firebrand. A patrol went out to search some old French trenches for any signs of enemy infiltration and Sid went part way with them to climb up to the observation post in the church tower. From here he could keep watch for any signs of enemy activity and cover the men from his company. If they came under attack they would fire signal rockets and Sid could raise the alarm with the company HQ. He saw nothing; the night was cold and dark, but peaceful. But when the patrol was due to return, firing broke out in the village on the other side of the wire. Automatics in some of the abandoned houses were sending stabs of flame into the main street and there were two blasts from grenades. Then more gunfire started up from the street. A German patrol had wormed its way into the far end of the village and set up an ambush. Sid couldn't see who was who in the darkness. Gun flashes were spitting fire in all directions across the street and someone – it turned out to be Chichester-Constable – ran up the street firing his Tommy gun while grenades exploded behind him. Sid fired a flare from the Very pistol and saw Chichester-Constable leaping over coils of barbed wire into the British sector. A soldier – Sid thought it was a German – lay in the road behind him.

The firing continued intermittently and the company HQ telephoned the observation post, asking if any more of the patrol had come in. They hadn't. Sid was told that Chichester-Constable was returning and that he should report any sign of the patrol. By this time the firing had stopped. Chichester-Constable and more men came back to Grindorff, and the first patrol gathered itself together at the other end of the village and made its way up the main street. Four of the men in the patrol had been hit and wounded. Private Whitehouse had shot the German soldier now lying in the street as he tried to kill Chichester-Constable with a grenade. Chichester-Constable decided to leave the dead soldier there, and waited quietly near the body in case the German patrol returned for their comrade. They didn't. In the iron-grey half-light of dawn Sid saw the big figure of his commanding officer, his Tommy gun held at the ready, crouched by the dead soldier waiting for more of the enemy to appear. He was, said Sid, 'a ruthless bastard. He hated the Germans.' Eventually a patrol went down to him and they carried the body back to company HQ. The dead soldier's pockets were stuffed with letters from his wife, photographs and, according to the adjutant, a pornographic anti-clerical drawing.

Two days later, C Company's position further along in Hartbusch was shelled by the Germans and there was a heavy raid on some French positions further south. Although the raid was successfully repulsed, twelve French soldiers were killed. On 14 April a large retaliatory raid by the French met a catastrophe and the entire party of thirty men were killed or captured; only one officer, who was very badly wounded, managed to get back to his own lines. Then on the 16th Sid heard the sound of very heavy shelling to the south. One of their sister battalions in the brigade, the Gloucestershire Regiment, was coming under attack. After the bombardment eased fifty enemy soldiers, backed up by mortars, tried to break through the lines. Four men of the Gloucesters were killed and eight wounded, while four others were missing and it was assumed the Germans had taken them. The enemy left six of their own dead.

These heavy, aggressive raids coming within a few days suggested that something was up. Were the Germans getting ready for a big push? Or were they also trying to blood new and inexperienced troops? No one knew, or if they did they weren't going to tell Sid. As far as he was concerned, his phoney war had ended a few weeks ago. It was now extremely noisy, violent and dangerous. He was relieved when on 19 April the battalion was pulled out and moved back to Metz to begin their redeployment back to their old billets at Le Forest on the Belgian border.

5

THE ENEMY'S PLAN

September 1939–February 1940

Sid was relieved to escape the intense and permanent conflict that marked the French border with Germany, but the constant shelling and the cross-border skirmishes were misleading. The area that Sid was leaving was really a sideshow in the greater German plan for war in Europe.

On 27 September 1939, a few weeks after Britain and France had declared war on Germany, Hitler made it clear that sooner or later he would attack western Europe, and the German Army High Command, or OKH (*Oberkommando des Heeres*), started to draw up its plans. The original scheme was for the main thrust to advance through Holland, Belgium and northern France, with the strategic aim of defeating the French and Allied armies, creating an occupied buffer to protect the vital factories and coal mines of the Ruhr and providing a jumping-off point to launch air and sea attacks against Britain. The plan produced in these first four weeks of the war provided for German forces to reach the French frontier, but was vague about the conduct of the campaign after that.

The plans were presented to Hitler on 25 October. He didn't like them. They would not deliver the decisive blow he dreamed of and they might well create circumstances like those that led to the debilitating war of attrition in France and Belgium that had proved such a disaster for Germany in the First World War. In fact, the first phase of 'Plan Yellow', a frontal assault through Belgium, was similar to the first phase of the Schlieffen Plan, the blueprint for the war with France in 1914.

The most important war aim, directed Hitler, was the defeat of the Anglo-French armies so that large areas of French territory could be seized. A repeat of the long, static trench warfare in Flanders against the Allies would only lead to disaster. The General Staff reworked the plan, coming up with the new formulation that the strategic aim was 'to engage and defeat as strong a portion of the French and Allied armies as possible in northern France and Belgium, thereby creating favourable conditions for the continuation of the war against England and France'. It was at best a slight modification of the original, but Colonel General Walther von Brauchitsch, commander-in-chief of the German Army, and his chief of staff, General Franz Halder, were committed to the concept of a main northerly thrust. As a result, German forces were assembled along their western frontier, with the most powerful in the north. This was Army Group B, under the command of Colonel General Fedor von Bock. Bock was a dour Prussian, the inheritor of a long family tradition of military service, who believed that there was no greater honour than to die for the Fatherland. His forces, made up of forty-three divisions formed into four armies, stretched from the Dutch border to that of Luxembourg. These armies would be responsible for the main attack, striking west through Belgium, then heading into northern France.

South of Army Group B was Army Group A, which was commanded by Colonel General Gerd von Rundstedt. This group's forces were considerably smaller, with twenty-two divisions formed into two armies. They faced the Luxembourg border and their task was to guard the southern flank of Army Group B as it advanced into Belgium. South of Luxembourg, the Franco-German border was dominated by the fortifications of the Maginot Line, and here Army Group C, under Colonel General Wilhelm von Leeb, with eighteen divisions, would make feint attacks to pin down the French forces along the frontier.

The commander of Army Group B, Rundstedt, who had arrived in post in October from the successful campaign in Poland, was unhappy with the overall outline of the planned offensive. Rundstedt was a successful and able soldier, the product of an elite Prussian military academy. Like most of the German generals, he had fought in the First World War. He had retired in 1938 at the age of sixty-three, but was recalled a year later to lead an army group in the invasion of Poland. Rundstedt, despite his age, was a modernizer. He had a better appreciation of the role of armoured divisions than some of his younger contemporaries and had the benefit of an intelligent chief of staff, General Erich von Manstein. Rundstedt argued that, overall, Plan Yellow was flawed because the operation would be successful only if the Allied forces were wiped out and cut off from any reinforcements. The frontal assault by Army Group B would not achieve this, but his Army Group A, if it were sufficiently strengthened, would be able to do the job. Brauchitsch disagreed, but made some concession to his subordinate by assigning an armoured division to his army group.

At this point – it was now November – Hitler again intervened, telling the OKH to create a group of mobile troops that would be able to advance through the Ardennes to Sedan. Brauchitsch responded by sending a corps of two armoured divisions, a motorized infantry division and two motorized regiments, under the command of General Heinz Guderian, to Army Group A. Rundstedt had not yet finished his own war of attrition, however. At a conference of army commanders held on 21 November he and General Manstein tried to demonstrate that Army Group A needed to be enlarged by the addition of another whole army. Brauchitsch held his ground.

The argument continued and, despite the movement of some units from Army Group B to Army Group A and the allocation of others from the reserves, Plan Yellow remained substantially the same: that the main offensive would be a frontal attack by Bock's Army Group B across the Belgian plain. It was these plans that were revealed to the Belgian and French High Command in January when the German reconnaissance plane flown by Major Hoenmanns got lost in fog and made a forced landing in Belgium.

While the Allies were debating the authenticity of the captured documents and placing their troops on high alert for a possible offensive on 17 January, the German plans were themselves coming under even greater attack from Rundstedt.

He had written a long document which he sent to Brauchitsch with a request that it be submitted to Hitler. He took up once again the argument that the existing plan was little more than a reworking of the old First World War Schlieffen Plan and that it would lead to the same stalemate. The offensive needed, in his view, to be decisive. The attack should annihilate Allied forces on land and in the air, and the aim was to eliminate 'the continental sword of the English and then to attack England by air and sea'. Plan Yellow still aimed for the occupation of the Belgian coastline and this was also, according to Rundstedt, not enough. The lessons of the First World War were clear. Britain could be defeated only by cutting her Atlantic shipping lanes, and to do this the whole of the French coast had to fall into German hands. The document produced by Rundstedt and his staff was more than just a critique of an existing plan. It was an attempt to clarify Germany's war aims in the west. It identified Britain as the ultimate adversary and argued that she had to be isolated from the continent, and from her empire.

Brauchitsch refused to submit the document to Hitler, but the arguments were achieving wider currency and were beginning to have effect. Hitler was impatient with what he saw as the conservatism of the General Staff, and he kept nagging away at the question of where the main attack should take place. It didn't make sense to concentrate the main thrust where the enemy was expecting it. In February 1940 Rundstedt's chief of staff, Lieutenant General Manstein, was promoted and given command of an infantry corps. Before taking up his post he had lunch at the Reich's Chancellery in Berlin with Hitler. Also at the working lunch were General Alfred Jodl, chief of operations (or supreme commander) of the High Command of the Armed Forces, or OKW (Oberkommando der Wehrmacht), and General Erwin Rommel, a young soldier, one of Hitler's favourites, who was shortly to assume command of a Panzer division in Rundstedt's Army Group A. Here over the dining table Manstein elaborated on Rundstedt's alternative views of Plan Yellow. It's unclear if this was the decisive incident behind the change of focus for the assault on the Allies, but Plan Yellow was now radically overhauled. The following day Brauchitsch reported to Hitler that the area of responsibility of Army Group A had expanded and that its forward units were to be significantly strengthened.

Rundstedt had achieved everything that he wanted. Brauchitsch, however, now that he had lost the argument, went further than any of his critics had suggested. The final Plan Yellow, produced on 24 February, saw a huge expansion of Army Group A, and with it the burden of the main attack. Two armies and most of the armoured formations were taken from Bock's Army Group B and given to Rundstedt. They would advance across Luxembourg and the Ardennes in the south of Belgium, then into France. The strategic aim of the plan was indeed to cut off the Allied armies in the north, surround them, and reach the French coast along the valley of the River Somme.

The forces aligned against the Allies in the west were now considerable. Army Group B in the north was formed from twenty-eight divisions, three of them armoured. Army Group A was now a massive forty-four divisions, seven of which were armoured. In addition, there was a very large reserve of another forty-five divisions, estimated to be three times the size of the reserve of the French Army.

German strength was not only in numbers. The armoured divisions, as we shall see, were equipped with better tanks, and their tactical use in battle was much better appreciated and developed. German artillery was better and more powerful. Moreover, the Luftwaffe, the German air force, was equipped and organized to play a key role in the battlefield, assisting the advance of the land forces. Assigned to cooperate with Army Groups A and B were two Luftwaffe fleets that numbered in total around 3,700 aircraft.

There was one other advantage possessed by the German forces that had been overlooked by the Allies. The German assault had been scheduled twice previously, once in November 1939, the second time in January 1940. On both occasions the forward units had begun the advance to their operational start line before the attack was cancelled. But the troops had not moved back to their original locations. They remained at the point at which they had received the order to stand down. Plan Yellow had originally allowed for six days' mobilization before the start of the battle. By the time the last Plan Yellow was disseminated, German troops were able to go into action with less than twenty-four hours' warning.

By the time Sid was moving back to Rumegies, the enemy's units and their plans were in excellent shape.

6

MOVING UP TO THE FRONT

10–13 May

Early in the morning on 10 May Les Clarke hurtled along a narrow country road. The exhaust of his 500cc BSA motorbike filled his ears and his battledress whipped in the slipstream. He took the bends wide and at speed. There wouldn't be any other traffic this early. In fifteen minutes he arrived at the brigade HQ. Telephones rang, typewriters were clattering – Les had never seen such activity so early, and the atmosphere was earnest and urgent. It wasn't long before he heard the news. Jerry was on the march.

Two hours later the news was confirmed and announced to the world. Throughout the BEF, in billets and in every unit's HQ, men listened to the wireless as the BBC broadcast on the seven o'clock news that Belgium and Holland had been invaded by heavy concentrations of German soldiers supported by tanks. By then Les had returned to his battalion at Ancoisne with a sheaf of orders and the first situation report of the day. He was waiting for more documents from the adjutant, more orders to take to the various companies, but the rest of the battalion's routine seemed unchanged by the sudden events on the German border. He had heard a great deal of anti-aircraft fire the previous evening, though not from anywhere close, but there seemed to be less enemy air activity this morning. The men were forming up for the normal trenching details and breakfast was served at the usual time. Later that afternoon a route regulation party was put together, ready to move forward and make a reconnaissance of the road into Belgium, but there seemed to be no sign of any urgent advance. News of what was happening was scarce.

Events, however, were moving at lightning speed, faster than anybody in the Allied armed forces was able to grasp. Very early in the morning of that Friday, the 10th, Belgian troops in observation posts along their border had become aware of large German troop movements and they soon saw that an invasion was imminent. At four o'clock the Belgian foreign minister was driven to the British ambassador's residence, where he formally asked the British government for help in resisting the invasion of his country. At 5.30 that morning German troops had crossed the frontiers of France, Belgium, Holland and Luxembourg. A report from the 50th Division HQ, in reserve, sums up the situation in the immediate hours after the German attack. British airfields had been bombed at Arras, Le Touquet and Abbeville, and French bases at Berm, St-Omer and Calais had also been hit. Two enemy bombers had been shot down and the surviving crew of one of them, a Heinkel 111, had been captured and taken to the British II Corps HQ. The northern part of

Brussels had been bombed, and reports were received that Antwerp too had suffered air raids and that buildings in part of the city were burning. The report also detailed the destruction of road bridges over the River Meuse, which ran close to the French border with Belgium and Holland, along with the demolition of other canal bridges by the Belgian Army to hold up the German advance. Belgian and Dutch troops were reported moving east to engage the Germans, who were seen to be building pontoons to lay a prefabricated bridge across the river at Groesbeek. German artillery units were assembling at a site east of Roermond, a Dutch town on the Meuse.

French Army HQ sent a message to all its units, and to the British Expeditionary Force, calling a general alert; then another message said that the Supreme Command had issued orders for Plan D, the long-prepared-for manoeuvre to meet the Germans along a line drawn up along the River Dyle in Belgium.

General Gamelin, commander-in-chief of the land forces, issued an Order of the Day in the afternoon at 14.05. It read:

> The Attack which we have been anticipating since last October has been launched this morning. It is the beginning of a fight to the death between Germany and ourselves. The watchword for all the Allies is: calm, energy, confidence. As Marshal Pétain said 24 years ago: 'Nous les aurons [We'll get them].'

When Larry Uren at Villers-au-Bois stood to after breakfast on 10 May, news of the German attack was of course circulating, but the 1/7th Queen's made no physical preparation for moving. They, like Les's battalion of the Durham Light Infantry, were part of the 50th Division and were held in reserve. As Larry's comrades had only recently arrived from the UK, and had moved forward from Rennes only a few days previously, it was a good thing that they were not expected to advance to meet the enemy. The battalion HQ was asked to forward to the brigade HQ preliminary plans for a move to Chelers, but most of the companies were forming up transport and provisions for the next day's exercise with the brigade, which would test the battalion on its efficiency and preparedness for a withdrawal.

The British forces in the front of the advance into Belgium were three divisions, the 1st, 2nd and 3rd, and in the lead was the 12th Lancers, a mechanized cavalry regiment, who arrived at the line of the Dyle first.

Stanley Chappell's 2nd Regiment Royal Horse Artillery was part of the II Corps artillery, in support of General Montgomery's 3rd Division, and they received orders on the 10th to move out immediately. The guns with their limbers of ready-use ammunition had been hitched up behind the quad tractors and by 13.00 they were on the road. Stan sat in the back of the quad, looking out. The village and the vehicle park in the grounds of the large manor house just outside it disappeared from view. The regiment had spent days digging in and preparing their positions, with carefully plotted firing lines, a series of worked-out range settings, and the fortified revetments for each gun connected by well-drained communication trenches. Now all this work was being abandoned for a rapid deployment to a country for which they had inadequate maps and absolutely no previous reconnaissance. It wasn't just the unnecessary labour that he and his mates had put in that concerned Stanley; it was the foolhardy abandonment of a well-sited artillery battery. He just couldn't see the logic in it. Surely a well-prepared position was better than a poorly prepared position? But he had no influence over anything. If he had put his opinions into words he might have found that the staff at the GHQ in Arras would have agreed with him.

The plan that they were working to, Plan D, had been worked up by the French High Command. It was based on the belief that the Dutch and Belgian forces would be quite capable of holding up the German advance for the three or four days needed for the BEF to establish itself properly along the River Dyle, deep inside Belgium. Back in the autumn of 1939 there had been some discussion about the best response to an expected German attack. The French High Command, in the shape of General Gamelin, assumed that the main thrust would come through Belgium and perhaps Holland. As we have seen, this was the original German plan. Gamelin and the rest of the French General Staff did not take account of any changes, however. They were fixed on the idea that the Maginot Line and the terrain of the Ardennes region were a sufficient barrier to an enemy advance further south. General Gort and his chief of staff, Lieutenant General Henry Pownall, contributed to these discussions, but under the terms of his appointment Gort had no power over the policy that was finally adopted.

The French decided that the Allies should advance into Belgium and meet the enemy there, rather than wait for them on the French border. The question was whether to establish a front along the line of the River Scheldt – or Escaut, as the French called it – or the River Dyle further east in Belgian territory. The alternative options were known, respectively, as Plan E and Plan D. There were disadvantages and benefits to both. The Scheldt was a longer line to hold, but it meant that Allied troops would need only a day to reach it. The Dyle line was shorter, and would free up the French Seventh Army with its seven divisions to try to link up with the Dutch Army at Antwerp and provide some cover to the Belgian Army in the north. An extra advantage was that, being further to the east, there were two other rivers to the west, the Dendre and the Scheldt, that could provide a deeper defensive position in front of the French border. The disadvantages were that it would take some of the Allied forces longer to reach the line. The British Expeditionary Force in particular would have to make an advance of over sixty miles without the benefit of any route reconnaissance. This is precisely what Stanley was doing.

There was also another assumption in Plan D, and it was about something that was beyond the control of the Allies. If it required several days for the French and British forces to reach the River Dyle and establish a defensive line, then the Belgium Army would, obviously, have to hold the German advance on their forward line for as long as the Allies needed to get into position. Whether it was possible for the Belgians to achieve this was unknown. The Belgian government's rigid adherence to its policy of neutrality meant that there had been almost no discussion about what plans to adopt if, as seemed likely, death and destruction swept once more through Europe.

Which of the two plans to implement was a decision that was going to be taken at the last moment, and the British General Headquarters had a full set of operational instructions for either eventuality.

As we have seen, on the morning of 10 May, just before six o'clock, the French Supreme Command issued orders for the immediate execution of Plan D, the advance to the River Dyle. It appeared on the face of it the most intelligent option to take – if the Belgian Army could stop the Germans close to their border, if the Dutch Army could hold out, and if the advance through Holland and northern Belgium was the main thrust of the German advance. All these were absolutely vital questions. The answers would not be long in coming.

So it was that the long column of trucks, quad tractors and artillery pieces of the 2nd Royal Horse Artillery wound its way through the towns and countryside of north-eastern France later that afternoon to enter the outskirts of Lille, just a few kilometres from the Belgian border. Stanley was struck by the hushed, sombre atmosphere of the town. The streets, it seemed, had been abandoned by the residents; there was not a living soul to be seen. The citizens of Lille had put up the shutters, with windows and doors closed, and not a single light showing. It seemed to be a fortress town, holding its breath in apprehension of what was to come. At the time, Stanley thought that the people of Lille were overdoing it. The Germans were still in Belgium and their advance would be stopped by the advancing French and British troops. If anyone should be apprehensive, he thought, it was him, heading for a battle with the German Army, which, from all that he had heard and learned about the previous war, he knew to be a ruthless enemy.

The artillery column stopped at night for food and rest, then continued at first light the following day. General Gort was prepared to risk the danger from air strikes for the sake of the greater speed the convoys could achieve by day. By

17.50 on the 11th Stanley had crossed the Belgian frontier and the regiment was making steady progress. Then they came to a halt. There was an air raid warning, so they all climbed out of the quads for shelter. Stanley was able to take cover in the hedgerow, but the leading part of the column, which was more than a mile ahead, was trapped in the narrow streets of the small old town of Aalst. German bombers were targeting the town, not the long column of guns and their tractors, but even so a member of I Battery was killed by a bomb and two other gunners were wounded.

The raid over, the gun batteries drove on through the town. It was the first time that any of the regiment had, even indirectly, come under fire. Stanley had been alarmed, though the raid had been some way ahead, and the blasted buildings, the rubble in the streets of the town and the dazed, shocked faces of some of the civilians as they drove past reduced them to silence, apart from the odd curse.

They drove on to reach Brussels, where the mood was completely different. The roads were lined with cheering, enthusiastic civilians and the houses were festooned with flags – Union Jacks amongst the French and Belgian colours. By two o'clock in the morning of 12 May Stanley's regiment had reached the outskirts of Louvain. The River Dyle passed through the western side of the town – a busy waterway, dredged and canalized for river traffic. The regiment's 25-pounders were going to be sited so that they could provide covering fire to both east and west banks of the river, as well as lending fire support to the 3rd Division's Guards regiments, which were advancing to make contact with the enemy.

Lieutenant Gibbons, Stanley's troop commander, had

selected an area to the west of Louvain, in a semi-rural district, with the four guns ranged up in front of the command post. The next morning Stanley saw that there were one or two isolated houses and a farmyard, but mostly rolling fields stretched east and south. It was a beautiful spring day in the countryside, but it was suddenly shattered by the shout of 'Gas! Gas!' Stan fumbled for his gas mask and cape, and for the next half hour he got hotter and sweatier as he struggled to make sense of muffled orders from the lieutenant and to talk to the rest of the gun crews. After thirty minutes in which there had been no explosions from shells or bombs, and no sign of any clouds of gas or chemicals, they took the masks off. Their faces were a deep red, with stark white crease marks where the rubber masks had pressed against their skin. Whether it was a genuine alert or just an exercise Stan never discovered, but no one ever shouted 'Gas!' again.

The nearby houses were empty and there was nobody in the farmyard. A cow, its udder swollen, had walked into the yard, lowing piteously and obviously in need of milking. Stan had never milked a cow before, and nor had anyone else in the troop. But Stanley, who served on the plotting table, didn't need to be on instant readiness to man a gun, so he volunteered to walk over to the yard. The beast was quite cooperative and after a few minutes fresh milk was hissing in a warm stream into a bucket. There were chickens in a run nearby. After filling a bucket with meal, he went into the chicken run and, after some frantic scrambling on the ground, the chickens squawking to raise the roof, he grabbed one and quickly wrung its neck. He stood there, the chicken twitching, its wings flapping spasmodically. He would never have done what he had just done at home, or even back in the billets in Ancoisne. But now it didn't matter. The rules didn't apply. He went back to the troop with fresh milk and a chicken for the pot. It looked as though the living was going to be good, at least for the short term.

While the chicken was cooking Stan decided to explore along the road towards Louvain. Everywhere was deserted. He came upon a large café and walked in through the front door down a short flight of steps. Everything was neat and tidy, as though it were just on the verge of opening – but the regular customers had fled. It was like a stage set. A door slammed in the back and Stanley realized that he was alone, unarmed, in a foreign country close to the front line. He waited, his heart in his mouth, as sunlight streamed through the windows and reflected off the bottles behind the bar. There were no more sounds, so he headed out of the door and walked quickly away, back to the battery. The chicken was cooking over a small petrol cooker; someone had thrown some vegetables into the pot and it smelled delicious. There was hot tea with fresh milk. This didn't seem like war at all. It was very different from the scene back at the barracks of the carnage at Néry. It was 13 May.

7

THE GERMAN OFFENSIVE BEGINS

10–16 May

Sid Lewis's 2nd Battalion Royal Warwickshire Regiment stood to on 10 May to be told that the German Army had invaded Belgium and Holland. They had been back from their posts on the border in the Saarland for just over a month. The news of the German invasion came as no real surprise to them, and, although their fights with the enemy had been vicious and nerve-racking, Sid knew that their recent contact had been little more than skirmishes. It could only get worse from now on.

The fighting that they did see on that day was in the air, where dogfights between British and German aircraft were played out above them. One ended, to the great satisfaction of Sid and his mates, with an evil-looking German twin-engined bomber crashing to the ground while two white parachutes slowly descended. Other than that, the first day of the German offensive was strangely quiet. The battalion was part of the 48th Division, and in the greater scheme of Plan D they formed part of the reserve for I Corps. The 1st and 2nd Divisions would advance up to the River Dyle, a move which was expected might take up to ninety hours, and then the 48th Division would go forward. So there was no real activity until the morning of 13 May, when the CO, Major Philip Hicks, left at ten in the morning with the French liaison agent to make a reconnaissance of the route into Belgium. A handful of men from the various companies went with them. Later that day the transport arrived, then Sid and the rest of his company were informed that they were to move out that night.

Ten trucks arrived at the company HQ at eight o'clock. They loaded up their kit into 15cwt trucks and climbed aboard the personnel lorries. At eleven o'clock that night they finally headed out, joining the long line of lorries from the division's three brigades that went through the French countryside, crossing into Belgium, where they passed through Tournai and onwards to their destination in some woods near Waterloo, south of Brussels. The lorries' head-lights were darkened, but there were small red lights attached to the rear axles for the following driver to see. Small lamps were also placed at strategic points along the route. The major hazard was fatigue; occasionally a driver fell asleep at the wheel, the lorry slowly coming off the road and toppling into a ditch or scraping through trees.

It was a rough overnight journey, past fields hidden in darkness and through seemingly deserted towns. Villages were filled with the sound of slow-moving lorries – it must have seemed endless to anyone living there. By six o'clock the next morning they had arrived, not at their destination but at a road junction near a small community called Hal. Sid climbed down, tired from his journey in the back of the lorry, where he had had an uncomfortable, intermittent sleep. The journey wasn't over, however – now he had to march another fifteen miles on foot. They were camped close to the Lion of Waterloo, a high mound topped with the statue of a lion, which commemorated the defeat of Napoleon at the Battle of Waterloo in 1815. Sid had time to climb the hundreds of steps up to the very top. An air raid on Brussels was taking place to the north and from the top of the monument Sid had the illusion that he was level with the dive-bombers circling over the city.

The battalion was to take up position along the line of the main road that led by the side of the wood, running south from Brussels to Waterloo. The wood, with tracks and paths marked on the map that might be usable by patrols or Bren-gun carriers – it was impossible to tell without investigation – was a difficult place to hold. Some patrols were sent off to reconnoitre the routes through the woods, while others went south-east to inspect fire trenches and anti-tank positions that had been dug by the Belgian Army. They seemed to Sid and others in the platoon to be badly built, almost useless. The weather was very hot and the sun shone. Belgian troops passed along the road, as did streams of civilians heading towards the city. Nobody was particularly friendly.

It was two o'clock in the afternoon of the 14th. The British Expeditionary Force was occupying a part of Belgium with a front line that stretched along the River Dyle for about seventeen miles. Stan's artillery battery, which was in support of Montgomery's 3rd Division defending Louvain, was close to the northern boundary of the British area of responsibility, where it met positions manned by the Belgian Army. Plan D called for the French Seventh Army to advance to join forces with them and with the Dutch Army as well. To the south of Louvain was the British 1st Division, then further south was the 2nd Division, whose edge met that of the French First Army.

Events were rapidly overtaking the Allies' plan. It had been assumed that the British and French forces would have ninety hours – almost four days – to advance to the planned lines along the Dyle and then to Antwerp. The BEF had done this, but the Germans were advancing much faster than anyone had expected. By Sunday, 12 May, German columns had made fierce inroads into Holland and the Dutch Army was in confusion. There were reports of a long column of German troops ten miles north of Arnhem and another column, almost a mile and a half long, on the road to Hertogenbosch. The bridges over the Albert Canal and the River Meuse at Maastricht had been captured and German troops were pushing westwards from here.

These bridges over the Meuse on the Belgian–Dutch frontier were of vital strategic importance for the Belgian Army and they had sought to secure the area by building a huge modern fort at Eben-Emael, just south of Maastricht, where the Albert Canal and the Meuse were connected by a series of locks. The fort was excavated out of a limestone hill and extended for almost a thousand yards in each direction. The gun turrets in the fort were placed so that they could defend bridges over the canal and river at three separate locations. Manned by over seven hundred men, it was believed to be impregnable and was absolutely crucial to the Belgian defence of their border with Holland east of Brussels and Antwerp. The Belgians had to hold this border for several days to allow the French Seventh Army to advance and link up with them and, they hoped, with the Dutch Army north of Antwerp.

The fort barely survived for twenty-four hours after the start of the fighting. On the morning of the 10th German gliders landed on the top of the hill that formed the roof of the fortress and seventy-eight airborne engineers spread out and set demolition charges that prevented the gun turrets from coming into action. The fort's garrison was trapped inside by the glider-borne troops on the roof, and this allowed follow-on forces of German parachute troops to land and capture the bridges over the Albert Canal without suffering any serious casualties. The following day German soldiers from an infantry division surrounded the fort and the garrison surrendered.

Next morning a situation report from the British General HQ, circulated to all the divisional headquarters, detailed the German advances. The enemy movements were mainly from Münchengladbach in Germany into Holland, and there was a column one and a half miles long north of Arnhem. The enemy columns had advanced over newly built bridges that crossed the Meuse at three separate places. Moreover, there was increasing enemy pressure westwards from Maastricht. The report identified the various units in German Army Group B, which was spearheading the northern advance. Ominously, in view of the Allied reliance on wholesale and coordinated demolition of bridges over the various rivers and canals that stood in the way of any advancing army, the report said that units with amphibious tanks had been observed.

The onward march of the German Army against the

Dutch and Belgian Armies was worrying enough for General Gort, but another, even more serious situation was developing to the south of the British positions, which was not mentioned in the situation reports.

The French had assumed for many years that the German Army would not attack across Luxembourg and the southern part of Belgium over the hilly, wooded region known as the Ardennes. The terrain in this area was thought by the French High Command to be unsuitable for tanks or motorized military forces. The frontier at this point was intended to be covered by the French Ninth Army, a force that was not considered to be in the first rank or at the same level of professionalism and training as either the Seventh Army or the forces on the border with Belgium to the north. General Gamelin, the French commander-in-chief, believed that this view was confirmed by the documents that had been captured in January when the light plane carrying them had made a forced landing in Belgium. So convinced was Gamelin that these documents revealed German plans that he had fully committed his best forces to advance into Belgium and Holland. German plans had changed in the meantime, however, and in May their formations were organized into two prongs, a northern and a southern one. The northern prong, Army Group B under the command of Colonel General Bock, was made up of twenty-eight divisions, three of which were armoured. This was the force that was now advancing across Holland and the northern part of Belgium.

The second prong of the German attack was in the south, Colonel General Rundstedt's Army Group A, and that too moved into action on 10 May. As we have seen, it was by far the larger force, almost double the size of Army Group B, numbering forty-four divisions, with seven of them armoured. It attacked directly through the hill country of the Ardennes and was to prove to Gamelin and the French High Command how wrong they were about the difficulties this terrain would pose.

A Panzer group consisting of the seven armoured divisions spearheaded this column. General Guderian, the German Army's leading proponent of tank warfare, commanded three of the divisions in III Panzer Corps. In another group was the 7th Armoured Division, commanded by Major General Erwin Rommel. At 4.30 on the morning of the 10th they started their advance. They moved through typical Ardennes terrain, with well-wooded country and many narrow defiles and steep hills. It was the sort of country where properly prepared demolitions and roadblocks could have seriously slowed the advancing German columns, but Rommel reported that many of the static obstacles could be bypassed by moving cross-country and by using side roads. Few of the obstacles were covered by fire, from artillery or infantry, and Rommel's division was never held up for any length of time. The same is true for the other armoured units in Army Group A, crossing the same type of terrain further south. They finally encountered the French forces of the Ninth Army a day later, on the 11th. The French cavalry could not withstand the German advance and Rommel reached the River Meuse, the natural border between Belgium and France, on the afternoon of the 12th. The bridges crossing this river had been destroyed by the retreating French, but Rommel set out to cross using inflatable rubber boats.

The Germans suffered heavy casualties at the beginning, but persisted in their attempt, covering the infantry trying to

These portraits, then and now, span more than seventy years: Larry Uren in the 1/7th Battalion Queen's Royal Regiment (**top**), Reg Beeston in the 224 Field Company Royal Engineers (**middle**) and Sydney Whiteside in the 144 Field Ambulance Unit (**below**).

(**Left**) General Viscount Gort VC, Commander of the British Expeditionary Force (BEF), was subordinate to the French General Gamelin, Commander in Chief of the French General Staff, who stands on Gort's left. French strategy relied on a line of massive forts along the border with Germany called the Maginot Line (**above**). But the German Army marching into Warsaw already had plans to bypass these defences (**below**).

Hitler, with Field Marshall von Brauchitsch next to him, leans over a map (**above**). Von Brauchitsch was in charge of the plans to invade France, Belgium and Holland but the strategy came under sustained criticism from Von Rundstedt (**right**), who believed the main assault should be through the Ardennes. General Rommel (**below**), was an ardent supporter of von Rundstedt's belief in the use of tanks.

Reservists were the first to be called up into the army (**above**), as the BEF formed up in France. It was a major operation and a whole army and its equipment had to be shipped across the Channel. A signals vehicle is unloaded at Cherbourg (**below**), and trains carry regiments of Matilda tanks across Northern France to the Belgian border (**right**).

Training went on throughout the long build-up. Stanley Chappell's 2nd Regiment Royal Horse Artillery is practising a rapid withdrawal (**above**), with their 25lb guns and tracked carriers lined up at La Bassée. Sid Lewis's 2nd Battalion Royal Warwickshire Regiment (**below**) continued their rifle practice at Rumegies even during the very harsh winter of 1939–1940.

The French believed the Ardennes were impassable. The German Army proved them wrong. A column of armoured personnel carriers makes its way through an unguarded road block (**above**). The German advance meant that British troops were marching into Belgium while columns of civilian refugees were heading in the opposite direction, fleeing the approach of war (**below**).

There were some German casualties. The tail plane of a shot-down Heinkel bomber is carried away by British squaddies at Tournai (**above**), but the German advances in the south were extremely rapid. German troops were able to cross the River Meuse near Sedan into France just two days after the start of the fighting. Here, machine guns cover the rubber dinghies ferrying men across the river (**below**).

The Belgian fort at Eben Emael was thought to be impregnable but this strategically vital position, which guarded several river and canal crossings, was captured on the first day by German airborne troops who used gliders to land on the roof. This photo shows the immediate aftermath (**top**). The Belgian army was not well prepared for war, and some units started to retreat in disarray before the advancing French troops could meet up with them (**right**).

The German advance to the south of the BEF was extremely rapid. Only a few things held them up. Rommel, in the van of the armoured columns, pulled back at Arras, and he was also delayed for two days at La Bassée Canal by the hundreds of barges sunk by the British. Specially large bridges had to be brought up to avoid the wreckage (**left**).

cross the river with gunfire from tanks spaced at fifty-yard intervals along the eastern bank. Other crossings also succeeded, and by the early morning of 14 May the first tanks had crossed the Meuse. The German bridgehead was fragile, but the French forces, reeling from the speed of the German advance, were not coordinated enough to take them on. Over the next twenty-four hours, with support from dive-bombers and infantry, the German armoured columns had created a hole sixty miles wide in the French front line. Rommel describes in his diary how, looking back from a hill some miles into French territory, he could see endless pillars of dust stretching into the distance as far as the eye could reach, dust thrown up by the tracks of his advancing tanks.

The German Army also made a rapid advance into Holland, with the 9th Panzer Division heading for Rotterdam. The French commander-in-chief, General Gamelin, had decided to commit his reserve forces of seven divisions to the Seventh Army, commanded by General Henri Giraud, for the defence of Holland. Once the fighting started, Gamelin's plan was that these troops would advance quickly through Belgium to meet up with the Dutch Army at the town of Breda near the Dutch–Belgian border. But the leading units of the Seventh Army were shocked to meet up not with Dutch troops but with the tanks of the 9th Panzers, who had charged through Holland and were already at the town of Tilburg, just a few miles further east. General Giraud ordered his French Army to fall back towards the Belgian port of Antwerp on the mouth of the River Scheldt. The port, however, was being bombed by the Luftwaffe, and streams of aircraft with black crosses on their wings were flying over the

French columns. Any prospect of the French reinforcing the Dutch Army had vanished.

It wasn't until 13 May that the British Cavalry of the 12th Lancers on the east coast of the River Dyle came into contact with the first units of German forces, the 19th Infantry Division, about ten miles east of Louvain. Units of the Belgian Army withdrew at this point, and continued to do so, and Montgomery decided that the cavalry would also pull back to the line along the western bank of the Dyle. So they crossed the river and the Royal Engineers started demolishing the bridges. By the afternoon of the 14th Stanley's battery was told that the cavalry was clear, and the 25-pounder guns opened fire on the enemy. The advance guard of the German troops were careless, perhaps assuming that there was going to be no resistance. Their reconnaissance patrols appeared on the far side of the river, in plain sight, disregarding the need for any cover. They were fired on first by British troops on the western bank, then suffered more serious casualties as they were targeted by Stanley's guns and those of other artillery units. German guns were brought forward and they in turn started firing on the British infantry now dug in along the river.

The exchange of fire continued, with Stanley sitting at the plotting table, in contact via the radio lorry with the battery HQ and the forward observation posts. The quiet country spot was filled with the crash of guns and the metallic rattle of ejected shell cases. Smoke and the smell of cordite filled the air. The German troops tried to float some pontoons across the river just south of Louvain, preparatory to bridging it, but artillery shells smashed them up. The Germans were at an impasse, getting hammered by fire from artillery, mortars and machine guns from across the river. Adrenaline surged through the men of Stan's battery: at last they were in action, the noise and fire from the guns filling their senses. They were working well, smoothly coordinated, the years of training paying off, keeping up a steady, regular rate of fire. It wasn't to last.

Later that evening orders came through to withdraw during the night, to pull back to positions further west, near to the small town of Beyssem, to provide more cover to the British defenders of Louvain. German units, who had at last succeeded in infiltrating the town, were attacking along the railway line and around the goods yard. Firefights were breaking out along the railway platforms and the passenger subways as men from the 2nd Regiment Royal Ulsters and the 1st King's Own Scottish Borderers struggled to hold them off. German artillery pounded the station and the area around it, smashing the glass canopy over the platforms.

Stanley's 25-pounders and the rest of the 2nd Royal Horse Artillery were brought into action again, pouring shells on to German positions on the west bank of the Dyle, trying to zero in on the German artillery that was bringing such grief to the British in Louvain. They were in action throughout the day and the night, firing at German gun batteries, then directed to other targets. Every few hours into the morning of the 16th the guns would blast off a salvo at a new target. The men worked with a rhythm that became mechanical, and the noise and concussion of the big guns seemed to become permanent, so that when, at 16.00, orders came not for another set of aiming points but for yet another move, this time much further west, there was confusion and dismay. Everything was going so well, yet they were retreating!

Stanley felt perplexed, and angry. Néry Battery did not withdraw! Going forward into Belgium, he had assumed that the territory of France behind him was as solid as the Rock of Gibraltar. But that afternoon they hitched the guns up to the quad tractors once again and moved out. They should have joined up with the 15th Hussars west of Brussels, but when they arrived at the rendezvous there was no sign of the other unit. After a wait, the orders came to keep moving and they retraced the route they had taken just a few days before. There were no waving crowds now and the roads were choked with traffic of all sorts – British army lorries, convoys of men and artillery, ragged groups of Belgian soldiers. Most disturbing of all was the tragic sight of civilians fleeing with bicycles, prams, wheelbarrows, motorcycles, horses and carts, all piled up with the personal belongings that had once made a home – mattresses, some sticks of furniture. Men, women and children fled for safety from war and an invading army.

The roads were so crowded that the convoy often came to a complete standstill. At one stop, Stanley heard some enormous explosions ahead and thought the road before them had come under fire from some really heavy long-range guns. Then, as the lorries slowly inched along, a runner told him that one of the regiment's despatch riders, Bombardier Brown, had been killed by a shell. They pressed on, in retreat, and Stanley was never told why.

They passed through Brussels again, then Ninove, finally ending up in Eekent, five miles west of the River Dendre.

On 14 May Sid Lewis woke at 03.30 to the sound of heavy gunfire in the distance. It was coming from the south-east and was probably still a long way away. He was called to form up

and ordered out on patrol to search for reported para-
troopers, but it was a wild goose chase. Moving along the
sides of the roads, from farmhouse to farmhouse, they
startled rabbits and pheasants, but saw no enemy troops.

The rest of the day was spent improving trenches and
maintaining watch on the road. Sid wasn't clear about what
they were intending to do, or what they were waiting for, but
he wasn't that concerned. It was enough to enjoy the
countryside and the good weather. In the afternoon another
patrol went out with the CO to look for possible company
positions in the wood itself. It was a large area of forest and
the densely growing trees presented a challenge to any
battalion trying to defend it. Movement was difficult and it
was impossible to see more than twenty feet in any direction.
It was hard to imagine that an enemy would choose to
advance through it either. On returning to the battalion HQ,
though, Sid was told that they were making another move, a
few miles south to the golf course at Waterloo. They marched
down the road and prepared to set up tents for the night.
German reconnaissance planes flew overhead and later a
bomber dropped a stick of twelve bombs along a road that
ran to Brussels through the forest, but they caused no
damage. Late in the afternoon Sid saw two battles between
German and Allied aircraft take place in the air over Brussels,
but it was impossible to understand who had come out on top.

Guards were being posted and the rest of the men were
falling out to sort out the bivouacs when the company
sergeants called them all to stand to again. Shouting for quiet
against all the cursing, the NCOs ordered the men to prepare
for immediate movement by transport. An order had come
from brigade HQ: the battalion was to go via Waterloo to the

town of Hulpe, which was on the south-eastern corner of the forest. In thirty minutes they were moving out in the 15cwt lorries yet again, slowly grinding their way through the dark night, past the now constant streams of civilians fleeing the invading Germans. They got to Hulpe at 1.30 the next morning, tired and hungry, and were assigned to some rough-and-ready billets. Machine guns and anti-tank guns had to be set up before the men could grab what sleep was possible before being called to stand to again at 3.30 a.m.

As the CO made his rounds, the sound of artillery firing was still coming from the east and French troops with horse-drawn transport were making their way past them. There was no breakfast, because the transport with the field kitchens and rations was still on the move in the rear. Sid was beginning to feel uneasy. Chichester-Constable, the company commander, seemed unhappy too. The men didn't see much of him. He was always attending conferences in battalion HQ. In the fighting that Sid had seen on the front near the Saar there had been some initial confusion, but the battalion had soon pulled itself into shape and the men had been confident that everyone knew what they were doing. This wasn't true of what was happening now.

The German invasion had happened six days ago, but they had yet to come into contact with the enemy and in the last two days had moved a few miles around a forest from one position to another. It seemed pointless, and it was tiring, disruptive. In the next few hours it got worse. At midday the battalion was ordered to positions they had reconnoitred the day before and which had been thought to be very difficult to defend in the middle of the forest. But they set out, marching overnight from Hulpe, and arrived at 7.30.

Like the rest of the company, Sid was extremely tired and he hadn't had any food for almost thirty-six hours. Fortunately, the rear echelon transport had finally arrived and dispersed among the trees, so the field kitchens fired up and the men had a proper meal.

They set to once more, digging firing trenches and machine-gun posts along the sides of a road that traversed the forest. Only an hour later the men were once more ordered to move, and they marched just two miles down the road to repeat the process of digging in. For two days they had marched almost in circles and seen no sign of the enemy, except for bombers that seemed to fly above their heads with impunity and a spotter plane that circled lazily, a constant companion to their chaotic moves.

8

LARRY UREN AND LES CLARKE MOVE UP

10–20 May

Larry Uren in the 1/7th Queen's – newly arrived and part of the BEF for just one month in the recently re-formed 25th Brigade of the 5th Division – was now billeted in Chelers, a small village south-west of Lille. They had moved there on the day that the German advance started, 10 May. The brigade had begun a major training exercise, which went as planned on the 12th and the 13th. Its purpose was to familiarize the men with the procedures for withdrawal. No actual withdrawal was expected; in fact, the plan was that the division was to advance into Belgium, and on the 16th Larry went with a party from the brigade to plan the route. The 5th Division was to form part of the General HQ reserve, based on the River Senne as part of a defence in depth of the front-line forces on the River Dyle.

Les Clarke's 6th Battalion Durham Light Infantry, part of

the 50th Division, was continuing to dig its line of anti-tank ditches near Seclin after the boxing tournament on 9 May. There was a lot of aerial action during the day, and D Company sent a detachment to guard an enemy bomber, a Dornier that had been shot down close to their billets. The crew were all killed, but some signals and code books were rescued and sent to the battalion HQ.

The first movement into Belgium by men from Les's battalion wasn't part of the general advance, but a more mysterious affair altogether. Four men and an NCO with good map-reading skills were ordered to the brigade HQ. They were given some street maps of Charleroi and told to make their way in two 15cwt trucks into the centre of the town, to the main office of a bank, where they would load up boxes of gold, share certificates and other securities, then bring them safely back to the brigade headquarters. News of the unorthodox mission spread quickly and some of the men started to offer odds on whether the two lorries and their crews would ever be seen again.

They left at 15.00, their route taking them past Lille airport, which late that evening was given a heavy pounding by German bombers. The sounds of the anti-aircraft fire and the exploding bombs travelled through the spring air to the men in their billets in Seclin. Les was kept busy on his motorbike, speeding between brigade HQ and battalion HQ, because that afternoon the battalion had received orders to ready itself for the move into Belgium, now scheduled for 16 May. There was time for some last-minute rifle and grenade practice on the 15th and then they moved out, climbing aboard the lorries and heading into Belgium. So far everything was going according to plan. Les, moving up and down the long column of vehicles on his motorbike, had no inkling of what had already started to go wrong to the south. A nineteen-year-old boy on a powerful machine, independent and carrying important despatches, he raced along and was one of the few men who could see the full extent of an army division on the move. He found it absolutely exhilarating. So too was the welcome that the young soldiers received from the civilian population. They too were still in the first flush of optimism about the outcome of the war, and Les was kissed by the young women, showered with gifts of wine and food. They were treated, he says, as conquering heroes.

Les's battalion was directed to the town of Grammont, astride the River Dendre. Here they established some positions on the eastern bank, with platoons guarding the approach to bridges a little way further north at the hamlets of Idegem and Zandbergen. This was originally intended to be their position as part of the general reserve, but it was now the interim line to which the front three divisions of the BEF were pulling back as part of their overall withdrawal to the River Scheldt. From acting as a general reserve, Les Clarke's battalion had in fact now advanced to the front line and would shortly experience the full firepower of German Army Group B.

There were two wooded areas to the east of Zandbergen and a patrol went forward to reconnoitre. They found nothing and were sure that the woods were empty. But all the time the patrol was in the woods two German planes circled above D Company, only flying off as night fell. Next morning the battalion started to dig in, while the sappers began to prepare bridges for demolition. There was a constant traffic of refugees over the bridges, along with an assortment of

Belgian soldiers, some on bicycles, others on foot. It was obvious to the men at the bridges that these were deserters, but there seemed to be a lot of them. Neither did they see any other Belgian units. An intelligence report was received by the battalion HQ that a bridge held by the French Army had been captured by German soldiers dressed as refugees. They had been let across the bridge and were then able to attack the French guards from the rear. Orders went out for checkpoints and a guard to be set up so that the traffic across the bridges could be controlled. They were to make sure that the civilians were genuine, and if this meant searching them then they should do so. Belgian soldiers who were stopped were also interrogated and they implied through broken English or gestures that they were retreating for fresh supplies or ammunition. This was very obviously a pretence. The men let them through anyway, but Les knew that they were really doing a runner. He thought it was peculiar that they could do that, and that there were so many of them, and he wondered what had happened to the Belgian Army further forward. The checkpoints caused congestion on the roads leading to the bridges and streams of traffic built up on the eastern bank.

Another report also came down from brigade HQ that enemy armoured vehicles had broken through the defences at Ath, a town further south on the Dendre, close to the line where the British Expeditionary Force met the French First Army. Brigade HQ was informed that German forces might be expected at any time and all the bridges were to be guarded by anti-tank weapons. This message led to a flurry of activity and Les was ordered to brigade headquarters. Five other despatch riders were there, all with orders to take the same message to the division. This way at least one of them would get through. The possibility that the enemy had advanced so far along the southern border of the BEF was catastrophic. If they broke through and headed north, then at least six divisions would be cut off.

From then on a blizzard of orders and counter-orders, statements of readiness and general instructions went from the battalion to the companies and vice versa. The battalion was moving, that was sure, but when, and what to do about the bridges they were meant to be guarding, were the big questions. The bridges had to be demolished to stop the enemy using them, but they were also needed to allow British troops to withdraw. Four hundred anti-tank mines to be laid along the approaches to the bridges were on their way and were expected around 16.00 that day, the 17th. They didn't arrive, but meanwhile orders were received to be prepared to move at half an hour's notice. Work was to continue on securing and fortifying the positions, but the troops must also prepare for a long overnight journey. Les thought that he was well out of all that and got back on his motorbike.

The drone of approaching aircraft and the wail of the hand-held sirens added to the sudden sense of danger. Les headed for cover, but the enemy bombers flew overhead, heading for another target. They flew over Grammont and hit the local airfield, the dull thud of the explosion carrying through the evening air. Three of the Stukas returned and flew at a few hundred feet over the two bridges guarded by the battalion. They had obviously spotted the British troops and one or two men fired at them with Bren guns. They had no effect, but the gunner of the rear bomber returned the compliment, spraying machine-gun bullets into the streets as the plane roared above them. It did little harm, but it added to the sense of confusion.

It seemed absurd to keep working on improving slit trenches and gun positions if they were to be abandoned in a few hours' time. Were some of the men going to be detailed to remain as a rearguard – always an unpleasant thought? Later that evening there was even more uncertainty when orders were received that all trucks were to be loaded and packed with kit and equipment ready for transit at midnight. While kitbags, ammunition and rations were being loaded, a lieutenant from the Bren-gun carrier section of the Cameron Highlanders passed through the men holding the eastern side of the bridge at Idegem. He was part of I Corps and had got lost. Before making his way to the battalion HQ for directions, he told the guards that I Corps to the south was retreating very quickly and that his battalion was acting as a rearguard. It didn't take much thought to work out that, if he was part of the rearguard, the enemy must be close.

Orders finally came that the withdrawal was to be at 6.00 the following morning. There was to be no night withdrawal and no one was to be a rearguard. That was some comfort, but the early packing meant that the night was going to be uncomfortable and breakfast would be pack rations. At 4.30 that morning confirmation was received, and the convoy started pulling out at 6.00. The battalion was moving back to the Scheldt.

Larry Uren's 1/7th Queen's Battalion had been dug in at a small village called Meerbeke, to the east of Ninove, the forward edge of the line along the Dendre and a few miles to the north-east of the 6th Durham Light Infantry. Their journey into Belgium had been fought against solid ranks of refugees heading west, all streaming away from the Germans. Halfway into the move there had been a change of plan, and Larry and his comrades now found themselves digging in along a line that crossed a river valley, the river running at right angles to the defenders' row of slit trenches and machine-gun posts. The battalion's orders were to set up anti-tank positions to control the road from Brussels.

Larry was ordered to head out with a mate and a Boys anti-tank rifle to find a good position down the road. He was horrified. He had never fired a Boys before, never seen a tank. His training in the militia had been very basic, and while other units had spent their time in France on training exercises, Larry had been in the strange limbo of an extremely extended, enjoyable route reconnaissance. While he had spent a lot of time with his CO, Captain Dickenson, and would often be chosen to drive him, he had been with the rest of the battalion for just over four weeks. But he was in no position to argue, so the two of them trudged down the road. The Boys rifle had a calibre of .5in and a magazine that held five rounds. The chamber was cleared and another round inserted by sliding a bolt back and forth, similar to the standard .303 Lee-Enfield rifle. The Boys was, however, much longer and heavier, and had a bipod to support the barrel.

Larry set up the rifle where he had a good view down the road and waited. All the traffic was civilian, mostly refugees on foot. Larry had never seen action, and the sight of the civilians struggling along was upsetting, but he assumed that this was just another stretch of boring guard duty and that he would be relieved in a couple of hours.

Then they heard the sound of engines and the clank of

tracks on the road. Larry felt sick. Down the road came three tanks, steadily advancing, the refugees quickly scrambling out of their way. He had no idea what they were. They got closer. 'Fire the fucking gun!' said his mate.

Larry straightened the gun and peered down the sights. It was impossible to miss. He squeezed the trigger. The recoil was so violent that Larry thought his collarbone must have broken. But the bullet just pinged off the front of the tank. He worked the bolt and fired again. The recoil lifted the bipod off the ground and sent another kick into Larry's shoulder, but again the bullet bounced off, flying into the air. He fired all five rounds to no effect. His mate, who should have loaded the spare magazine, had dropped it in his haste and anxiety as the tanks rumbled closer and closer. The first one halted, its turret turning slowly towards them. Larry and his mate scrambled to their feet.

The hatch opened and the commander climbed out. 'You stupid little people,' he said, in the accent of a toff. Larry still remembers with some heat the contemptuous tone in which he spoke to them. 'Don't you know the difference between a British and a German tank? Give me your names and numbers.' They gave him false ones, of course. He wrote them down in a little notebook and then, before turning on his heel, he said, 'I'll have you on toast!'

Fortunately the battalion's orders changed soon after and Larry avoided questions about the five rounds that he had fired. They moved to secure a bridge over the river at Ninove, as well as a footbridge, the Pont de Lust, that crossed the river south-west of the town. The orders were to hold the bridges on both banks of the river prior to blowing them up. When they were demolished they were to take control of the west bank from the edge of the town at Ninove to the Pont de Lust. As the time came to retreat from the eastern bank, the men urged the crowds of refugees across as quickly as they could. There would soon be no possibility of retreat. They had to hold them back as the road bridge was blown up. It was a sad sight and Larry found it difficult to bear. Where was the luxury of Monsieur Dubonnet's chateau now? A loud crack echoed from the building behind them, a puff of black smoke appeared from the span and the bridge collapsed into the river.

The echo of another explosion told Larry that the footbridge had also been destroyed. Then they started digging in again. A British spotter plane, a Lysander, was circling above them, a welcome change from the usual enemy aircraft.

To their left at the rear, in an orchard, was a battalion of the Royal Irish Fusiliers, who had been the rearguard to the north and were now trying to regroup. At around four o'clock in the afternoon a flight of German Messerschmitt fighters appeared from the east and flew low over Larry, the roar of their engines sending a spine-tingling surge of fear through him. They swooped on the Lysander, shooting it down; it crashed to the ground a mile or so away. Then they turned and started to fire on the ranks of the Fusiliers, the aircrafts' guns blazing, sending cannon shells smashing into the fruit trees. No one returned the fire.

Later that evening the company commander walked along the trenches. Orders had been received, he said, that they were to deny the line of the river to the enemy 'at all costs'. Those were orders directly from General HQ. The CO knew that the men had never seen the real face of war. He hoped his presence would help steady them a little for the fighting that would soon be upon them, but what he had to say was hardly reassuring. The men listened in silence, staring straight ahead. Batteries of a Royal Artillery regiment, the 92nd Field Regiment to their rear, started firing, the shells whistling over Larry's head to land on the crossroads and other targets east of the river. The harassing fire continued throughout the night, intermittent salvoes of five shells sending gun flashes into the sky, then a shrill whistle overhead, followed by a faint echoing boom as the shells exploded in the distance.

At 3.00 on the morning of the 19th, the battalion received new orders for a withdrawal to the line of the Scheldt. They were to move out at around nine o'clock. The question was whether it would be too late. The enemy was now very close. The shellfire from the 92nd Field Regiment had not stopped German tanks and other units from advancing. It would have been normal practice for the battalion to start thinning out before the withdrawal, reducing the number of men in various positions so that some defensive fire could be kept up while the battalion gathered at the assembly point. This would be a risky business if there were a full-scale assault in the middle of it, however, and the battalion CO decided to hold on and then at the last minute pull out en masse across the railway line that ran behind them.

He was right in his assessment. At 7.30 a.m. shells started landing on their positions. The shelling was heavy, accompanied by machine-gun fire and sniper fire into the rear areas. Dive-bombers also appeared overhead and attacked the columns of the 92nd Field Regiment, which was already withdrawing, as well as some of the transport for the Royal Irish Fusiliers. Larry remembers that the first rush of fear at the start of the bombardment was almost overpowering. The battalion had never seen this before. 'Some of the lads were bomb-happy. It's impossible to describe how frightening it is. Lads just lay there shivering. You couldn't blame them. The German 88s were also blasting the life out of us.'

The dive-bombers targeted the roads behind the 1/7th and hit an ammunition depot at a crossroads on the route to Ninove. Larry thought that they would in fact fight to the end. It seemed as though they were surrounded. German troops were advancing to the east bank of the canal and appeared to have crossed it to the north of him. There was machine-gun fire and heavy fighting from the Royal Irish Fusiliers' positions to the left and behind him. The shells were spewing shrapnel through the trees and shrubs and there were cries for stretcher-bearers and screams from the wounded men. His .303 Lee-Enfield seemed inadequate against this onslaught. They were going to pull out at 9.30, but Larry knew it was going to require a real effort to leave the comparative safety of his slit trench and cross over the railway line behind him.

The time came, however, and he climbed out, keeping as low as he could, feeling horribly exposed as the shells continued to fall and bullets whistled through the air. He saw someone to his right fall to the ground, then he was running, over the railway tracks towards the rest of the company. There were no clear orders about what to do. The attack on the ammunition dump had blocked the start of the route to Audenarde. There just weren't enough lorries anyway. Some of the men had started to take over any civilian lorry or car they could find. Alternative routes existed along country lanes, but nobody was sure what they were. But there was no time to wait, so sections set off heading west. Larry was with about sixty others, with Captain Dickenson in charge, and they moved off in several vehicles. Shells were still falling behind him and he knew that the Germans would not be held up by the river for long. Audenarde, however, had been heavily bombed and as they reached the outskirts they saw that the town was destroyed. A heavy cloud of smoke hung over it and many of the houses were burning, but what most sickened Larry was the sight of dead bodies still lying in the street. There were no medical orderlies, no fire services. There was also no sign of the battalion. They drove on through the night and at ten o'clock the next morning they finally managed to reach the new rendezvous, a wood near Bellegem south of the town of Courtrai, where they joined up with the rest of the battalion. Many men were still missing. Larry learned that Lieutenant Candy, a young man whom he thought a decent officer, had been killed by a sniper in the final withdrawal to the railway line. Soldiers arrived in dribs and drabs over the next few hours and the battalion remained in the Bellegem area for most of the day, recuperating before preparing to move to a new area on the La Bassée Canal.

Further north, Stanley Chappell's L (Néry) Battery 2nd Royal Horse Artillery was dug in in fields outside Eekent. While the line of British troops pulled back from the Dendre, Stanley's battery kept up a barrage on to the advancing German Army. As the day wore on, one troop would move back while the other kept up the covering fire, leapfrogging each other to give some protection to the rearguard as they moved west. Stanley hardly knew where he was. It didn't matter. It was just a question of firing, limbering up, firing, then moving again. He was quite exhausted, and there was a profound sense that the endless retreat was wrong. They were hungry, the food they could find in the abandoned farms and villages they went through was getting scarce, and they hadn't shaved. Their faces were blackened from the gunsmoke. While Larry's 1/7th battalion recovered at Bellegem, Stanley's regiment continued to move back, skirting Audenarde, then to a town called Dottignies from where they were able to cover the troops holding the River Scheldt. They dug in there for the night of 20 May.

9

THE 48TH DIVISION PULLS BACK

16–19 May

We left Sid Lewis in the 2nd Battalion Royal Warwickshire Regiment near Waterloo on 16 May after their advance into Belgium. That evening the battalion was ordered to move again, another two and a half miles down the road. The battalion diary records that after this move there was a conference of company commanders at 11.30 that night in the battalion HQ. Every commander fell asleep before the meeting started. Woken, they heard that the battalion was due to move out in two hours' time.

Sid Lewis was also feeling dead from fatigue, but with the rest of 7 Platoon he climbed to his feet. The carrier section and transport headed out, then the men marched first to the village of Rhode-St-Genese on the main Brussels–Charleroi road, just north-west of Waterloo. Split up into sections, the companies finally assembled there at four o'clock in the morning – but the night was not yet over. They were to press on to Pepingen some fifteen miles away, where there was a bridge over a canal. It would be a long, arduous march, dead tired as they all were. They set out at 6.00 a.m., heading across country, avoiding the roads because the battalion officers thought it would lessen the risk of air attack. Sid and the rest of his section cursed them for this as they walked across fields, struggled over fences and through gates, their boots getting heavier with mud, but it proved to be a wise decision. From the shelter of the hedgerows they could see squadron after squadron of German dive-bombers blitzing the nearby road, leaving behind burning lorries and screaming wounded men.

They trudged on through the morning, getting hotter, hungrier and thirstier, until at midday they reached Pepingen, where they finally got a hot meal and could rest, in between setting up observation posts and digging in. They remained there for a few hours, with no idea about what the next move would be. Would they stay here and hold the hamlet, or start marching yet again? In the afternoon, hand-held air raid sirens started wailing and Sid dived for the nearest cover. A formation of twin-engined Junkers bombers came over in a low attack, the explosions evenly spaced as their sticks of bombs fell across formations of troops. Nobody from the battalion was injured, but men in other units were.

At six o'clock that evening they received more orders to move. Fortunately the battalion's transport was available, so they travelled to another village where billets had been found for them in houses and in the village hall. Orders were received for the next day, with reveille posted for 5 a.m. and breakfast at 6. Sid looked forward to a night's sleep, unrolling the palliasses and blankets, easing his feet out of his boots and lying down with a Woodbine and a brew of tea. He should have known better. At 21.30 a liaison officer drove up to the battalion HQ with orders to start marching again at midnight, this time to an area near Herinnes. Once more Sid formed up and the battalion, its trucks in the lead, most of its men marching on tired, swollen feet, headed in a southerly direction.

Even for the regular soldiers in the battalion, the permanent movement and the seemingly wilful denial of sleep was far beyond what even the army was justified in getting away with. But however much the soldiers cursed the incompetence of their officers, the men in charge of the 48th Division had little choice. They had been presented with a fait accompli by the French liaison officers when they were told that the French First Army to their right was moving back to the west as a result of the German breakthrough in the south. Sid had appeared to move in circles around the woods near Waterloo because the French were already moving back to the road that ran south-west from the Lion of Waterloo and would soon be several miles further west, at the town of Braine-l'Alleud. But after this decision had been communi-cated to the General Staff of the 48th Division by the French General Damme, the commander of the French 2nd Infantry Division, no other information was forthcoming about French plans. It seemed to the Division that General Damme and his men were also in the dark about what the French High Command intended to do. It was not until the move by the 48th Division had got under way that a messenger from the French brought the information that the line they were expected to hold had already been abandoned. A gap was opening to the south between the British and French forces, which the Germans were already beginning to exploit. The division had to move back to the line of the Dendre, and do it fast.

The roads were now seriously congested, not only with fleeing civilians, but with other British troops moving back to the River Dendre. After making increasingly slow progress for an hour, Sid's battalion came to a complete halt. Two upturned field guns and a huge jam of civilian vehicles that couldn't, or wouldn't, manoeuvre their way past them blocked the road ahead. The battalion drivers in the transport struggled to turn round in the narrow road, fighting against the press of people and traffic behind them, but finally they did, and started to head back the way they had come to find an alternative route. Sid and the other men on foot edged through the crush, shoving and cursing, bursting through hedgerows to get past the tangled guns and cars.

They marched on and on and on. It seemed for ever; there was no respite. There had never been a route march like this. At occasional stops for a rest, men collapsed in a heap and fell instantly asleep. Riflemen, sergeants, even some younger officers. Only the hardened souls like Chichester-Constable kept their eyes open, and roused and kicked the section corporals to get back on their feet, who in turn kicked awake the men. But Chichester-Constable knew what was at stake. There was gunfire to the south. It was keeping pace with them and the soldiers to their south, whoever they were, were taking some heavy punishment. The most dangerous thing would be if the gunfire got ahead of them.

At 6.00 in the morning, exhausted, unshaven and hungry, they stopped. Some cooks' lorries had managed to rendezvous with them and a breakfast was served, but orders quickly came to form up once again. They continued on their march. Sid's A Company was in the rear and the line was beginning to stretch out as some men collapsed and stretcher-bearers stopped to pick them up. Fatigue was now so strong that Sid dreamed he was asleep and woke to find that he was still marching like an automaton.

Later that day, in the afternoon, a despatch rider appeared with orders to make the maximum possible speed. The sergeants shouted encouragement and abuse in equal measure. But it was urgent, desperately so. A bridge over a canal ahead at Papignies was ready to be demolished by the Royal Engineers and the sappers were waiting for the battalion to cross. It should have been blown an hour ago. The men marched on at the very limits of their endurance. They crossed the bridge finally, then Sid started digging in with the rest of A Company to hold the bridgehead. Anti-tank guns were set up, and houses on the left and right of the bridge were strengthened, their windows pushed out and loop-holes knocked through the walls. The charges on the bridge finally exploded and it collapsed into the canal.

The men took it in turns to get a few hours' sleep in the dugouts and houses along the canal and some pack rations were brought round. Finally they could take the weight off their feet, but their level of fatigue was very high. Sid found that even after a couple of hours of sleep he still had to struggle to keep his eyes open as he stared across the canal at the darkening Belgian countryside. Alertness returned, how-ever, when at nine o'clock at night the sounds of machine-gun fire came from Sid's left. B Company was there, further along the bank. He couldn't see what it was or where it was coming from, but then some shells started landing. There was no sign of any enemy troops or tanks approaching and after a while the shelling stopped. Nothing moved.

At ten o'clock a runner brought orders that the battalion was to form up yet again and move out. It was hard to believe. The men on the canal bank moved out of the houses and went back to the village in the rear, where they stood on parade in the village square. It was only a few hundred yards but there were a lot of stragglers, particularly from B Company. At five minutes to midnight they were once more on the march. It was dark and Sid knew the battalion was starting to break up. The gaps between the sections and the platoons were getting bigger and bigger. Fatigue was causing many sections to get lost or left behind. The adjutant and intelligence officer went back and forth along the line of marchers, urging the men to keep up, but the column was becoming badly stretched out. The sound of shellfire was heard once more on their left, and they knew that the Germans were advancing. They needed to make much faster progress. Bren-gun and machine-gun fire could be heard coming from far along their flanks and there was a danger that they would be cut off. The bridgehead that they had just left was still being held by a small section of armoured cars, but they too were going to pull out at dawn. Dawn was not far away. Transport for the battalion, to carry them to their next destination, had been promised to the CO but it just didn't appear. The riflemen were more like a rabble now as they staggered along, too tired to keep formation. When a halt was called everyone, even the officers, immediately fell asleep. They were drunk with fatigue.

At 5.00 in the morning the personnel transport finally appeared and the 15cwt trucks formed up for the men to climb aboard. Sid could barely hoist himself on to the back, where he sat, drained and light-headed with exhaustion and hunger. He no longer cared where he was or where he was going.

The battalion's route to their posting at Hollain on the River Scheldt – the last line of defence before the French frontier – went through the town of Tournai. The drivers of the transports met an almost impenetrable traffic jam as they got closer. The numbers of trucks and marching troops heading west were just too much for the narrow roads. Then squadrons of German dive-bombers appeared in the grey dawn, swooping on the mass of British troops below them. Air raid sirens wailed and shrill whistle blasts announced the attack, but the men needed no urging to leap from the lorries and seek shelter in ditches by the side of the road. The nerve-racking scream of the Stukas caused Sid to try to bury himself in the earth, then the detonation of the bombs made the ground shake like jelly. He heard six or seven planes dive down like banshees, then after an excruciating interval when everyone knew that the bomb was going to kill them, it exploded elsewhere and there was another few minutes' reprieve. One bomb did fall close by, followed by a few desperate shouts and then a huge blast came after the first explosion. It completely overwhelmed and deafened Sid, and debris seemed to fall out of the skies for ever. He raised his head and saw that the burning remains of an ammunition truck lay on the road. A tyre was bouncing away and bodies lay strewn about. By now the bombers seemed to have gone and men began rushing towards the rest of the trucks to clear them from the remains of the burning lorry, but suddenly bullets were ripping dust up from the road and flying off bonnets and through the windows of the transport. Men were running everywhere to take cover from the strafing attack as a Stuka hammered past. When it was finally over, Sid picked himself up and climbed once more aboard a lorry. The attack had left men dead and dying in the road, buildings and vehicles burning, thick smoke pouring up from yellow leaping flames into the fresh morning air.

They continued on their way, turning south, heading along the Scheldt until they came at last to the town of Hollain. They climbed down, wearily. The battalion had lost a lot of men. They had left behind some casualties, and various sections had been abandoned by the transports or had become caught in the town of Tournai – or, more accurately, in the ruins that the Luftwaffe had created.

Hollain was a small town on the banks of the river, which had been tamed and looked more like a wide artificial water-way as it coursed between houses and factories built of Flemish red brick. A Company was set up in a disused ware-house on the western bank. There was some information that the enemy was rapidly advancing, so observation posts and mortars were placed, then a hot meal and tea were served up at last.

To Sid's astonishment, some of the villagers hadn't taken the chance to get away, and sections of riflemen were detailed off to round them up. Everybody believed that if they were to stay in this place they would soon be in the thick of a battle. But most of the civilians wandering around were not all there. One of the residents they found sitting in an empty café claimed to be Napoleon. He was locked up at battalion HQ until his papers, if he had any, could be checked.

For the rest of the day they dug in and made preparations

for the fighting that would soon be upon them. They were facing east across the river and set up an observation post on the roof of an old factory by the riverbank, from where the countryside was swept constantly with binoculars for any signs of the advancing enemy. A Lysander spotter plane droned overhead all day, but word got around that no one at battalion HQ could gather any information about it or what it was doing. But it circled with impunity and everyone believed that it was in the hands of the Germans. It would have accurately plotted all the artillery and mortar positions by now. But the day wore on and nothing was done about the plane, and the Germans didn't come. Night fell and Sid turned in for a sleep before his turn at watch. It was very welcome. It was 19 May.

10

THE GERMAN DASH TO THE COAST

15–20 May

The Germans had made extraordinary gains in a very few days and, while they had thrown the Allies into confusion, the German commanders were concerned about how exposed their own forces were becoming. By 15 May the southern flank of Army Group A was considered, according to their war diary, vulnerable to a counter-attack from French forces in the south. These French troops were in reality extremely disorganized, but this was not appreciated by the German staff at Rundstedt's HQ. Consequently, on the 16th Rundstedt ordered the advance to be slowed so that reserve infantry could be brought forward to defend the flanks and further consolidation could take place to allow the next attack to be carried out on a broader front. The advance units of the German Fourth Army had crossed Belgium and were now in touch with the French fortifications on their border, or had smashed across it already. Generals Guderian and

Ewal von Kleist wanted their armoured corps to push ahead and were sure that they would meet little resistance as they stormed over the border. As far as the armoured divisions were concerned, this was certainly true.

General Rommel, at the head of the 7th Panzer Division, was surging forward, maintaining fire from traversed tank turrets at possible enemy positions in woods and villages, always keeping up momentum in order to intimidate and shock. It was having an effect. Prisoners were giving themselves up in large numbers, French vehicles were being overrun without any opposition, and everywhere the enemy seemed to be totally disorganized and demoralized by the shambles.

But while these generals who had an immediate sense of the state of the French forces were eager to press on, those in the rear thought differently. In theory there was the possibility of French counter-attack and this was to be avoided at all costs. The French Ninth Army, which had to face the assault of Army Group A, was crumbling, however, and while Brauchitsch was pressing Rundstedt to strengthen his flanks, Rundstedt grasped that the French Army was struggling to create a more effective defensive line, probably as far west as the line of the Somme. The possibility of a French counter-attack was extremely remote. So on the 18th Rundstedt issued orders for Kleist to push forward towards the town of Cambrai, which was on the River Scheldt thirty miles inside French territory. The order, however, had already been overtaken by events on the ground. Rommel had pushed forward regardless and was so far ahead that communication with some of the regiments in his division was sporadic. His tanks had already reached the French town of Le Cateau, just fifteen miles from Cambrai. He had collected his Panzer commanders together on the 17th and given them his own ideas of their line of advance. It fully echoed Rundstedt's plan that had been incorporated into Plan Yellow. From Le Cateau they were to advance to Arras, Amiens, Rouen and then Le Havre on the coast. Rommel was extremely competitive and was quite prepared to advance, leading from the front even if it meant that he lost contact with his divisional HQ. He wanted to be the first to complete the encirclement of the British.

The southern thrust of Army Group A, because of their pace, was always one step ahead of the Allies. The British Army had not been broken on the Dyle line at Louvain, despite the street fighting near the station and the intense artillery bombardment from the enemy. General Gort had instructed his forces to pull back because the French Army to their south was retreating. Now they were leapfrogging back to the line of the Scheldt, but the danger was that the Germans were already consolidating for a further push before the Allies were able to regroup. The British troops had not been broken, but they could be outmanoeuvred.

On the eastern front the situation was less dynamic but equally severe. Dutch forces had capitulated on 15 May and the French Army was in retreat, as were the British, and Bock's Army Group B was pushing at an open door. Brauchitsch ordered him to focus on the southern part of his front to assist in the advance of Army Group A, but Bock had other ideas. His orders would have meant moving towards Lille, a large town which was heavily defended, and this was bound to delay his advance. Bock too wanted to get to the coast, and he thought that the quickest way to do that was to strike at the boundary between the British and Belgian

Armies near Audenarde. The two prongs of the German pincer were tightening.

Just as serious for the Allies was the fact that German forces had also attacked in the night to the north of Brussels and had broken the link between the British and Belgian forces. German armoured cars were moving west on the morning of the 18th, and the British troops who found themselves in contact with the enemy, rather than with their Belgian allies, had to fight very hard to get back to the River Dendre; some of the units involved sustained very heavy losses. The 4th Battalion Gordon Highlanders lost almost a company, the 14th Anti-tank Regiment lost seven guns, while the 15/19th Hussars lost almost 80 per cent of its numbers.

The withdrawal back to the line of the Scheldt that had affected Stanley Chappell and Sid Lewis was finished by the evening of 18 May, but this did not necessarily solve the problem that it was intended to. The German armoured advance through the Ardennes was outside Lord Gort's responsibility, and the chain of command that linked him with the French Army was now unnecessarily extended. Gort received very little timely information about the state of the French armies to his north and south.

The French First Army wasn't holding up the German advance, and as the fighting moved westwards the dangers to the British southern flank were growing. This threatened to surround Gort's General HQ, which had been set up in Arras, and, if the German advance continued, would also threaten to cut the rail and road links that brought supplies from the western ports such as Cherbourg and Le Havre.

On the night of the 18th the French General Gaston

Billotte arrived at Gort's HQ to brief him on the situation. It was clear to Gort that the French did not have much hope of stopping the enemy in the south; he formed the view that they did not have enough forces south of the German columns to counter-attack and close the gap. He then had to think about what could be done if in fact the German advance proved unstoppable.

There were only two options. In the first, the British forces would have to make a rapid and wholesale retreat to the west, moving back to the line of the River Somme. This would mean that their supply lines would be kept open and would be somewhat shorter; they would also still be working with the French. It meant also that the Belgian Army would have to fall back and abandon their country, and there wasn't any reason to think that Belgian soldiers would be prepared to do that.

The other course of action open to Gort was for the BEF to pull back to the coast and prepare for evacuation. He knew that this would be a difficult withdrawal, in which a lot of men and equipment might be lost. It would also cause an abrupt break in the joint actions with the French at a time when France was in the direst need.

Gort was faced with a momentous choice, but he was helped by the briefing that he got from General Billotte. He had shown Gort a map of the situation, which revealed that nine or even ten German armoured divisions were taking part in the thrust to the south, that they were already within just twenty miles of Arras, and that there were now no French troops between them and the sea. If they continued their advance then they would do so unopposed, making it impossible for the British forces to withdraw to the west. Pulling back to the sea was the only realistic option.

This was not a decision that Gort could make on his own initiative – the consequences for the conduct of the war would be far too grave. So on the 19th his chief of staff, General Pownall, telephoned the War Office in London, revealed the awful truth to the Director of Military Operations and Plans, and started to sketch out a way forward.

Meanwhile, the withdrawal to the Scheldt had been completed by 19 May and there were seven divisions holding a line that stretched for thirty miles. Each battalion was responsible for about a mile of riverbank. The enemy advanced in pursuit and their artillery was quickly in action. The town of Audenarde had already been heavily bombed and a further major attack was expected there.

In the south the enemy armoured columns had made further gains and were now only fifty miles from Abbeville, which stands at the mouth of the River Somme on the English Channel. The Official History sums up the gravity of the situation succinctly: 'The British Expeditionary Force was outflanked and the sensitive lines of communication on which its life depended stretched out, practically undefended, across the path of the German Armour.'

On 20 May German attacks on the defenders along the Scheldt were very heavy. The men had to suffer continual sniping, artillery and mortar bombardments, and air attacks. In many places there were attempts to cross the river, but they were all repulsed. Ammunition supplies were running low; II Corps had such seriously depleted stocks of artillery shells that guns were restricted to five rounds a day.

General Gort had very few resources left. There were two

divisions, however, that he could order to try to stop the German race to the sea. These were the 23rd Division and 12th Division, both of which were made up of battalions of Territorials who had travelled across the Channel in March and had been put to work improving the railway supply facilities around the ports of Le Havre and Cherbourg. They had also had a programme of training, but they had never, up until then, been equipped to fight and had never seen the enemy.

While they were moving into place, Arras was coming under attack by the German 7th Armoured Division under the command of Major General Rommel. The garrison held out, but Rommel continued his division's advance, attempting to outflank the town to the west. The SS Totenkopf – the 'Death's Head' Division – went forward as well, to the left of Rommel's men. The 6th and 8th Armoured Divisions also moved forward, taking on the Arras garrison and other British units trying to prevent their advance north, while the German 2nd Armoured Division pressed on to Abbeville, where they met the British 12th Division and Jack Haskett's 2/6th Battalion Queen's Own Royal Regiment.

The War Cabinet was told about the conversation that the War Office had had with Gort's chief of staff about the growing need to pull the BEF back to the ports along the Channel coast. The Chief of the Imperial General Staff, General Edmund Ironside, thought that such a move was unacceptable. It was his opinion that Gort should instead move his troops back and, with the French, organize a counter-attack to take advantage of what he thought would be a tired, worn-out enemy who had overreached himself. The Cabinet agreed, and Ironside repeated his view when he spoke to Gort on the phone. Gort knew that the men in London had no idea of what was happening on the ground. He himself didn't have the complete picture any more, but he knew that the French were completely disorganized and incapable of mounting any sort of coherent offensive, and that the Germans were far from tired. Ironside listened to him, saying nothing as Gort explained that the only course open to him now was to withdraw northwards. This at least would keep his forces in touch with the Belgian Army and prevent the BEF becoming surrounded.

As it was, the Germans were directing their armoured divisions at Arras and were also within striking distance of Abbeville. This town's position at the mouth of the Somme meant that its capture by the Germans would have cut France in two and completed the encirclement of the BEF. Was there a way to stop them?

11

LES CLARKE AND THE BATTLE
OF ARRAS

19–24 May

Les Clarke's 6th Battalion Durham Light Infantry had been pulled back to create a defensive line along the River Scheldt. This move had been far less arduous for Les than it had been for Sid Lewis, as Les had his despatch rider's motorbike and the rest of the rifle companies in the 6th Durhams were provided with motor transport. They faced the same problems of huge numbers of refugees blocking the roads as did all the BEF units that were moving back, but the roads got clearer as they approached the Scheldt. The convoy was followed for its entire journey by two spotter aircraft.

In the late afternoon the battalion halted for a break close to a village. Les went along the small main street to see if he could find any food that might make a change from his pack rations of biscuits and tinned fish or chocolate. The village was shuttered up. It was, he reflected, a big change from the cheering crowds that had greeted him when they first drove into Belgium. In many of the towns they had passed through today the Union Jacks and French tricolours had disappeared, and white sheets were now flapping from the windows.

He walked back towards the battalion, but just before he reached it he heard the sound of aircraft engines and almost at the same time the NCOs and air raid pickets were blowing on their whistles. Les dived for cover against a wall. The planes roared over, followed by a series of explosions, much louder and higher pitched than normal. They sounded like giant firecrackers, and his ears were ringing. The planes flew away; it had been a short and sweet attack. Les continued back to the battalion. The bombs had been anti-personnel weapons and shrapnel had blasted everywhere. Several lorries had caught the blast and were peppered with holes, their tarpaulins ripped across, their doors punched in. Then Les saw his motorcycle. The magnificent 500cc BSA lay on its side, leaking petrol, the frame shattered. If he hadn't been so angry he would have been close to tears. Every swear word he could think of was hurled at the German pilots, their families, their country. With a casual flick of a switch in a cockpit, Les's freedom had been destroyed.

He made the rest of the journey in the back of a 15cwt lorry. They moved twice after they crossed the Scheldt, first to a disused factory east of Lille and then to an evacuated hospital in La Bassée on the junction of two canals. The French armies in the south had crumbled against the onslaught of the German attack and the BEF was in danger of penetration on its southern flank. General Gort was proposing to set up a defensive line along the canals that ran through Béthune and La Bassée. When Les arrived with the rest of his battalion at La Bassée at 3.30 in the morning of the 20th they marched to their billets in the empty hospital, unrolled their palliasses and crashed out before the next stand-to. Then the orders changed again.

The General Staff of the BEF had been established in the old town of Arras in 1939, but that was no longer in the British area of responsibility. Lord Gort still held it, however, and a force made up of the 1st Welsh Guards, troops from the Royal Artillery depot, men from Searchlight and Royal Engineer units, and crews of armoured vehicles from the Light Armoured Reconnaissance Brigade headquarters made up the garrison. It may well have been thrown together from whatever men and equipment were available, but when the town was attacked on 18 and 19 May by Rommel's 7th Armoured Division, the Germans were repulsed. This did not, however, prevent the enemy from continuing to sweep west, heading towards the coast. In order to take the pressure off the Arras garrison, the General Staff decided to send a force south in an attempt to cut off the German communications from the east. Information from the French had at this point been almost non-existent, so the British General Staff had no real inkling of the size of the German forces involved. Neither was there any appreciation of the fact that they had moved so far west as to have almost reached the coast.

Two infantry divisions, the 5th and the 50th, were available to carry out this mission, along with the 1st Army Tank Brigade. These three units were all much reduced in strength, a result of the last few days' fighting. Each infantry division had two brigades rather than three. Of the two brigades left under the command of the 5th Division, one of them, the 13th, was already under orders to move to the River Scarpe to replace the 23rd Brigade and a French cavalry unit. The 5th Division's other brigade, the 17th, was going to be held in reserve until later in the operation. This left only the 50th Division to take part in the first stages of the attack, but one brigade, the 150th, was going to separate off and enter Arras to strengthen the garrison. After all these units had been peeled off for different tasks, only the 151st Brigade was left to make the assault. With a battalion kept in reserve, it was down then to the two remaining battalions, Les Clarke's 6th and the 8th Durham Light Infantry, to go in to mop up the German forces and cut their lines of communication to the east. It was a very tall order.

The men of the Durham Light Infantry would, of course, have the support of the 1st Tank Brigade, but here too the British were much diminished, with the brigade deploying just fifty-eight Mark I and sixteen Mark II tanks, two different versions of the same Matilda tank. Normally the brigade would have had a total complement of seventy-seven Mark Is and twenty-three Mark IIs. It wasn't only a question of the number of tanks, however, but of their speed and the weapons that they carried. The Mark I had very thick armour, but it was slow, able to move at just eight miles an hour. Its tracks were not well protected against enemy fire and its crew of just two men was kept very busy driving, maintaining awareness of the situation in the battlefield, operating the hull-mounted radio and firing its inadequate armament of a .5in machine gun. In truth, it was an armoured infantry-support vehicle. The Mark II had a gun firing a 2-pounder shell and was a more modern and effective design, but there were just not enough of them compared with the size of the German armoured units that were threatening Arras.

The General Staff, and the staff at the divisional HQ and at brigade level, had seriously underestimated the opposition that their attack was likely to meet. The orders passed from 151st Brigade staff to the battalions of the Durham Light Infantry said that German infantry and tanks were known to be operating south and south-west of Arras, but 'in numbers not believed to be great'. Yet a column of tanks from Rommel's 7th Armoured Division had launched an attack against Arras on the morning of 20 May. Rommel himself had got as far as the town of Beaurains, on the south-east outskirts of Arras, before turning back to bring up more support. There were reports of columns of enemy lorries moving west, and strong columns of infantry and tanks travelling west on the road from Cambrai towards Arras on the 20th. Another column of tanks was observed between two road junctions that put them more or less where the Durham Light Infantry and the Tank Brigade would be forming up on their start line.

The mission was slow to get started, stuttering and stalling because the logistics of the BEF were failing under the pressures of the rapid ad hoc withdrawal from the east. At 5.50 on the morning of the 20th a party of men from each company of the 6th Durham Light Infantry was assembled and went to brigade HQ to organize transport for the battalion to make its way to Arras. The four men, under the command of Lieutenant Cookson, returned with the hopeful message that there were no troop carriers at brigade HQ but that they would be sent as soon as they turned up.

D Company and a Bren-gun carrier platoon headed off south, where they took up a position on Vimy Ridge a few miles north of Arras. Meanwhile, the majority of the battalion remained on the La Bassée Canal waiting for their replacements, in the expectation that the transport that arrived would then be used to take them to Arras.

In the interim D Company had started digging in and had built three weapons pits per platoon, linked by communicating trenches. They had camouflaged them and spread barbed wire in front of them. A few hours later they were reinforced, not by the rest of the battalion but by troops from a platoon of a motorcycle battalion of the Royal Northumberland Fusiliers who were going to support the attack. They carried out reconnaissance patrols along the front of D Company's lines.

Meanwhile, back at La Bassée, the rest of the 6th Battalion had seen their replacements arrive, but the transport had left immediately. Time was now pressing and the battalion formed up and marched off. The lack of transport was galling for Les, who, now without a motorcycle, found himself in the mortar section of B Company, carrying the base plate of a 2in mortar on his back.

They passed various units of French troops, who seemed to Les and his mates to be a bit of a rabble. They lacked discipline or a sense of purpose. When the battalion stopped to rest for tea and some tinned rations at a small village, some French troops without warning set fire to a nearby haystack. It contained ammunition and after a few minutes it exploded, sending bullets whistling through the air. No one was hurt, but there were angry shouts and abuse about the reckless approach of their allies. Even more alarming, although in a different way, was the sight of French gunners destroying four of their own artillery pieces. Why these guns were not going to be used along the line of the La Bassée Canal was a question that would clearly get no answer, but Les remembers the sight of it and how it struck him forcefully that the French had thrown in the towel.

The break for tea extended for hours. They were told to stand down and wait for the troop carriers, but they didn't arrive until ten o'clock that night. Les climbed aboard at last and they continued their slow journey in the dark towards Vimy Ridge, reporting to the battalion HQ of the Northumberland Fusiliers. Les didn't finally arrive at their lying-up areas in Thelus Wood until 3.30 the next morning. The men had had an uncomfortable night, but there was not going to be any let-up, because two hours later they had to stand to and prepare for another move of eight miles before the attack could begin. But there was thick mist, with visibility cut to just a few yards, so they had to wait until it had cleared. Men went foraging, entering abandoned farms to find what eggs they could, and milking the complaining cows for their breakfast. A force of twin-engined bombers flew over the woods, but they couldn't be seen through the layer of mist; all that could be heard on the ground was the throbbing roar of their engines. It was nerve-racking, and Les remembers that the men moved quietly, as though the bomber crews above could hear them. There was a horrible feeling that at any moment bombs would start exploding amongst the trees.

The mist finally cleared and they moved off at 11.30, having been awake for eight hours already. D Company was in the lead, followed by the battalion HQ, then B and C

Companies. The carrier platoon, then the mortar platoon and the artillery and anti-tank batteries followed, and finally A Company brought up the rear. Parts of Arras had been hit by air raids and artillery, and smoke drifted into the sky. Their approach route was slightly west of south; they passed through the little towns of Anzin and St-Aubin, then turned east along the bank of the River Scarpe. At this point they stopped, climbed out of the transports, unloaded their weapons and prepared to advance on foot. Les now had to shoulder the mortar base plate, the heaviest and most cumbersome part of the weapon, and struggle along with it. Once more he cursed the German pilot who had done for his bike.

D Company started to advance at 2.30 p.m., a battalion of tanks from the Royal Tank Corps moving ahead of them. Les was in the rear of B Company and as they approached Wagnonlieu he could hear the sound of incoming artillery shells bursting a few hundred yards in front. They were hitting D Company and the tanks. Shouted orders to get into artillery formation followed and Les moved over to the right of the advance, while C Company went to the left. They continued forward, and Les felt very vulnerable walking towards the explosions and the sounds of gunfire. But the presence of tanks of the 4th Battalion Royal Tank Corps in the lead shocked the German infantry. This was the first time that they had faced the heavily armoured British Matildas. It was also the first time that the Germans had encountered any serious resistance to their advance, and they started to retreat. The tanks shot up a lot of German equipment and transport, without any opposition, and the German units were scattered. Their withdrawal had been extremely hasty and men were left behind. These enemy stragglers were still lurking in the houses in Achincourt and Agny when Les's company reached them. Some were prepared to give themselves up, but others tried to fight and there were several skirmishes as the battalion tried to clear the villages. B Company advanced through Agny with their bayonets at the ready. The mortars had been set up and Les went through the village to check some of the houses. One had been smashed with grenades and there was a wounded German soldier lying outside it, a bullet through his pelvis and in great pain. There wasn't much Les could do for him. A machine-gun post held out for some time in the village of Beaurains but was finally silenced by an attack with grenades. The battalion war diary says that the total number of prisoners sent back to A Company and the battalion HQ totalled around four hundred. Les thinks this is an exaggeration; he doubts that he saw many more than a hundred Germans taken prisoner. 'Nobody knew what to do with them. We had as much to do looking after ourselves. I saw lots rounded up, but we took their weapons and ammo off them and told them to scarper.' By three o'clock that afternoon the battalion had established its HQ in Achincourt and pickets and observation posts were set up overnight in Beaurains.

The German retaliation was not long in coming. The advance and success of the two battalions of the Durham Light Infantry had caused alarm in the German command. They were aware that their lines of communication were stretched and that the rapid drive to the French coast had left their flanks unguarded, but now the counter-attack at Arras made Rommel and others acutely aware of the danger they faced. The attack that day had pitted 1,800 British men and

74 tanks against German forces amounting to 7,000 infantry and 740 tanks, and they had initially overwhelmed the German forces. Rommel assumed that this was the prelude to a much greater attack and quickly called for counter-measures.

At six o'clock that evening German dive-bombers appeared over the three villages that the battalion had occupied. Wave after wave of Stukas dived on them. Les had experienced nothing like it. 'You're in some foxhole, any-where you can get. Foolishly, you think that if your head is covered you're safe. You turn into a sort of animal.' The hellish screams of the diving planes, followed a heart-stopping two seconds later by the crash of their exploding 500lb bombs, seemed to go on for ever. Once they had dropped their bombs the aircraft returned to machine-gun the area. 'We had no anti-aircraft fire. You can't shoot down a plane with a Lee-Enfield rifle.'

When the last of the three flights of warplanes left – Les estimated that there must have been about 150 aircraft in the extended attack – artillery fire started to fall on them. Stretcher-bearers were running from shelter to shelter with the wounded, runners were dodging between the battalion HQ and the company positions as shells whistled through the air and threw up huge gouts of fire and earth. The villages were quickly turning into rubble. The brigade had no attached artillery with which it could target the enemy guns and help to suppress the relentless shelling. 'The shelling got very nasty,' says Les. 'Then the tanks moved in.'

At eight o'clock the battalion diary records that reports from the forward company suggested that enemy tanks were working their way round the right flank of the village of

Agny and moving between C and B Company positions. At the same time, some of the men in the forward positions had spotted German artillery observation posts as little as sixty yards from the eastern edge of the village.

The two companies were ordered to withdraw to Achincourt to avoid being surrounded in the night. A Company took up a position along a railway line east of Achincourt to provide some covering fire for the troops of D and C Companies as they pulled back. German tanks, however, had also moved into position. Most of the British Matilda tanks that had led the advance of the Durham Light Infantry had by now been knocked out by heavy artillery and the 88mm anti-aircraft guns of Rommel's 7th Panzer Division, and the few that were left had moved to Arras to reinforce the garrison.

Five German Panzer tanks now appeared up the road from Beaurains and, on seeing the rearguard positions of the two companies fanned out into line abreast, they started firing. Caught out in the open, the men had no defences against the advancing tanks. 'They really got to work. They meant it. When they fired, they were going to get a hit. They didn't fire and hope.'

Soon dead and wounded were scattered over the fields, while others tried to run for cover. The bloodshed would have been even greater but for the appearance of four British tanks that took on the enemy, and in the ensuing battle the rest of C and D Companies were able to move back. Les thinks that over a hundred men died or were wounded that day in the German counter-attack.

The battalion pulled itself together at Achincourt, climbing aboard whatever transport was available, and moved back to Petit Vimy, where its shocked and exhausted remnants bivouacked for the night.

At stand-to the following morning the scale of the casualties became all too clear. 'You stood there, hearing men's names called who you had shared food and cigarettes with for months, and there was no response.' Almost a third of the battalion was missing, either taken prisoner, dead or wounded. 'Some of the lads were in a bad way mentally too. They were close to shell-shock from the dive-bombing and the tank attack.' Many officers were missing and second lieutenants were given command of the HQ Company and three other rifle companies. D Company, which had suffered the most casualties, was placed under the command of a captain; it was better for morale to have a more mature presence. 'We were nineteen years old, so a captain was an old man to us. Talking to a twenty-seven-year-old made you feel better. "What's going to happen to us now, sir?" Even if you were told rubbish, it helped.'

Les and the 6th Battalion Durham Light Infantry stayed at Vimy for the next two days as confusion reigned over where the German forces were and what counter-attacks, if any, could be mounted. They were dug in finally along the edge of a wood between Vimy and the village of Thelus, with the 9th Durham Light Infantry to their right. There were air raids the whole time. Then the Germans broke through in the south and crossed the River Scarpe, and their heavy artillery was moving within range of Petit Vimy. On the afternoon of the 23rd shells started hitting the high ridge in front of the battalion's positions, then more salvoes fell into Thelus Wood. All the time the men were digging in and improving their trenches. Soon shells started to come in from both the south-west and the south-east as the Germans moved up from Arras.

There was a serious problem now with supplies. Food and ammunition were low, but little was coming in from the ports to the west. Men went out to find what they could in the villages and farms, but this source was rapidly being stripped bare.

A severe air raid took place in and around the village of Vimy in the afternoon, with Stukas making machine-gun attacks after dropping their bombs. The village, which was full of refugees, was devastated and casualties were high. Parties of men from the battalion were organized to go to dig graves for the dead, picking up women and children where they lay sprawled. Les remembers that some were hideously wounded while others appeared to have been killed without a scratch. The dead horses, dogs and the odd cow were piled up on to pyres, and the oily black smoke from the flames drifted over the ruined buildings. Everyone was too exhausted and stunned by the events of the past days to shed any tears, but the party returned to their billets in utter silence.

Orders were received from the division that the ridge and Vimy itself had to be held at all costs. 'An officer came along. He was waving his pistol to emphasize what he said: "We will hold this position to the last man and the last bullet." He could tell what the feeling among us was. We didn't have to say anything. We'll see who's got the last bullet.'

The Germans had advanced as far as the town of Lens, which lay almost behind them. Just one road out to the north was still in Allied hands and it was in danger of being cut. Heavy shelling could be heard from the rear of the town and fires lit the low clouds in the night sky. The enemy was launching another assault. The sound of heavy machine-gun fire came from the right flank and they were using search-lights to direct their aim. Bullets swept through the woods and mortars crashed down – Les recalls that they were like hailstones on a tin roof. You didn't know whether to run or hide. Men were horribly wounded by bullets and shrapnel, and stretcher-bearers dodged between trees trying to get the casualties out.

It really did seem as if this would be their last stand, but at eleven o'clock that night runners came along the line to tell them that they were pulling out. It was a ragged, chaotic withdrawal under intense fire. Transport was waiting further up the road. They pulled out heading back to the canal line at La Bassée, taking a circuitous route in the dark to avoid an encounter with the enemy. It was slow progress and B Company, many of them on foot like Les, got lost. An officer driving an Austin 7 guided them through goods yards and over railway crossings until they finally caught up with the rest of the battalion at daybreak and were able to climb on board the overloaded troop carriers.

It was a cold morning. Their journey took them through towns and villages that had been heavily bombed. Large numbers of civilians had become casualties, dead or dying, lying at the side of the roads, in hedges or in the rubble of collapsed houses. Les was becoming immune to the sights and smell of death, but the long depressing journey out of Vimy was enough to break anyone's spirit. He felt personally in despair. Could it get any worse, he wondered?

On the morning of 24 May the scale of their losses became apparent. They had halted overnight in Don, a small village by the canal two miles east of La Bassée. Ten officers and just

192 other ranks lined up for the roll call, from a battalion of nearly eight hundred men. Another two hundred arrived throughout the rest of the day, but there were too few men to keep the old companies so the battalion was reorganized into a Headquarters Company and two others, called simply 1 Company and 2 Company. There was very little food available and not much ammunition left. What there was was redistributed amongst the two companies, along with the remaining weapons.

Two officers were sent to Lille to see if they could find some rations. Later that day there was a heavy air raid on La Bassée to their right. There was no end in sight. It was just a matter of waiting for the start of another terrible onslaught of artillery and dive-bombers as the enemy inexorably advanced.

12

LARRY UREN AT LA BASSÉE

20–29 May

Larry Uren and a group of men from the 1/7th Battalion Queen's Royal Regiment had pulled back from the River Dendre under intense fire and had got lost. They had been instructed to make their way via the Belgian towns of Audenarde and Coteghem to Belleghem Bosch, a forested area north-east of Lille. There were about sixty men of B Company with Captain Dickenson. Larry had been driving the captain in this withdrawal; fortunately not in the lead, and so not responsible for the lengthy diversions. The maps were hard to read and, as it turned out, inaccurate, with the result that they had taken several wrong turnings, driving through strange towns and villages all darkened and closed up. There was, Larry remembers, an enormous movement of people and vehicles going in completely different directions. He and the group finally arrived, but the war diary records that, even after they had joined up with the battalion, out of the five companies only two were up to strength. Two platoons were absent from A Company, two from C Company and the HQ Company was still waiting for its transport to arrive. It took two more days before the battalion was finally up to strength.

The opportunity to rest while the battalion re-formed was extremely welcome, but it ended when on 20 May the battalion received orders to move south-west to take up positions at La Bassée. The threat from German Army Group A in the south, and now in the west, meant that it was imperative to defend the BEF against attack from the southern flank and in the rear. Various units were moving to hold a line that stretched from Gravelines on the Channel coast, west of Dunkirk, through Béthune and La Bassée in the south, extending all the way to Lille. La Bassée was on the northern bank of a canal that, with others connecting the various towns along the proposed line, provided a natural barrier against the German armoured columns. The 25th Brigade was given responsibility for holding a length of the canal that stretched east for fifteen miles from Béthune, and the Queen's were in the middle at La Bassée with the Royal Irish Fusiliers on their left and the 2nd Battalion Essex Regiment on their right.

La Bassée was the largest village on that particular stretch of the canal and on either side of it, to the east and west at the rear of the battalion, were hamlets with the intriguing names of Givenchy and Salome. On the south bank the country was flat, with lines of poplars and hedges providing the only cover. The day that they arrived was peaceful and they were able to start locating observation posts, digging in machine guns and establishing battalion and company headquarters. There were several bridges over the canal and sappers were already starting to lay charges to bring them tumbling into the water. The men didn't know it, but they were to get two days' respite here. The fighting at Arras in which Les Clarke in the Durham Light Infantry had taken part had alarmed the Germans, who were also worried about their stretched lines of communication. Their advance was halted at the La Bassée Canal by orders from Rundstedt. The German armoured divisions were told to close up to the canal and use the pause for repair and maintenance.

The canal that ran through La Bassée was connected to miles of waterways that eventually took traffic to the great ports of Antwerp and Rotterdam. The war had brought most of this traffic to a halt and the canal banks at La Bassée were lined with barges two or even three deep. Their owners lived on board with their families, presenting an incongruous sight to Larry and many others in the battalion as they prepared their defences. Washing was hung out to dry, children and dogs played on deck and smoke drifted out of the stove pipes in the rear-deck housing. The arrival of the soldiers had caused some alarm amongst the barge community; so too had the sight of the sappers working on the bridges over the canal. There had been some friendly suggestions that the bargees should move out of the way, that things would be very hot soon, but they had nowhere to go. The bargees were of all nationalities, some Dutch and Belgian as well as French, all of them marooned by the war.

Larry was sympathetic – one of the greatest shocks to him and his mates had been the sight of civilian casualties, the dead and wounded, innocent victims of the fighting. Unfortunately, however, the barges were seen by the company commanders as a real danger. They were moored so densely in the canal that it was possible to walk across them from bank to bank. Demolishing the bridges was pointless if the Germans would be able to use the barges as ready-made pontoons. In the stretch of canal covered by the brigade there were over 250 of these vessels.

At a battalion commanders' conference at brigade head-quarters on the evening of the 21st, all the commanders voiced their concern about the barges in their areas. They wanted permission to get rid of them, if necessary by destroy-ing them. The brigade staff felt that this was a decision that could only be made by the division. It was a thorny issue, as the owners were certain to object, and the brigade was to be reinforced with some French units who might take a different view of destroying their countrymen's property. So the battalion commanders left the meeting with orders that the bridges could be destroyed at the company commanders' discretion if it was clear that German forces were advancing and that their capture was imminent; and also that a sergeant from the Royal Engineers could set the charges off if there was no time to wait for a commander's decision. But there was no decision about the barges.

The following day a French regiment, the 131st, went into the Queen's positions and added their strength to the defence. A British field regiment and two anti-tank regiments also moved in to add depth to the defensive positions. Towards the end of the day the orders arrived allowing the demolition of the barges in the canal. Larry went down to the water's edge with a section of Royal Engineers on the morning of the 23rd. They carried straw and cans of petrol to set fire to the wooden barges, and the sappers were going to blow holes in those with metal hulls.

The bargees were already highly agitated about the situation. Further up the canal, members of the Irish Fusiliers had broken up some of the biggest concentrations of barges by climbing on board to untie them and tow them upstream with their Bren-gun carriers. The shouts of protest and screams from some of the women had spread news of the assault all along the canal. When Larry and his fellow soldiers arrived at the barges the skippers – big, broad-shouldered men, many with wives as tough as they were – were waiting for them on the bank.

It was a dreadful situation. Here they were, armed with rifles and bayonets, setting out to destroy these people's property and ruin their livelihoods without any warning. Sent to fight German soldiers, they were now turning their guns on the French civilians they were meant to be defending. Not one of the soldiers wanted to be the first aboard, but after some barked orders from the NCO they leaped on to the deck and the fighting started. Larry climbed on to a barge, followed by a couple of men with hay bales. They splashed petrol on to the bales and the tarpaulin over the hold and the whole thing went up with a whoosh of yellow flame and heat.

Fire started on more barges, and the screams were now anguished and full of fear and anger. Larry leaped off the barge and ran along the side of the canal with his can of petrol, his mates following with more bales of straw. There were other barges to deal with. Fights had broken out all along the canal, and on the iron-hulled barges where the Royal Engineers had to set their charges in the hull the owners were being physically manhandled on to the bank of the canal and held at bayonet point. Larry thought it was horrible at the time, and still does so now. 'They were fighting to protect their homes. It was a dreadful thing. But we were hardened. We had seen death and destruction by then and we no longer cared. The war had done that to us very quickly.' Passing the groups of civilians, some with children in their arms, he could hear women crying and he caught the hatred in the curses hurled at him.

The demolition charges in the hulls of the metal barges started exploding. It was utter chaos. Flames went licking along the canal, lighting the black smoke of the burning barges from underneath, as everything – wooden hulls, tarpaulins, fuel – was consumed by the fire. The faces of the soldiers and the civilians flickered red in the firelight and the echoing explosions of the demolition charges turned the night into a giant, hellish bonfire party.

Now working methodically, the soldiers fired barge after barge. Flames shot high into the air and acrid black smoke swirled over the surrounding villages and fields. By the next day 250 barges had been destroyed. Fifteen miles of the canal had been turned into a giant conflagration and its banks were covered in ash and soot, the canal itself filled with the wrecks of sunken and burned vessels. The smell of burning carried on the wind for miles. The lives of 250 families had been ruined and they were now part of the ever-growing army of homeless refugees.

After the initial fight Larry had carried out the work like an automaton. Once the first five or six barges were burning, the fight had gone out of most of the bargees, and Larry's section had run from barge to barge with cans of petrol and bundles of hay. He felt disgusted at what had happened. He didn't care that there was a war on, or that the Germans were just a few miles away and would soon be on them. The whole event seemed to be part of the madness that had seized the world.

The following day there was the constant drone of spotter aircraft above them. Nothing seemed to be done to get rid of these planes, which were recording their every move. No fighters were sent to shoot them down and there were no anti-aircraft guns with the division. There was a strange atmosphere. The weather was fine and warm, but the reek of the huge fires that they had started on the barges still hung in the air, and with it was a sense of waiting for something to happen. As far as Larry was concerned, there was always that sense of anxiety, a sickness in the stomach about what might lie ahead. It was not until he was involved in immediate action that the adrenaline kicked in and the fear was forgotten.

By midday it was possible to see the enemy manoeuvring into position. The German armoured divisions might have been ordered by Rundstedt not to cross the canal, but reconnaissance units and infantry were on the move. The artillery that was in place behind Larry's battalion, the 25-pounder guns of the 74th Field Regiment, opened up, dropping shells on crossroads and areas where enemy troops might seek cover to assemble. The first contact, however, was on their right, when German tanks approached to a distance of a thousand yards and started firing on the 2nd Battalion Essex Regiment. Shortly after, a squadron of Stuka dive-bombers appeared and launched an attack on the Essex positions, killing a lieutenant and wounding some soldiers. The Germans were advancing rapidly and along the canal the sound of exploding demolition charges punctuated the sound of artillery fire as the bridges were blown up.

By the early hours of 24 May all the routes over the canals had been cut. Three hours later, at six o'clock in the morning, enemy shells started to fall along the length of the 25th Brigade's position. As the shelling intensified, the villages and towns along the canal started to burn and were slowly reduced to rubble. Infantry and armoured personnel carriers advanced across the open country to the south of the canal, where they were caught in machine-gun and mortar fire from the Queen's and the Royal Irish Fusiliers' machine guns. German casualties were high – men dropped in the stream of bullets and their advance stopped. The shelling continued, however, and areas in the rear now began to feel the force of the Germans' relentless bombardment. They hit the Queen's transport park and the 15cwt lorry that Larry had been driving went up in flames, along with several others.

The canal was thinly defended, so Lord Gort had ordered the 46th and 2nd Divisions to move as quickly as possible to help bolster it up. Their forward units now started to arrive, but they were held up by the German shelling of the approach roads and weren't able to get into place until two that afternoon, when men from the 7th Worcesters and the 2nd Camerons started to take up forward positions along the canal. The Queen's and the Irish Fusiliers had to stay in place. At the Pont-à-Vendin, to the east of the Queen's positions, a German armoured column made a determined effort to advance to the canal edge, but anti-tank artillery firing point blank set fire to the leading armoured cars and that attack was defeated. But the shelling continued, with the enemy offensive augmented by mortar fire and repeated attacks by Stukas.

Casualties in Larry's battalion were mounting and he

found that the strain of the dive-bomber attacks drove him almost to breaking point. The shelling was frightening enough; he worked on the old soldiers' rule that if you could hear it, it wasn't for you, but no human being could control the involuntary flinching that followed the whistling shell and the crack of the explosion. The Stuka dive-bombers, however, were truly terrifying. The siren-like howl they generated as they plunged earthwards to release their bombs seemed to bring death closer every second. You would shelter under a blade of grass if you could.

He stayed in his scrape and the shelling went on. The whole area had been reduced to a smoking wasteland. Destroyed bridges lay broken in the canal. Hundreds of barges had sunk and a thick, oily scum covered the water. The houses in La Bassée, Salome and Givenchy were now jagged walls, without roofs or windows, and piles of red-brick rubble blocked the roads. Carriers and lorries burned with flickering dark-red flames. Larry hadn't shaved for days, and his vest and khaki shirt were stiff with dried sweat. His horizon had shrunk to surviving the next salvo, the next air raid. It seemed presumptuous to think about the next day.

As evening approached the shelling lessened and he was told that the Cameron Highlanders were to relieve most of the battalion, though A Company and one platoon of C Company were to remain in place. Larry was lucky. He was going. They pulled out under cover of darkness and prepared to move to the town of Aubers a few miles to the north. Their numbers were much reduced. The shelling and bombing had whittled them down, and Larry was almost done in.

General Rommel, whose 7th Panzer Division had stopped south of the La Bassée Canal, received reports that the

British defenders could be seen pulling back. He signalled to his corps HQ for permission to cross the canal and this was given. He chose to make the attempt near to Givenchy, where one of his rifle regiments managed to get some troops across the canal by evening, despite fierce firing from the defenders and the presence of a large number of sunken barges. The next day, the 27th, the German engineers had not managed to get a pontoon bridge across the canal, largely because of the wrecks blocking it. Moreover, ten British tanks from the Tank Regiment had moved in to support the Cameron Highlanders, who were still laying down sniper and machine-gun fire. The situation was critical for the crossing, but Rommel managed to persuade his engineers to build some bigger pontoons and a Panzer tank made the precarious crossing. This tank, working in collaboration with others on the south bank and with some 88mm howitzers that had been brought up, stopped the British Matilda tanks in their tracks. Their presence, however, had allowed the Camerons to get away.

There had been plans for the Queen's to move forward once again to help extricate the Camerons, and in preparation the battalion marched out of Aubers to set up some defensive positions in a line that ran west of Nieuw Chappelle, a mile to the north of La Bassée. Their objective was to be the villages of Givenchy and Violaines, the point where Rommel was now directing his offensive. Larry had been told of the orders for a new advance when he had been sheltering with a crowd of other men in the ruin of a bar in Aubers. It caused consternation amongst them, and a couple of men climbed out of a rear window to escape forming up. The battalion moved back to the front with great reluctance. But the

Matilda tanks, which should have coordinated their assault with the Queen's, failed to join up with them, heading instead directly for La Bassée, where, as we have just seen, Rommel's tanks and artillery brought them to a sharp halt. The Queen's counter-attack was called off. Larry had had a lucky escape. The battalion was then ordered to dig in as the remnants of the 5th Division retreated through their lines.

The day before, on the 26th, Lord Gort had received a telegram from Anthony Eden, minister for war in the British Cabinet. It said that the French were not able to carry out an offensive against the German Army in the south. The safety of the BEF must be the first consideration. 'In such conditions only course open to you may be to fight your way back to West where all beaches and ports east of Gravelines will be used for embarkation. Navy will provide fleet of ships and small boats and RAF would give full support.'

The decision to evacuate the BEF had effectively now been made. First raised in a phone call to the War Office on the 19th, the independent realization by both Gort and the War Cabinet that the French Army had failed and the French government had broken made the evacuation inevitable. Later that day, at three minutes to seven in the evening, the Admiralty made the signal: 'Operation Dynamo is to commence.' Admiral Bertram Ramsay had not waited to be told. At three o'clock that afternoon the first ships had already left Dover for Dunkirk.

The British Expeditionary Force was now trapped in an enclave the shape of a rectangle, like a shoebox, with one of its shorter sides, the northern one, running along the coast from the Belgian border to the port of Gravelines in the west.

The other three sides were under attack. In the east General Bock's Army Group B had slowly advanced across Belgium. The southern and western sides were under more dynamic attack from the armoured columns of Rundstedt's Army Group A. Part of these – Rommel's 7th Armoured Division and others – had broken the canal line in the south at La Bassée and were moving north. In the west the 2nd Panzer Division had taken Boulogne and other divisions were now heading east from Abbeville.

Larry Uren had no appreciation of this greater picture, but he knew that things were very serious indeed. The men were now on half rations and were low on ammunition. They had been pulling back for days, their numbers were dwindling, and they were tired and hungry. He knew that he had been lucky to get away from Ninove and from La Bassée. Now the battalion was acting as a rearguard for the rest of the division to fall back to another river, the Lys, as a defensive line. Once again there was a massive artillery bombardment as the 5th Division retreated through their lines. Under the protection of a section of Bren-gun carriers they raced across a bridge, which was promptly blown up, and then the battalion was ordered to Dollieu, where they dug in on a line a mile to the west of the town to defend it from the south-west. They were dive-bombed heavily during the day and at around four o'clock in the afternoon they received news that German tanks had broken through the 2nd Division line and were approaching through the wood at Nieppe, a mile to their west. Moreover, German airborne troops had landed at the airfield just south of the town of Merville on the south side of the river and managed to seize a bridge over the Lys.

As darkness fell there was no clear dividing line between

the various forces and fighting started in the streets of Neuf-Berquin. Groups of soldiers held on to their positions, fighting for every village and building until they could pull back. It was a stubborn resistance and it slowed the Germans down considerably – they suffered heavy casualties. But this couldn't stop the battalions of the 2nd Division being carved up by the German armour, and the defensive line of the Lys was now in shreds.

An order came down from brigade HQ for the Queen's to move back yet again to another line that ran west from the town of Poperinge to the village of Watou. They moved out at two o'clock on 28 May. The battalion was barely managing to keep together. Much of their transport was lost or destroyed and it was impossible to organize any from divisional resources. Any vehicle available was being commandeered. 'There was very little discipline left, because there was almost no organization,' remembers Larry. 'Communication had broken down. Company and platoon were moving quickly and runners just couldn't find them. It was a case of sometimes just following the crowd.'

It was a mere twelve days since Larry had advanced into Belgium to meet the German Army along the line of the River Dyle. Now it looked like a rout. The battalion moved north for about a mile, but the roads were completely clogged with refugees – thousands walking; some, the luckier ones, in cars or lorries; some using horse-drawn transport of every conceivable description. All were piled with bundles of bedding and pieces of furniture that looked as though they might topple over at any minute. The roads were completely blocked. The 2nd Battalion Essex Regiment, ahead of the Queen's, had to abandon its motor transport and go ahead on foot.

Larry's company came to a halt and dug in for the night, mounting a guard on the road to the south. Gunfire could be heard from the west and the south, and it sounded not very far away. Brigade HQ ordered the motor transport to press on to try to find a way forward by going east of the town of Bailleul. The streams of refugees never stopped throughout the night, the noise of thousands of thudding feet, the cries of children filling the darkness. Larry and his friends in his platoon stuck together; they felt that they were barely floating on an ocean of complete chaos. The battalion's war diary records: 'Traffic, including French horse-drawn transport, beyond description. Roads blocked for miles on end.'

At 6.30 a.m., as the battalion tried to organize itself amongst the tide of fleeing people, the brigade commander arrived in a staff car. There was a huddle of battalion staff and company commanders. The orders were to proceed individually to Dunkirk, by company if possible, in small groups if not.

The battalion was dissolved. It was every man for himself and Larry, who had trained, travelled to France and fought in Belgium as part of the 1/7th Queen's Battalion in the BEF, was now in a broken and defeated foreign country on his own.

He had no map, no compass, no rations, just a rifle, a dozen rounds of ammunition and his haversack with his gas mask and cape. The first thing that sprang to his mind was 'Where is Dunkirk?' The second thought was 'How will I get there in this crowd?'

13

Sid Lewis on the Scheldt

19–26 May

We left Sid Lewis on 19 May in the village of Hollain on the western bank of the River Scheldt three miles south of Tournai. The war diary of Sid's battalion describes the village as quiet and peaceful.

The Scheldt at this point was a broad river, joined by two canals, and just south of the village were several locks with two large basins where river traffic could wait to pass through them. It made a very effective obstacle and was the last natural barrier before the defences of the French border to the west. While German Army Group A had been sweeping all before it to the south, Army Group B had been steadily advancing west from Brussels, snapping at the heels of the BEF as they pulled back.

Reg Beeston, the sapper who had spent the winter building pillboxes along the Franco-Belgian border, was now part of the 144th Brigade, along with Sid's 2nd Battalion Royal

Warwickshire Regiment, and all were now under the command of the 48th Division. Reg had joined in the retreat and his more destructive skills had come to the fore. He and his mates from 224 Field Company Royal Engineers had been blowing bridge after bridge as they pulled back in the face of the German advance. It wasn't, as he remembers, very difficult or challenging work. The metal bridges were destroyed by fixing slabs of TNT to the main girders, which were then detonated by time fuses or set off by an electrical charge. The charges were connected only at the very last moment, 'and then you had to run like buggery.' They also tried to create other obstacles. 'You could make deep craters in the roads with decent-sized charges of amatol. They would go up like a big bomb; the whole point was to shift tons of earth. But nothing seemed to stop Jerry for long.'

A railway bridge and a separate road bridge crossed the river at Hollain, with another road bridge further south near the docking basins. The sappers had destroyed all these by the time that Sid's battalion had started to dig in along the river-banks and establish company headquarters further back in the village.

They stood to at 4.45 in the morning and were issued with some rations. The food was basic, with some tea and tinned fish; Reg Beeston remembers that there was no hot food any more. The rations also included biscuits and bully beef. The biscuits were three-inch-square ship's biscuit – or hardtack – which Reg found quite tasty but which took a long time to eat.

Sid's section, meanwhile, was in reserve, not directly on the front of the river but near to a railway halt along the branch line that went into Hollain; the river was about a hundred yards away. The day was quiet so far, but Sid was alert, well aware that the enemy would eventually attack. In the early morning light a group of German tanks was seen in a far-off field, at a distance of about two thousand yards. Everyone rushed to their posts until the intelligence officer, who spent a long time looking through his field glasses from the observation post set up in an old factory along the side of the river, noted drily that they were actually cows.

The sun rose, burning off the morning mist, and the battalion spent the time improving their defences, adding sandbags to the machine-gun posts and ensuring that everyone had adequate reserves of ammunition. At two o'clock in the afternoon Sid heard some firing towards the left, where D Company was dug in. Then a runner brought information that German troops were some five hundred yards away, and the slow, dull fire of Bren guns picked up, soon becoming continuous. More German troops could be seen across the battalion front along the banks of the river, then the first enemy shells started landing with huge explosions in the village and the trees to their left along the river.

A unit of German troops and pioneers infiltrated close to the eastern riverbank at the nearby bend and tried to cross it in some inflatable dinghies. It was a brave but desperate effort. They soon pulled back under concentrated machine-gun fire, leaving some dinghies and bodies floating in the river. Perhaps in an attempt to take advantage of this crossing, large numbers of German soldiers established themselves in a wooded area on the far bank of the river. They set up machine-gun posts and bullets started to wing their way across the river at A Company positions. The battalion's mortar platoon was directed to lob mortar bombs on to the trees and the noise of exploding shells and mortars as well as the fire of machine guns filled the air. Sid was soon on duty as a stretcher-bearer, ducking and weaving from cover to cover to pick up the wounded, some hit by a shell splinter or, worse, the victim of a direct hit, a tourniquet tightened around a limb, the blood still pumping out of a severed artery.

Another attempt was made by the Germans to cross the river. Under cover of very heavy shelling they tried to manoeuvre some barges out into the stream. But mortars landed on them and they gave up the attempt, a few bodies left lying where they had been hit. All along the front the shelling was severe. Reg Beeston, further north than Sid's battalion, remembers the large-calibre shells going over his head constantly. He was sheltering in a foxhole about three feet deep and it was possible to look up and see the shells going over. There was almost nothing to be done.

After two and a half hours of this heavy gunfire, the Germans had managed to move close to the river and start digging in. Telephone wires linking battalion HQ with company HQs were cut by the shell blasts and the observation post on the riverbank was now unusable. Mortars and machine-gun fire had smashed it apart, its windows now just jagged holes in the walls, and the streams of bullets that crisscrossed it meant death for anyone who raised his head.

It was now very frightening to move about in the open. Ferrying the wounded back to the village meant dodging mortars and shellbursts, and the village was unrecognizable from the quiet, peaceful place of just a day ago. It was shelled to pieces, with few houses still intact, the roads covered in bricks and slates, and pitted with shellholes.

At six o'clock in the evening there was a fierce fusillade of shells against battalion HQ, located at the rear of the village, and simultaneously there was a new onslaught on the positions of D Company to the left, with the men just going to ground to avoid the streams of machine-gun fire directed at them. Under this relentless covering fire, German troops had managed to cross the river – no one was sure how they had done it – and were working their way to the rear of D Company's positions. The battalion sent a despatch rider to brigade HQ asking for help in taking the pressure off D Company, but none was available. There were no reserves. All along the front line the Germans were pouring men and armour at the British positions, and the whole front, from Tournai to Maulde, was badly stretched.

Darkness brought some relief from the fighting, but the German artillery kept up an intermittent fire throughout the night, wearing down the men and destroying any chance of sleep. Sid was exhausted. The battle had been preceded by that arduous route march back from Waterloo and they had had very little in the way of sleep or food. The shelling had gone on for hours, and his perilous journeys to the aid post had caused a cold sweat of fear to trickle down his back at times. After his first experience of shelling in Sedan, Sid's nerves had settled down and he had stopped ducking at the sound of every exploding shell, but here on the banks of the river it was different. The Germans were moving in and it seemed to him that it was only a matter of time before he was taken prisoner or killed, or perhaps savagely wounded like one or two of the men he had carried on his stretcher, so badly hurt that their bodies arched in pain. Every shell blast set his nerves jangling.

Casualties had been mounting, D Company had been really beaten up and there were rumours that they had been overrun. Sid crouched in the ruins of the cottage that they had moved into the day before, grabbing sleep every now and then; towards the morning he finally nodded off, even when another German salvo screamed in.

Daylight on the 21st brought no relief, although the enemy had come to a standstill along most of the river. The battalion was still holding out, but sniper fire came from behind their position, from the embankment of the railway near the river, where a few German troops had managed to cross. Reg Beeston was also kept pinned down by sniper fire, this time coming from across the river. Sometimes a bullet's passage could be heard before the report of the gun that fired it. One whistled past his mate's head, making him throw himself to the ground. But amongst his group of men taking shelter in the orchard the most damage was caused by mortars. There were five or six fatalities and a lot more were injured by shrapnel from the bursting mortar bombs.

The brigade HQ had finally responded to the request for help and men from the Oxford and Bucks Light Infantry arrived to reinforce them to the south. A Bren-gun carrier section also arrived and went into the area behind Sid's company. The sniping stopped then; two hours later, however, the shelling started again and the battalion HQ was hit. The Bren-gun carrier platoon also received a direct hit from a salvo. The shells wounded the second lieutenant, killed a platoon sergeant and destroyed six of the Bren-gun carriers; their crews were also badly wounded.

Despite the seemingly permanent sense of being under fire, the men kept going. It was almost a matter of honour not to give in to the endless pounding. Sid's mate Chalky White weaselled out into the wrecked village and managed to scrounge some tea and sugar, a tin of condensed milk and the makings of a fire. When the brew was mixed up in a big Dixie, it wasn't long before everyone was looking forward to a hot drink. They were just about to serve it out when a salvo of mortar bombs made them dive for cover. One scored a direct hit on the Dixie of hot tea. Sid had never heard so many oaths strung together.

The shelling picked up again in the afternoon. Sid reckoned that it was all to do with the Germans' supply lines – more ammunition would be brought up and then they would start again. There was nothing that could be done except seek shelter and endure, for what seemed to Sid a lifetime. The nerve-sapping shriek of incoming shells and the crash of explosions were worse today than they had been yesterday. The salvoes creeping in seemed ever nearer, before at the last minute they relented and life could continue for another few minutes. Men huddled in slit trenches or, in the rear areas, crouched by the walls of shattered houses, searching for any-thing that might bring some illusion of shelter.

The 144th Brigade had also pulled back from Waterloo and 144 Field Ambulance Unit, in which Sydney Whiteside was a medical orderly, had set up casualty posts in their rear. The retreat had been energy-sapping. The unit could only move at night, and by the time that Sydney had reached the area of the Scheldt he hadn't slept for six nights in a row. The ambulances of the unit took the wounded from regimental aid posts to casualty posts, and if necessary took them further on to advanced dressing stations. The casualty posts at Wez-Velvain, a village to the rear of the brigade which was a reserve area, was heavily shelled on the 21st and the casualty post had to be evacuated. Throughout this day the ambulances operated under what Sydney describes as 'very unpleasant circumstances'. Three ambulances were hit by shellfire. The war diary for the field ambulance unit records that 254 casualties were evacuated through the advanced dressing stations during this bombardment, although other casualties who were more seriously wounded and needed surgery bypassed the advanced dressing station and were taken directly to a medical dressing station, where operations or amputations could be carried out. The unit buried six men that day.

The rain of shells falling on the 2nd Battalion Royal Warwickshires eventually slackened and men slowly gathered their wits, expecting another attack from infantry or tanks, but nothing happened. Sid eased himself up from behind a wall. Again, there was no hot food, just another issue of biscuits and tinned meat.

The following day, 22 May, started with the familiar mortar fire and artillery shells. It seemed quieter, however. The Germans attempted to cross the river to the north of the 2nd Battalion's lines, but mortars and intense machine-gun fire nipped that in the bud. There seemed to be a stalemate along the river at Hollain. The artillery bombardment continued intermittently, straining nerves, causing casualties, but there was no new attempt by the Germans to move forward and cross the river. Then that evening, to the great joy of Sid and the rest of the battalion, orders came through that they were to be relieved by the 4th Battalion Oxford and Bucks Light

Infantry, and they were to move out to Wez-Velvain. The journey was slow and the transport took ages to arrive, but finally they were in the rear area, where there was some hot food and where Sid could sleep.

Next day they had another jolting journey through jammed roads to the place where Sid had been billeted six months earlier, the town of Rumegies. Here they took up positions in pillboxes and trenches that they had built during the winter. Rumegies was deserted and houses that six months ago had been part of the life of the town, with families and a welcoming cup of coffee, were empty. Several of them were also reduced to rubble, demolished by the sappers to improve the firing lines from machine-gun emplacements.

Sid spent a quiet day there before once more moving westwards in a series of hops that saw the battalion transport, including the cooks' lorries, used to transport the men because there was nothing available from the brigade. Sid had to march for several miles before the lorries returned to pick him up, but finally he arrived at Aubers.

The French had decided that the line along the Scheldt was too vulnerable; they wanted to shift the defence west once again to the Franco-Belgian border. Lord Gort was now concerned about the safety of the British Expeditionary Force. Arras had been abandoned, the garrison fighting its way north, and a southern defensive line was going to be created along the line of canals that stretched from St-Omer in the west to Béthune in the east. The vulnerability of the British Army was already seeping down the ranks. The staff at 48th Division HQ heard on 23 May that the Germans had captured Boulogne. It didn't take a great deal of thought to realize that the BEF was now almost completely encircled.

The division then received orders to send a brigade group to defend the town of Dunkirk. Sid was grabbing sleep where and when he could. He had arrived in Aubers at four in the morning and by six was in a truck in a convoy heading for Dunkirk. The towns and villages that they passed through had taken a pounding in the few days since they had last been there. The German bombers had caused plenty of damage and the rural towns and villages were empty, with the wreckage of houses littering the streets. It was a sight to which Sid had become immune after seeing the devastation of Hollain and Tournai.

At midday on the 25th the convoy was halted. They were not to continue to Dunkirk, but to head west and make for a village called Nouveau Monde. The instructions that were sent down to the companies were that they were to make their own way to the battalion rendezvous. The only maps that they had were a very inaccurate quarter-inch scale, and the roads that crisscrossed the border were narrow and twisting. Eventually, however, after more than three hours, the first company reached the town. Nouveau Monde, Sid discovered, was a road junction on the banks of the River Lys, with small terraced houses built around a large church. There was little in the way of food left in the village, but Sid killed a chicken in one of the nearby farms. He and a few mates lit an open fire to cook it, but as he tried to fan the flames with his tin helmet the leather lining caught fire. Now his helmet didn't fit properly, so he had to tie a large yellow handkerchief round his head. Chalky White remarked that it would help to keep the sun off his head when they got to the beach at Dunkirk.

Many of the transport drivers got lost along the route, so it was another two hours before the last men to arrive had climbed down from the lorries. They were still a few miles from Dunkirk, but they had to abandon the transport now because it was urgently needed elsewhere. Sid wondered if any of the vehicles would find their way back. The men sorted themselves out, making themselves as comfortable as possible in the empty houses while they waited for fresh orders. Several hours went by before, at eleven o'clock at night, Sid was ordered to form up. Some basic rations were doled out – mainly more biscuits and tins of fish and corned beef. Another night march lay in front of him.

At six o'clock the next morning, on 26 May, Sid with the rest of the battalion arrived in the small country town of Wormhout, built around a small square with six roads radiating off it. Just to the east of the square was a brook crossed by an old stone bridge. It looked to Sid like an old market town. It seemed untouched by the war, and there were still plenty of civilians living in it. The battalion was there to defend the town against German troops advancing from the west. Dunkirk was not far away.

14

JACK HASKETT MEETS THE GERMANS

18–21 May

So far the description of events has followed the veterans who moved up into Belgium after the start of the fighting on 10 May. But there were more troops in the British Expeditionary Force than in just those nine divisions that were sent forward as part of Plan D. The British rear echelon stretched all the way back to the disembarkation ports of Le Havre, Cherbourg and Brest, and the depots at the railheads in Rennes and Le Mans. There was another group of soldiers, though, who were formed into fighting units but had not, originally, been considered fit for the front line. However, as the situation worsened, this changed and they were to come into direct contact with the enemy.

Jack Haskett, who had spent four years in the artillery as a Territorial and then had been conscripted into the infantry of the 2/6th Queen's Royal Regiment, was in his billet near

Amiens when the Germans invaded on the 10th. It had not disturbed Jack's battalion greatly, although there had been a lot of air raid warnings early in the morning and throughout the day as the Luftwaffe bombed the Royal Air Force base at Abbeville. The 12th Division, of which the 2/6th Queen's was part, was in the rear areas carrying out labouring work, because most of the soldiers were raw recruits and still needed a lot of training.

The situation changed with the German breakthrough in the south. That the French had been unable to stop the advance of German Army Group A under General Rundstedt meant that Lord Gort and the British General Staff were not only concerned with the German advance on their eastern front, but they also had to concern themselves with protecting their southern flank. The move to support Arras was part of this, but Gort also had to guard his lines of communication to the rear. The 12th Division, including Jack's battalion, were ordered to guard four key towns in the west: Albert, Doullens, Amiens and Abbeville. By 18 May they were being mobilized. They had stood to in the morning, formed up and then later that morning marched towards Amiens.

The Official History compares the strength of the 12th Division with the strength of the approaching German army group. The 12th Division had only a troop of four field guns from a Royal Artillery school. Their signals and administration units were not fully up to strength and they were not properly armed. Their total numbers were barely more than half a normal division. In comparison, the five armoured divisions that spearheaded Rundstedt's Army Group A were made up of seventeen tank battalions armed with over nine hundred pieces of artillery. There were fifteen motorized infantry battalions and twelve batteries of field guns. Lord Gort had no inkling of the size of the German force at the time, but he knew that they were powerful enough to have overcome any French resistance. He must have known that the deployment of the 12th Division, and the 23rd Division further east, was an act of desperation. He had, however, no other choice. Units were already being rushed from the eastern flank to hold the canal line in the south-west. There were no other reserves left.

Jack Haskett arrived at the main railway station at Amiens and entrained with the rest of the battalion, climbing on to a waiting troop train. They went first to Abbeville, where Jack thought they were to get off, but the train halted and remained in a siding for a while. Men climbed out of the carriages to stretch their legs. Then suddenly, without any warning, the train broke into movement again and steamed slowly out of the siding, with men hopping back on to the coaches and section leaders shouting at them to catch up and get on board. The battalion stayed on the train for another twelve hours. It travelled slowly through the night, making frequent and sudden stops. There was nothing to see in the pitch dark. Normally there would be an extra issue of haversack rations for a train journey, with planned stops for at least one hot meal and tea on a journey as long as this. This time there was nothing and the men were hungry and thirsty when at last the train steamed, slowly, into another siding.

The doors crashed open and Jack saw a sign on a signal box that he thought read Lens, a place of which he had never heard. The men climbed out to relieve themselves and look around. It was early morning. An aeroplane flew overhead, loud and low. There had been no air raid warning and one of the lads behind Jack blurted out, 'It's OK – it's a Norwegian hospital plane!' It was in fact a twin-engined German bomber, with black iron crosses on its wingtips. Jack thought, 'Christ, what sort of a unit am I in?' He dived for cover under the carriage. The bomber ignored them, but the sound of anti-aircraft fire and whistling, exploding bombs could be heard close by and the raid on the town went on for another fifteen minutes.

When the bombing stopped, once again there were frantic orders and whistles as everyone was urged back on to the train. It reversed down the tracks, the way they had come, and the journey continued, this time making good speed, as though the engine driver wanted to get away as fast as possible from the air raid.

During the night and day that the 2/6th Battalion had been on the train, further east the battle around the perimeter of Arras was engaging Rommel's 7th Armoured Division, who were to meet some unexpected opposition from Matilda tanks of the Royal Tank Regiment and lose several villages to the men of the Durham Light Infantry. At the same time, the two brigades of the British 23rd Division, who had been sent to the Canal du Nord east of Arras, were outflanked by the German 8th Armoured Division. While the 69th Brigade was able to pull back and regroup, the 70th was met by the tanks of the 8th Armoured Division and was wiped out. Just fourteen officers and 219 soldiers survived out of three infantry battalions and some engineers.

The German 1st and 6th Armoured Divisions split from the southern flank of this large armoured spearhead and pushed further west, heading for Albert and Doullens, the towns defended by the brigades of the 12th Division. Meanwhile, the German 2nd Armoured Division struck a line of march directly for the town of Abbeville on the coast.

Oblivious to all this, Jack and the rest of the battalion sat on the train as it steamed through the French countryside at a good clip. At last it slowed, then with the brakes screeching came to another halt. Now there was plenty of encouragement from the NCOs to get out and form up. Kit was unloaded from the wagons – this was clearly the right destination. Jack looked around and realized that they were back in Abbeville once more. What, he thought, was all that in aid of? There was, of course, no explanation given to anyone. Some rations and tea were rustled up for them, then after they had assembled into their various companies the battalion marched out of the station, through the town and down the main road.

Jack was in D Company and would normally have been bringing up the rear of the line of march, but now found himself in the lead. He had no idea where the headquarters company was, but the company CO knew where he was heading. They had passed the outskirts of town when they heard the throb of aircraft engines. Whistles blew and this time there were no more remarks about Norwegian hospital planes. The battalion rapidly took cover and Jack scrambled into a nearby field. It was a cow pasture, covered in cowpats. The cows were still in the field and as the Stukas went into their attack, the animals became panicked at the sound of the diving sirens and the crash of the bombs. They charged around the field, bellowing in fear, and Jack thought that he had come all this way to be trampled to death by a mad cow.

The dive-bombers were not targeting Jack's battalion but

Abbeville airfield which was close by; the Stukas circled malevolently around it, like a swarm of angry hornets. They were giving the airbase a real pounding and seemed to be having it all their own way.

At the end of their raid the enemy aircraft flew away and the battalion pulled itself together. They formed up on the road again, setting off with D Company still in the lead and Jack's 16 Platoon at the head. Word came up that they were to stop at the next crossroads and set up a roadblock. They kept marching, with the line starting to spread out, but they came not to a crossroads but to a fork, with the main road continuing and a narrower country road heading off at an angle. Jack's sergeant told them to keep moving down the main road. Another half mile along it was a parked lorry – a British 15cwt loaded with supplies. There was no one in the cab or in the back and the engine seemed quite cold. After milling around with no sign of anybody in charge of the vehicle, they started helping themselves to bars of chocolate and cigarettes. The sergeant allowed them to stock up before calling them back to their duty and urging them to keep going. There was still no sign of the crossroads, so they continued a little further along the road until they came to a farm building. This too was deserted and the sergeant, who felt that they had marched a long way since they passed the fork in the road, told them to set up the roadblock across the stretch of the road where they were. A couple of men went forward as lookouts while two Bren guns were set up under cover on each verge. Others went to the farmhouse to search for food and water.

They waited there for an hour, but no traffic came down the road. Jack thought that there should have been more runners taking messages back up the road to the company HQ, or to the battalion, but no one seemed bothered. He thought that the battalion had become completely split up. In fact, Jack was certain that they had gone too far ahead of the rest of the column and that they should have set up the roadblock where the two roads forked, which was now about two miles back down the road. One of the men who had been sent forward came back down the road to report that they had seen a tank emerging from the edge of a wood down in the valley to their left. A shell had landed close to it – he had no idea where it had come from – and the tank had moved back into the trees. The sergeant said that he would go back and tell the company HQ. That, thought Jack, was a runner's job, but never mind.

The sergeant went up the road and disappeared around a corner while the rest of them stayed by the side of the road, the Bren guns manned, two men crouched in the verge further up and the rest of the platoon spread out in sections on either side of the road. They waited. It was going to be dark soon. The sergeant returned – he could find no sign of the rest of the company, nor of the battalion. He told them to form up and that they would march back the way they had come.

Jack didn't like it. They were on their own, lost most likely; they would be marching in the dark and there was a chance that the platoon would get split up. When they got back to the battalion they would be in trouble. But the sergeant was right – there was nothing else for it, so they marched raggedly on. Then they heard the noise.

There were tanks behind them, on the road. Jack looked back and saw the silhouette of one rear up over the crest of a hill before crashing down and disappearing into a dip. They were heading their way. Jack needed no orders from the sergeant, and the platoon dived for the ditch at the side of the road.

They waited as the tanks – there were several of them – clanked and ground their way down the road. It was night now, but with a good moon. Jack's heart was in his mouth. The tanks came closer, then stopped. Jack eased into position. There was a tank almost right in front of him with an officer standing in the turret. It wasn't an easy shot; he had to get his Lee-Enfield at an acute angle. He had no qualms about firing, but was uncertain about the rest of the platoon. They were young and inexperienced. Would he be the only one firing? Was it better to do nothing and hope that the tanks would go past? Where had the rest of the battalion gone?

Before Jack could get his sights on the German officer or make a decision about whether to squeeze the trigger, the tank captain turned and shouted directly at him and pointed. Two German soldiers charged up, shouting loudly. They carried sub-machine guns and the muzzles of both swung towards Jack. He let go of his rifle and slowly raised his hands with his palms open. He was very frightened, so frightened he found it difficult to move. As he slowly stood up, keeping his eyes fixed steadily on the barrels of the guns, the sound of machine-gun fire came from the direction of the fork in the road. Had there been a fight with the rest of the company? But there was no more gunfire after those first bursts.

The whole of the platoon was now lined up by the side of the road. They were being made to hand over their ammunition and everything else in their pockets and packs, including the chocolate and cigarettes they had 'liberated' from the supply lorry. Nobody had fired a shot. The officer that Jack had tried to get in his sights was talking to them, in English. He wore a black jerkin and tan trousers. 'Where are your officers?' he asked. 'Where are the rest of your troops?' The answer 'We don't know' sounded pathetic to Jack's ears. Worse, the German officer obviously believed them.

Then the soldiers told them to hand over their jack knives. Jack had his on a lanyard and couldn't get it off, so one of the lads opened his own and cut it. They were herded down the road with their hands on their heads. They passed the fork from where the sound of gunfire had come, but there was no sign of any dead or wounded, no sign of any fighting at all. Jack was now very anxious. He didn't know what was going to happen to him – it was very uncomfortable to be under the guns of the German soldiers. He was now a prisoner, and it was only just sinking in that he would not get home again, not for a long while if at all. He felt mentally stunned. The thought of trying to run crossed his mind, but they would shoot him for sure. There was too much moonlight for him to get away easily.

They were marched towards a low building on the other side of a gate in the hedge. It had a rough, whitewashed wall and there were no windows in it; Jack assumed it was a barn or some other sort of farm building. The soldiers guarding them ordered them against the wall and a sudden spasm of fear went through Jack as he realized that they were going to be shot. He shouted out, 'They're going to kill us.' Two Germans with sub-machine guns were standing to one side.

There was some murmuring, then Jack said loudly, 'When one of them gives the signal to open fire, rush them.' He isn't sure where the courage came from. He knew that he just wasn't prepared to stand there and wait to be shot in cold blood. Although he would probably die, he wanted to put up some last show of resistance.

The moment hung in the air, Jack's nerves ready to break, when the officer who had first spotted Jack ran through the gate shouting an order. The two soldiers with the machine guns stepped back, then ran out of the field. The officer shouted to Jack and his mates, 'Go! Keep your hands in the air. Down the road – go, go!' He was waving a pistol in the air and pointing it at the gate.

They shambled out and started to walk down the road. Jack knew that they were going to be mown down and that his shouted suggestion to charge at the gunmen had made the Germans change their minds about how to kill them. He cursed himself for shouting out.

They kept walking, Jack's back squirming in the anticipation of a bullet, his mind frantically working out whether he would have enough time to make a jump for the ditch. The mind goes through any mental gymnastics to hold off the certainty of death.

They walked. It seemed to be for ever. Then he heard someone singing behind him: 'Daisy, Daisy, give me your answer do.' For an instant Jack thought he had gone mad. Then the sergeant slowly cycled past singing the rest of the song. He laughed, and Jack turned round and saw that the Germans had gone. There were no tanks, no men with sub-machine guns. 'They've scarpered,' said the sergeant.

The lads gathered around. Jack felt almost like flying, he had been so certain a few minutes ago that he was going to die. Now he was free to live again. The sergeant said that they should go back to the fork in the road and wait until daylight to search for their weapons, and that maybe the battalion or the company would turn up.

Jack thought this was madness. He had only just escaped with his skin and he did not want to chance it again. Several men thought the same as him and the sergeant realized that his authority was not what it used to be. The question was taken even further out of his hands when from up the road, at speed, came an RAF ambulance. Jack waved it down.

The driver told them that he was heading for the port of Boulogne, that everybody was evacuating from there. Jack and some of the others, about seven of them, decided that they were not going to wait. They climbed up into the back of the ambulance and it drove off through the night, leaving the sergeant and the rest of the platoon in the road. Jack learned, much later, that they had all been taken prisoner.

The ambulance took several hours to reach Boulogne and when it drove into the port area it was already daylight. Jack searched for the Regimental Transport Office, but when he found it the staff there were in the process of packing up to depart. They couldn't give him any advice about where the rest of his battalion was. He wandered back to his small group of comrades. In his opinion they had become very demoralized and listless. They were very tired and hungry and the corporal who had come with them lacked initiative. At the back of Jack's mind was a fear of falling into captivity again. There was no chance, it seemed to him, of getting in touch again with the battalion, and the port was full of army and air force personnel who were preparing to leave for England. The only solution was to get out of Boulogne. So Jack and his companions found some shelter in a bombed-out warehouse and spent the rest of the day looking for food. In between times, Jack returned to the port to see if there was any ship that he could get on, but nothing came in. There was the occasional air raid, but he and the rest of the lads stayed sleeping in the warehouse overnight.

The next morning a train pulled into the railway siding along the dockside. It was an ambulance train carrying wounded men, some of them walking but many lying on stretchers. Jack walked once more down to the dockside, where a ship had come in overnight. Soldiers were disembarking from it, lining up and marching off out of the port. He had no idea who they were.

When the disembarkation had finished, groups of wounded men arrived and climbed up the gangway on to the ship. Medical orderlies also carried some of the stretcher cases on to the quayside, where they were picked up and carried up the gangway. Two officers were standing nearby and Jack listened to their conversation: they were discussing how many stretcher cases there were to get on board, and the need to get the ship away as quickly as possible. Jack didn't need to hear anything else. He rushed back to the warehouse and roused his mates to their feet. 'I'm going to get you out of here, lads,' he said. He told them to go to the train and get hold of a stretcher case, carry it to the dockside and when they got there, instead of putting it down, they should go to the gangway and ask where they were to take it. 'Carry the stretcher case on board and then don't get off! Find somewhere to hide – a cupboard, anywhere – and hide 'til the ship's moving.'

The men were slow to respond, but with some urging they did as they were told. Jack went first with another lad.

They were not challenged by anyone. Arriving at the ship's gangway he was directed into the saloon, where he handed over the patient to a medical orderly then walked purposefully away. Once in a passageway he and his mate went down gangways as far as they could. Then he found a storeroom and went into it. After a few hours the ship started to vibrate and they could tell by its motion that they were at sea.

Jack stayed in the storeroom until he thought the ship was docking again, then came out and climbed up to the deck. He went down the gangplank and was given transport, first to Aldershot and then two days later to Guildford, the Queen's depot. It was there that he started to have problems. The 2/6th Queen's hadn't yet returned from France and his story of how they had become separated from the battalion wasn't believed. Jack and the rest of his mates had to answer questions for some time about what had happened. In the end they were given permission to return to their depot, but suspicion continued to hang over them and they were confined to barracks, kept as virtual prisoners. Jack was finally released and allowed home on leave when the rest of his battalion returned from France and the loss of contact with D Company was confirmed.

The German 2nd Armoured Division occupied the town of Abbeville on the night of Monday, 20 May. The German Army had reached the coast and the BEF was now encircled.

15

STARTING 'DYNAMO'

19–26 May

By the time Jack Haskett and his mates had left Boulogne, Abbeville was securely in German hands. The bold plan to drive for the coast and outflank and isolate the British, French and Belgian armies to the north had succeeded. The armoured divisions of German Army Group A had raced through Luxembourg, Belgium and northern France in just ten days, brushing any opposition aside, and had reached the sea.

Tanks from the 2nd Panzer Division, which Jack Haskett must have encountered on the road out of Abbeville, had seized the town on the evening of the 20th. After a day's recuperation and maintenance the 2nd Division headed north towards Boulogne. There were no British troops stationed there, apart from, on the 20th, a searchlight regiment, eight 3.7in anti-aircraft guns and eight machine guns to provide some anti-aircraft cover. There were also some other troops, stragglers like Jack from the various attempts to hold up the German armoured columns, and French and Belgian soldiers in a similar position.

So far we have followed events as the various units fell back on to ad hoc defensive lines, along rivers and canals, as Lord Gort struggled to adjust to the German advance. The rapid collapse of the French Army and the precarious situation of the BEF were also focusing minds in the UK.

The telephone call made by Lieutenant General Pownall to the War Office in London on the 19th, outlining Lord Gort's view that evacuation had to be considered, had several repercussions. One, as we have seen, is that General Ironside, Chief of the Imperial General Staff, flew to France to tell Gort that he should consider an attack towards the south.

The call had also started other men working, because in the event that the German advance was successful but the BEF remained in France, then alternative supply ports would need to be identified. A meeting was held at the War Office which included Vice-Admiral Bertram Ramsay, the Flag Officer Commanding Dover. Ramsay had been responsible so far for an effective blockade of the Straits of Dover, which had pro-tected the supply ships crossing the Channel from any attacks by U-boats or German warships. Ramsay had also overseen the rescue of the Dutch gold reserves and the evacuation of the Dutch royal family, prime minister and Cabinet from Rotterdam before the country fell to the Germans. The Dover command had also sent destroyers to carry out demolition work in the port of Antwerp in order to deny the docks and oil facilities to the Germans. In the course of this operation HMS *Valentine* was sunk by German bombers and two other ships were badly damaged.

The meeting on 19 May at the War Office had several things to consider. The German southern advance had reached a point where it would soon be able to cut the supply lines from the western French harbours currently in use. Calais and Boulogne would have to be used as much as possible for this traffic now, because Dunkirk was more difficult to defend against air attack. The second item on the agenda was how to organize the orderly evacuation of members of the BEF who were no longer required in the present circumstances. This number might amount to about two thousand men a day after 20 May. It might also be necessary to plan for the emergency evacuation of base-unit staff, hospital orderlies and other non-combatant staff, which could reach fifteen thousand people, and this might need to be done from the night of the 22nd. The men at the meeting, however, did not think that the emergency evacuation of very large forces was likely. One factor that had to be considered was that the seas between Dover, Calais, Boulogne and Dunkirk were very shallow in places, so large ships would not be able to use the ports.

Within twenty-four hours the situation had changed for the worse and on 20 May, a Monday, a conference was held at Naval Headquarters in Dover. The HQ was housed in huge galleries dug into the face of the white cliffs themselves. Here, suddenly, the emergency evacuation of very large forces was definitely up for discussion, and estimates were made that ten thousand men might be got away from each of the three ports of Calais, Dunkirk and Boulogne.

What vessels might be available to carry them? The naval staff proposed the requisitioning of all passenger ferries along the Channel; they identified ten available in Dover with another six operating out of Southampton that would be quickly available. Some fishing boats were also handy, and as many as forty Dutch coasters that had fled to Britain after the fall of Holland could be pressed into service. Sea transport officers in ports along the east and south coasts were also told to record the details of all small ships up to a thousand tons, including paddle-steamers and pleasure craft.

The staff to organize the evacuation were accommodated in the conference room, which, during the First World War, had housed a dynamo for auxiliary electrical power. So the plan for the evacuation was given the name 'Operation Dynamo'.

Before the ports of Boulogne and Calais could be used to send in supplies, they would need a greater army presence and the War Office had already taken steps to give them one. On 21 May the 20th Guards Brigade, which was undergoing training in Camberley, was ordered to Dover. Here they embarked on two cross-Channel steamers, *Biarritz* and *Queen of the Channel*. Their destination was Boulogne. They steamed out of the harbour escorted by two destroyers, *Whitshed* and *Vimiera*. Brigadier William Fox-Pitt, commanding officer of the brigade, had received orders to set up defences around the town. He was also told that an infantry regiment and an armoured regiment would arrive from Calais to supplement his forces. These would be vital, because his brigade was composed of just two battalions, the 2nd Irish Guards and the 2nd Welsh Guards. There was also the brigade anti-tank company and a battery of the 69th Anti-tank Regiment. It was almost impossible for them to hold a perimeter around the town even with the promised reinforcements, but these did not arrive anyway. Even so, on 22 May they managed to hold off several attacks from the

German 2nd Armoured Division, which arrived on the outskirts of the town at around five o'clock in the evening. A
French infantry division was on its way to form a defensive
line to the south of the port, but its troop trains came into
contact with and were attacked by German tanks. There were
heavy casualties and its extra support for the Guards Brigade
never materialized. The situation for the Guards was not a
good one.

The 2nd German Armoured Division attacked again on
the morning of the 23rd, from all sides now, and after some
hours of heavy fighting the Guards battalions were withdrawn to the edge of the town. The cross-Channel steamers
had left Boulogne with the wounded – and also with Jack and
his comrades on board – but the destroyers had stayed to give
gun support to the troops on land. A party of Royal Marines
had been landed to create some order in the port area and a
demolition party had also come ashore. Four other destroyers had arrived – *Vimy*, *Venomous*, *Wild Swan* and *Keith* –
along with some French warships. They shelled enemy gun
sites and machine-gun posts, but were themselves being hit by
enemy artillery that had moved on to the high ground around
Boulogne. A French destroyer, *Orage*, was sunk, the captain
of *Keith* was killed and the captain of *Vimy* was wounded and
later died.

The German tanks were held at bay for several more hours
by the vastly outnumbered Guards battalion, but then at
about five o'clock the Luftwaffe arrived to attack the
destroyers and the troops in the town. The raid was partly
frustrated by the arrival of RAF fighters, but at 6.30 that
evening a signal was received from the War Office to evacuate
the port. As the warships manoeuvred to enter the narrow

harbour – only two could do so at one time – they came under heavy shellfire from the advancing German armour. The ships fired back at very short range, and while this duel between German tanks and naval gunners took place, the troops boarded the ships. Taking around a thousand men each, the destroyers took it in turns to berth. There was another large air raid from the Luftwaffe on the port and the ships waiting outside to enter, and this was coordinated with a massive push by the 2nd Division on the now very close perimeter. All of the ships suffered some damage from the battle, but kept their guns firing while the troops were embarked. Tanks had now entered the town and HMS *Venetia* also tried to enter the port. Another massive bombardment came from the artillery on the hills and one of *Venetia*'s guns was hit, killing the crew. The bridge was hit and the captain and others wounded; the ship, now out of control, ran aground. *Wild Swan*, alongside the jetty, fired on the tanks approaching the quay. *Venomous* opened fire with her pom-poms at columns of infantry trying to infiltrate the streets around the quays. *Venetia* managed to refloat herself, and the three ships got out of the port at around nine o'clock in the evening.

Another ship, HMS *Windsor*, was ordered into Boulogne later that night and managed to pick up six hundred more men and some wounded.

The final ship to attempt to get men off, *Vimiera*, arrived on her second trip at 1.40 in the morning. The port appeared deserted, but after a small party was sent ashore, around 1,400 men appeared and rushed aboard. She was so overloaded that there was barely enough water under her keel for her to pull out of the harbour.

Some Guards were left behind and they, with French troops, managed to hold out for another thirty-six hours.

As we know, the initial response of the War Office to Lord Gort's request for the evacuation of the BEF brought the Chief of the Imperial General Staff, General Ironside, to see Gort with instructions that the BEF was to move south to take up its position on the left of the French Army. When he got to the headquarters he was told that German armoured divisions were already attacking Arras from the south. Gort was planning to send some units to help the Arras garrison, but it quickly became clear to Ironside that that was the limit of any move to the south that could be achieved. He then went to see the French General Billotte to get his forces to support the plan.

Meanwhile, the French General Maxime Weygand, brought back from retirement in North Africa to replace General Gamelin, met King Leopold of the Belgians. Gort wasn't told of this meeting. At it Leopold agreed that the Belgian and French forces should pull back even further to the old pre-10 May defensive line along the border between the two countries. Gort, belatedly learning about the meeting, made his way to join it. Weygand had already left by the time he arrived, but Gort heard from General Billotte that the French First Army was too tired to take part in any fresh offensive. He also gathered that, beyond the reluctant agreement of the Belgian king to pull back to the frontier, the meeting had come up with no new initiatives. That night Pownall started the process of planning the evacuation of the BEF.

A decision to evacuate wasn't expected until 24 May at

least, but so rapid was the German advance that by Thursday morning, the 23rd, Ramsay could see from his office window the shellbursts from the attack on Boulogne by the 2nd Panzer Division. The number of ports available from which to get the BEF out of France was being reduced in front of his eyes.

In the preceding days, the dangers from enemy submarines and aircraft had been clear. Supply ships trying to dock at Dunkirk had been bombed. Five French ships – a destroyer, an oil tanker and the rest cargo ships – had all been sunk and damaged by air attack as they tried to leave the port. The lock gates on some of the harbour basins had been damaged, so could not be used. Later the Germans had set up artillery on high ground to the east of Calais and they shelled a supply ship sailing along the coast to enter the marked passage into Dunkirk harbour.

By the 25th casualties had already been evacuated in several trips made by hospital ships, and so too were 1,500 civilian evacuees. On this day another 1,246 troops were evacuated, mainly base personnel not involved in the fighting, but including as well the first significant number of men from the rear echelons of the BEF. Supply ships were still arriving, and all of this took place under the threat of heavy air raids. In two days, four destroyers had been sunk and six others put out of action.

While Vice-Admiral Ramsay and his staff might initially have calculated that there were three ports in northern France from which they could try to evacuate the BEF, he was not in any position to ensure that that would remain the case and the fall of Boulogne demonstrated how quickly circumstances could change. As far as Calais was concerned, it too was transformed into a garrison by the arrival, as late as 22 May, of the 1st Battalion Queen Victoria's Rifles and the 3rd Royal Tank Regiment. The Queen Victoria's Rifles were a motorcycle battalion, but they landed without their motorcycles, any transport, or any mortars. The Royal Tank Regiment came with the fuel for its tanks carried in tins stored as deck cargo. It was originally intended that the Tank Regiment was to journey by road to Boulogne, but it was given conflicting orders when it arrived in Calais. The commander of the Boulogne garrison, Brigadier Claude Nicholson, sailed with the 30th Infantry Brigade and landed at Calais to discover that the Tank Regiment had already had a battle with a German armoured division and had retreated back to Calais. The town was being shelled and was surrounded. Further chaotic orders followed, instructing the brigadier to get thirty-six thousand ration packs to troops in the Dunkirk perimeter, and the forces in Calais were yet more seriously depleted in trying to carry out this order.

On the morning of 24 May the brigadier was told that, in principle, the port was to be evacuated. This was followed several hours later with another signal that said that the French commander, who was nominally in charge of the area, 'forbids evacuation'. The signal continued, saying that, as the harbour was now of no importance to the BEF, Brigadier Nicholson should select the best position to fight to the end. Rear Admiral James Somerville, Ramsay's deputy, went to Calais to see the situation for himself and found Nicholson in a cellar under the railway station lit with a few candles. It was filled with exhausted officers and men, fast asleep except for the few telephonists and staff officers actually on duty. Somerville brought the sad news that there was not to be any rescue, and said that the destroyer *Wolfhound*, which had remained in the port acting as a signals relay station, ought to leave because shells were landing all around the harbour. Somerville said that he had been telephoned by the prime minister before he left Dover, saying that it was essential for the garrison to hold up the advance of the Germans, which was threatening to cut the BEF off from its last remaining base at Dunkirk. Brigadier Nicholson told Somerville that he had anticipated these orders and showed him plans for retreating to the old citadel to hold out as long as possible. A further message was sent to the brigadier by Anthony Eden, the foreign secretary, later that day, telling him that 'The defence of Calais to the utmost is of highest importance to our country as symbolizing our continued co-operation with France.'

Nicholson did pull his forces back to the citadel and there the garrison held out in extremely tough conditions for another two days, refusing offers of surrender. It finally fell late on the 26th after a day of intense shelling and dive-bombing. Three thousand men were taken prisoner, and there are seventy-five bodies in the War Graves Cemetery at Calais from this last stand, although many more died in German captivity either of their wounds or of illness. One of them was Brigadier Nicholson himself, who died in prison in 1943, aged forty-four.

With Boulogne and Calais gone, Dunkirk was the only port left for Operation Dynamo. The question was, how long would that survive?

16

SID LEWIS ON THE WESTERN FRONT

26–29 May

The 26th of May was quiet, for which Sid Lewis was thankful after the fighting at Hollain. Arriving at Wormhout, the battalion marched west, crossing the small bridge over the stream into the centre of the town. It was six o'clock in the morning. The mayor and the local chief of police knew that fighting was taking place in the east, but no one had told them that the Germans might appear from the west. French civilian organization on a national scale had practically disappeared. The arrival of the troops had caused a stir, and the small village square was crowded with local residents anxious to find out what was happening and where the troops were going to go.

General Andrew Thorne, commander of the 48th Division, had been called to a meeting at Dunkirk on the 24th to make plans for the defence of the western flank of the shrinking pocket occupied by the BEF. The Germans were pushing eastwards along the line of the coast, but the French 68th Division was managing to hold the line at Gravelines. The greatest weakness was further south on the western flank. The French had captured some German documents suggesting that the next assault was going to be directed at the town of Wormhout. There were no forces guarding this part of the flank. The 48th Division was by now reduced to just two brigades, the 144th and the 145th, and General Thorne could not make contact with his corps headquarters. He took a decision to use the forces that he had available to defend the main towns along the right flank, from Hazebrouck in the south to Wormhout and Ledringhem in the north. At best, these defended towns could act as strongpoints; the German armour might easily penetrate between them. They were, however, all that could be put together. Even if they held the enemy up for just one day, it would allow more soldiers to move north to the Dunkirk perimeter, from where they might be evacuated.

So Sid Lewis and the 2nd Battalion Royal Warwickshire Regiment found themselves in the small rural town of Wormhout that late spring morning. Nobody had told Sid, or anyone else in the battalion, that the town appeared in some captured German plans as the target for a major offensive.

On their arrival Sid's platoon was sent to fields on either side of a road that ran due west from Wormhout to the next village, Esquelbecq, which was about 1½ miles away. Midway between them they started digging in, setting up Bren-gun and Vickers machine-gun posts to cover the road, and establishing a defensive line across the fields. The regimental aid post was set up close to the town square, near to the battalion HQ and close to where the transport lorries were parked, hidden from the air under some trees bordering a field. The work of digging in went on without interruption from any enemy attack. And surprisingly, there was no air activity either.

Sid stood to the next morning at 4.30, an hour before it got light. This was the best time to launch an attack, although no tanks appeared across the wheatfields and no German bombers appeared in the sky. Orders had been received by the battalion that they were to move the front out to Esquelbecq. C Company was told to assume responsibility for this area, and their move forward entailed the remaining companies moving their positions because they now all had wider fronts to cover.

At about ten o'clock these manoeuvres had been completed and there was still no sign of any German advance, so the battalion stood down and a pay parade was called. Rations were now very short and the battalion decided to issue pay so that the men would be able to go into the town to buy food. As far as Sid can remember, the instruction was to stock up on any food they could, because no one knew when rations would be arriving. He was dubious about this, having seen the numbers of refugees in the town when he passed through it the day before and having already experienced the unwillingness of any shopkeepers in other towns to sell anything to the British troops any more.

Still, he went into the town because it was plain that there would be little in the way of meals served up by the field kitchens. He was heading towards the square when the peace was shattered. A formation of German dive-bombers appeared from the south and circled Wormhout. Air raid sirens had already sounded, and Sid and his companions scrambled into a ditch as the sinister-looking Stukas flew overhead. Then the leading bomber flipped over and started its howling dive. The familiar knot of tension in Sid's stomach tightened as he lay there, face down, the first explosion a few hundred yards away, blasting at the square and the refugees desperately seeking shelter. Then another and another Stuka went into their screaming dives, each one ending in the explosion of a bomb. Shrapnel and pieces of earth and rubble fell from the sky and bounced off the cobblestones of the square. An army lorry loaded with petrol was lifted into the air by the blast from a 500lb bomb, then dropped back on to the edge of the crater. Save for shattered glass in the headlights and windscreen, it suffered no other damage. Others hadn't been so lucky. By the time the Stukas departed, Wormhout had been blasted, the smell of smoke and rubble and the screams of the injured filling the air. Rising to his feet, Sid looked to the south. Another aircraft was flying in, very low. He recognized it as the British Lysander, a single-engined observation plane that had been following them for days, like some baleful albatross. It was gliding in to land, across the fields, its propeller almost visible. It jolted to a halt close to a hedge and a figure in German uniform stepped out. If he'd had his rifle Sid could have shot him. He watched as the man disappeared behind a row of pollarded willows and the aeroplane turned and took off again.

Sid had no desire to stay in the town any longer. Besides, the idea that any shop would be open with a shopkeeper prepared to sell food was now absurd, so he walked back empty-handed. Later, C Company were ordered to move from Esquelbecq to defend the brigade headquarters at

Bergues, five miles up the road to Dunkirk, and the rest of the battalion moved yet again to fresh positions. Sid was relieved to see that two machine-gun platoons from the Cheshire Regiment had arrived and were moving into the line along the northern edge of the Esquelbecq road. Sid's A Company was now looking out over fields to the south of Esquelbecq, which was out of sight in a dip in the landscape. To their north was a large house that Sid thought of as a manor house, with a high wall round the grounds that extended to the road. An old brick archway was cut into the wall and had obviously in earlier times formed the entrance to the estate. The Esquelbecq road formed the right edge of Sid's platoon, so that the machine-gunners flanked him. He was grateful for their presence. He had just five rounds for his Lee-Enfield rifle. A good shot he might be, but he was not going to do very much with that.

German activity was increasing to the south-west and the noise of gunfire was growing louder. The bombing meant that an attack was imminent. At Hollain the dive-bombers had been followed by shelling, then tanks and infantry moved in; but nothing else happened for the rest of that day.

At daybreak on 28 May everything changed. There was a ripple of distant gunfire to the west. A few minutes later artillery shells screamed over and exploded on the nearby manor house and woods. Fifteen or twenty rounds landed, then there was a lull. Sid sat down to have a scrap of breakfast with a mate, Fred Blansdale, another rifleman, whom Sid describes as a pleasant chap. They both had some hardtack biscuits and were sharing a tin of jam. The sergeant major called for volunteers from the section to climb on to the top of a haystack further down the road with a Boys anti-tank rifle to keep watch for any advancing armour. Fred Blansdale and somebody else, whose name Sid no longer remembers, volunteered and they walked off, keeping close to the side of the road. Half an hour or so later the second soldier returned, distressed, with the news that they had been spotted by a sniper and Fred had been killed with a bullet through his head. Nobody in the area where Sid was had heard the shot.

Sid shuddered, thinking that some effort ought to be made to recover Fred's body, but before they could plan anything a machine gun opened fire from the woods in the manor-house grounds, sending out a burst of tracer bullets. They zipped into the haystack, setting it on fire. Sid watched as it blazed, burning Fred's body with it. It was horrible, even though they believed that Fred was dead. But of greater concern was that the Germans had got as close as this without anyone really noticing. They must have been creeping up throughout the early morning. Everyone was very alert, but again everything went quiet. The fire in the haystack crackled away. No one suggested sending out a patrol. They were thin on the ground. Anyway, Jerry was out there and would move against them in his own time.

An hour later another air raid warning sounded as a flight of bombers appeared. The target this time was not the town but A Company itself. As they huddled in their foxholes, the earth shuddered with every explosion. The battalion war diary reports that fifteen bombers were engaged in the attack. Sid doesn't know; all he can remember is that the dive-bombing seemed to go on for an eternity, with explosion after explosion. The men were so stunned at the pounding they had received that it took some time for them to raise their heads after the sound of the bombers had disappeared. There were cries for stretcher-bearers from all over, and Sid staggered out of his trench, his ears ringing, to see a cratered field that still seeped smoke from the blasts, men lying, or crawling for help, covered in blood. For the next hour he ferried some of the wounded to the aid post near to battalion HQ. Meanwhile the company commander, Major Chichester-Constable, went from platoon to platoon, doing what he could to encourage his men, but there were a lot of casualties. Sid's section was now down to four men, and the German ground assault had not yet started.

Shelling followed the air raid, but the intermittent salvoes fell on the town and around the battalion HQ. The next change in the pace of the battle was the sound of mortar bombs, their detonations coming from Sid's right, where B Company had set up a roadblock. They had been checking the identity of refugees who were trying to get to Wormhout and there was a crowd of civilians there who had fled from Esquelbecq. Several cars carrying German soldiers raced down the road and came to a halt behind the crowd of civilians. The men of B Company on the barricade immediately opened fire on them and a 2-pounder anti-tank gun in position at the roadside also pumped shells into the leading cars. They burst into flames, and so too did the barricade. It was a scene of utter mayhem, the Germans in the cars leaping for cover, running to a house near the roadblock and returning fire with machine guns. The civilians suddenly trapped in the midst of a pitched battle ran for whatever cover they could find, terrified out of their wits. Some lay where they had fallen.

German infantry also tried to advance up the road from

Esquelbecq, but they had to make their way along the wall of the estate. This was covered by the two machine-gun platoons from the Cheshire Regiment, who fired relentlessly, and Sid recalls that the German casualties were heavy. The machine-gun crews would cease fire and wait until a number of German troops had passed through the archway in the wall, then they would rip into them with another hail of bullets. The Germans responded by sending some light tanks up the road and this provided some cover for their infantry. The tanks slewed off the road, over the ditch and then clanked their way north to outflank the machine guns and the B Company platoons that were covering the road. The tanks kept up their fire on the troops who were dug in along the roadside, and this started to cut into the men of B Company.

After an hour or so the pressure from the Germans was having its effect. A Company had pulled themselves together after the Stuka attack, but mortars were landing on them and, like Sid, most men were down to very few rounds of ammunition. The Bren gun of one section was out of ammunition, and mortars were forcing a section on the left to pull back. The machine-gunners of the Cheshires were now coming under attack from the side and they were also running out of ammunition; they started to withdraw under heavy fire. The remainder of B Company stayed in place and did what they could to hold off the attack. Five more German light tanks came up the road, stopping at the barricade. Before they could fire, the 2-pounder anti-tank gun scored a direct hit on the lead tank and the others reversed, taking cover in some trees by the side of the road. But this was the last of the anti-tank gun's ammunition, and the

German tanks in the woods now started shooting at the centre sections of B Company, while German infantry moved round to their left.

When the machine-gun fire from the Cheshire Regiment stopped, Sid realized that his A Company would soon be overrun. German tanks and infantry continued their advance on Wormhout and a group of tanks was also heading up the narrow lane to their left. There was so little ammunition that the fire from the slit trenches and strongpoints went unnoticed. The town itself was being struck by shells and many of the houses were on fire. The lorries that had been parked close to the casualty clearing station were also burning fiercely. Sid had taken several wounded cases for treatment but had been forced to give up – the journey was now far too dangerous. Shells were falling thick and fast, and the battalion HQ had moved under heavy fire to a different location further back. Communications between the company command post and the battalion had failed some time ago. Sid saw more tanks moving up the road from Esquelbecq and heading into the village.

Then the company CO, Chichester-Constable, ran over to Sid's slit trench and grabbed a rifle. To Sid's amazement, he ran towards the German tanks approaching from the south up the lane. The leading tank came to a stop. The major stood there, aggressive and larger than life, and Sid recalled the night when he had seen Chichester-Constable sit by the body of the dead German in no man's land in the Saar, waiting for the arrival of another enemy soldier that he could kill.

The machine gun in the tank's hull moved slightly and Sid saw flame and smoke spit from the muzzle.

Chichester-Constable crumpled, hitting the ground before the sound of the machine-gun burst reached Sid's ears.

He knew it was time to make a run for it. He was not alone. The platoon sergeant called the four remaining men together and said, 'Let's get back to the company HQ.' There was nobody there. They continued on to Wormhout square, which was now scattered with dead bodies lying amongst the rubble of half-destroyed buildings.

A group of wounded soldiers, eight of them, lay by the side of the road, some with head wounds, others on stretchers, more seriously hurt and unconscious. Mortars were falling on the town and the sound of gunfire could be heard a few streets away. Sid had no idea what was going on, and neither had the sergeant, but there was a 15cwt lorry parked nearby. The sergeant climbed in and started it up. They felt trapped, in imminent danger, but they placed the wounded as comfortably as they could in the back of the lorry, the sergeant all the while telling them to hurry and get a move on. At last he engaged the gears with a grinding judder and the lorry pulled out on to the road. Sid sat on the running board, his feet on the mudguard, as they slowly edged out of the town. They crossed the small bridge over the brook and then turned north, to Dunkirk. The road ahead was blocked by refugees, their carts and smashed vehicles. It would be death to get trapped in with them. The sergeant swung the lorry into a road that forked to the right. It looked clear ahead and they were able to keep moving, trying to keep the pace as slow as they dared to avoid shaking up the wounded men in the back.

As they drew clear of Wormhout, Sid realized that for the last two days he had never stopped feeling afraid. The adrenaline, and the deep anxiety that had started eating away at him with the first raid by the Stukas, had never left him. Now, driving north, he started to come down. The lorry was passing other British soldiers and he felt that he had at least put some distance between himself and the advancing Germans. In an hour they reached a British roadblock and were directed to a brigade military hospital where they could unload the wounded. To Sid's eyes a couple looked close to death. The sergeant said they should try to press on to Dunkirk, but they had gone only a few hundred yards when they were stopped by another roadblock at a crossroads. This one was manned by military police. The redcap told them to get out: 'No vehicles past here. It's got to be destroyed. You make your way on foot from here on.'

They set light to the lorry, then the four of them headed off down the road. Sid can't describe what he felt when he saw the flames eating into the canvas cover of the truck and the glass of the windscreen shattering in the heat. Burning a lorry like that seemed hopeless. As if there really was no future. He didn't know that he had been extremely lucky to get away from Wormhout.

The German unit that had spearheaded the assault on Wormhout was an SS regiment, the Leibstandarte SS Adolf Hitler (LSSAH), a unit that was originally created to be the personal bodyguard of the Führer. They were dedicated Nazis, now, in 1940, part of the German Army but still separate from it, owing their allegiance to the party and to Hitler. They had seen action in Holland after 10 May and had fought hard, advancing 134 miles in just four days. After the British counter-attack at Arras, the LSSAH joined the advance of the German 20th Motorized Division, which, with the 10th Panzer Division, was advancing from the west to cut off the retreat to Dunkirk. They had suffered heavy casualties and continued to do so in their attempt to take Wormhout.

By the late afternoon of the 28th, the surviving men of the 2nd Battalion Royal Warwickshires were finally overwhelmed. Many were dead or wounded and some, like Sid, had managed to withdraw, but around ninety prisoners were held by soldiers from the LSSAH, who had reached the centre of Wormhout. About fifteen men of the Cheshire machine-gun platoons, who had killed so many of the enemy as they tried to move up the Esquelbecq road, had also been taken prisoner earlier. Two men from the 2nd Battalion saw them lined up against the wall of a hut and shot dead. These two had evaded the SS troops and had gone into hiding.

The rest of the British prisoners of war were force-marched along a road, growing increasingly fearful and intimidated. Their guards showed no compunction about bayoneting any prisoner who was unable to keep up because of wounds, and would shoot any who protested. The ruthlessness and brutality of their captors was obvious. Finally the men of the 2nd Battalion were roughly herded into a cramped barn. The German soldiers set up a machine gun and shouted for five prisoners to come out. When they did so they were lined up and machine-gunned. Then a second batch of five was ordered out. The machine-gunners killed these men too. The prisoners refused now to leave the barn, shouting at the guards, and an officer demanded that they be treated as prisoners of war. The response was a bullet fired into his stomach. Then the guards followed this by hurling several grenades into the barn, and fusillades of machine-gun bullets were fired into the press of screaming, wounded men. Afterwards a bullet to the head was the treatment for any prisoner who seemed still to be alive.

Miraculously, five men survived the massacre and got away from the barn. They were later taken prisoner and treated for their wounds by a different unit of German soldiers.

Sid Lewis had escaped death by the skin of his teeth.

17

STANLEY CHAPPELL AT MONT DES CATS

28–29 May

Stanley Chappell's 2nd Royal Horse Artillery had forced their way from the line of the Scheldt in Belgium west to where the BEF was defending itself against the German forces in their rear. Since 25 May they had been dug in to the north of the Bois de Nieppe, from where they had provided covering fire for the 132nd Brigade of the 44th Division. The division itself had also been hurtled west in an effort to plug the gaps in that now extremely vulnerable flank. They were defending the southern part of the flank that ran south-east from the town of Hazebrouck. At the same time as Sid Lewis was facing the Germans at Wormhout, so Stanley was directing his battery's 25-pounders against German tanks further south.

The enemy had pressed forward, relying on their preponderance of artillery and greater supplies of ammunition.

They stormed several strongpoints and then were pushed back, but were able to advance more easily in the undefended gaps between them. On 27 May riflemen of the 132nd Brigade had withdrawn through the guns of Stanley's battery and the whole regiment pulled out. Stanley and the rest of the gunners raced to hitch up the field guns, while mortar shells exploded and machine-gun bullets flew over their heads.

The next day they were in action again a few miles further east and once more coming under intense artillery fire themselves. The regiment had seen its ranks diminished over the last few days. Three men had been killed and several wounded when an enemy shell had hit the battery, and others were missing, either wounded or just lost in the increasingly chaotic withdrawals. During the day on the 28th one troop of each battery withdrew, and then at nine o'clock that night the regiment was ordered to form up and move out yet again. It was obvious to Stanley that the Allied war plans hadn't survived longer than a few days, and that their situation was desperate; but the perpetual retreat that they were carrying out still rankled.

The column of trucks, quad tractors and field guns made as much speed as they could along a country road. It was dark and they showed no lights. A good distance was kept between the lorries in case of air attack, so the drivers had to concentrate hard not to lose sight of the lorry in front. If they did, then there was a good chance they would end up miles from the rendezvous point. Stanley was exhausted, and as he looked around the men in the back of the lorry he realized that they were all filthy, covered in oil and soil, and black from powder smoke. Half of his mates were already asleep, leaning on the men next to them.

A despatch rider drove down the line of vehicles. The convoy came to a halt and there was a huddled command conference by the side of the road. There had been a change of orders: the regiment was splitting up. Headquarters, along with H/I Battery, was to continue to the coast. All personnel and regimental transport and equipment, except the guns and ammunition, was to be abandoned and they were to head for Dunkirk. Stanley's battery, L/N, was going in a different direction – to a prominent hill known as Mont des Cats. The 44th Division was going to hold it overnight. It dawned on Stanley that his battery might have been selected for this task precisely because of the gallant stand they had made at Néry in the First World War. Would he be called upon to emulate his courageous predecessors?

Mont des Cats is a small hill, about 530 feet high, but with a commanding position over the surrounding countryside. German units had advanced to the villages to both the north and the south of it. The 44th Division, under the command of Major General E. A. Osborne, who held positions in front of the Mont, wanted to fall back to the Dunkirk perimeter. In order to do so with any safety, Osborne wanted to carry this out in coordination with the French forces on his left flank. But when he went to visit his French opposite number, General Benoit de la Laurencie, the French general told him that his III Corps was going to withdraw not the next day but at eleven o'clock that night – just two hours away. This was a severe shock to General Osborne, who realized that his troops would have no protection on their flank and so would also have to move that night. Osborne thought that he had two choices. He could pull back to Dunkirk straight away – but his men had been fighting hard all day and were exhausted; he didn't think that many of them would make it, as the withdrawal would inevitably be overtaken by daylight. The alternative was to move back to Mont des Cats, hold it overnight and the next day, then withdraw the following evening to take maximum advantage of the hours of darkness to conceal their movements.

There were already several hundred men on the Mont. A field company of Royal Engineers had been fortifying the hill and there were detachments of the 52nd and 65th Field Regiments, whose guns had kept the German tanks at bay. The Germans had approached to the foot of the hill several times, but had withdrawn as darkness fell. General Osborne was sure that they could be held off for another day and would again pull back at night. He decided that he would concentrate the division on the Mont, then head out a day later. But many of the units didn't make it back that night and by morning only the divisional HQ had reached the Mont, along with some other divisional units.

The German General Guderian decided that his tanks should take no part in any further advance – the ground was too boggy and they were suffering too many losses. He felt that the western army could wait for Army Group B in the east to move forward. But this decision did not mean that the British on the Mont would be able to escape. There were still plenty of artillery and aircraft to keep up the pressure.

When Stanley and his troop reached Mont des Cats, he found a wooded hill about half a mile in diameter topped by a large monastery. It offered a panoramic view of the countryside, hedges, woods and farmland, which must have been a beautiful pastoral scene in peacetime, but was now ravaged by war, with German infantry and artillery swarming across it. The Mont was a highly defensible position, but not with the limited resources and ammunition that were available. The field regiments were low on ammunition, as was Stanley's battery, and the force holding the Mont was in a desperate situation. They dug in as best they could and the remnants of the withdrawing 44th Division tried to cover the approaches as much as their limited numbers would allow.

At daybreak German artillery started a bombardment. Columns of infantry moved through the cover of hedges and trees, advancing up the hill. All the British artillery opened fire with the big guns, but were unable to prevent the enemy's remorseless advance, and the range got shorter and shorter.

An air raid of Stuka dive-bombers tried to wipe out the artillery. Stanley's battery was widely spaced and the quads had been parked under the trees. They suffered no damage. Then another artillery barrage fell on them and during this onslaught the enemy infantry pushed forward. In the last few hours of the engagement the 25-pounders were firing directly at the enemy over open sights. There was no need for Stanley's plotting skills in this battle – he was hauling cartridges and shells to the guns. The Germans were just a thousand yards away down the hill in open countryside, and could be seen moving about. The battery sergeant major, Tyrrel, was coolly and determinedly indicating with his arm and pointing out targets. The gun-layer was looking down the optical sights, then stepping back to pull the firing handle. For twenty minutes the guns crashed and belched smoke as men in the battery fell, hit by sniper fire or machine-gun bullets. Then the order came to cease fire. There was no accompanying order to limber up; instead, the battery was told to destroy the guns. The weapons must not be allowed to fall into the hands of the enemy.

A shell was loaded in the breech of each gun as usual, then another was placed in the muzzle. The sergeant tied a long lanyard to the firing handle and the men in the battery all retreated to take cover. There was a shouted 'Fire!' and the concussion of the double blast shook dust into the air and thumped their chests. The guns were ruined, their barrels blasted apart like blackened banana skins. It was a sad sight. Destroying a gun went against all their training as artillery-men. It was a piece of machinery that they had looked after and cleaned with loving attention. Now it was smashed. There was no time to mourn, however.

German artillery had started to get the range of the now useless battery on the hill, and their 105mm shells landed on the wood. Stan ran for his life and dived for cover just as the next salvo hurtled in. The shelling went on for another ten minutes, then ceased.

Stanley and another bombardier walked up to a road that ran along the top of the hill. The trees were blasted and blown apart by the shelling and Stanley saw a body lying on the ground. His face was covered with blood, his battledress stained a dark red. The wounded soldier could hardly speak and couldn't move. Stanley's companion picked him up and carried him in a fireman's lift to the top of the hill to find some medical help, but bedlam had broken out. Trucks and vans were roaring down the road, the drivers grinding the gears in their haste to get away. The Mont was being overrun by the Germans. One lorry slowed slightly and Stanley heard a voice shout 'Grab hold!' A hand snatched at his and pulled him into the back of the vehicle. It was the head mechanic of his troop, Bombardier Trevor Luff. The back of the lorry was crowded with men from the battery and, as they hurtled at breakneck speed down the road, Stanley was bounced about, but he didn't care. There was only one road open to the coast and the driver, like everyone in the lorry, was desperate to get out before the advancing Germans closed it.

After several miles, Stanley thought they had managed to avoid the enemy. It was getting difficult to make any progress along the road ahead, however. It was filled by the tide of humanity that was fleeing the advancing Germans and they were spilling out on to the fields on either side. Soldiers – French and British – army vehicles, civilians with cars, bikes, lorries, horses and pushchairs blocked the way ahead.

Two days earlier, Sydney Whiteside, the medical orderly in 144 Field Ambulance Unit, had driven with his unit to the small town of Wulverghem on the Belgian border. The ambulance unit had not motored west with the rest of the 144th Brigade to hold Wormhout, Hazebrouck and the other strongpoints facing Army Group A. Sydney's unit was now attached to the 5th Division, which was facing Army Group B on the eastern flank, south of Ypres.

They had seen an increasing number of casualties and had moved to a different location every night in the past four days. Sydney was extremely tired. On the afternoon of 27 May he was detailed as an ambulance orderly to go to a regimental aid post to pick up some casualties and bring them back to the main dressing station where their wounds could be bandaged properly and they could be given morphine. The unit was preparing to move and before they left they were given the map reference of the place where the unit would be that night. Sydney and the driver set off. They had not gone more than half a mile when the driver turned off the road and started to drive down a bumpy track running along a field. It was the driver's job to know the route, but Sidney asked him why they were going off the road; the driver replied that he had been told to avoid it. They drove across several fields before turning on to the metalled road again. A hundred yards in front of them was a British machine-gun post. The crew were preparing to fire across the field.

They had stumbled into the front line. Once again they turned off and drove up to the regimental aid post. They loaded the four stretcher cases on to the back of the ambulance, then drove off to a main dressing station, where the wounded would be given fresh bandages and morphine before being taken further back from the line to a casualty clearing station. By the time that Sydney's ambulance arrived at the main dressing station it had closed. The staff had packed up and were preparing to pull back with the rest of the 5th Division.

Sydney decided that the only thing to do was take the wounded to the casualty clearing station where they would get some treatment. So they set off once again, heading north, driving through Poperinge where Sydney saw a crowd of soldiers walking through the town carrying white flags. He couldn't tell whether they were French or Belgian – the uniforms were similar – but it was an ominous sight.

Finally they reached the casualty clearing station, which had been established in a village church, and they pulled up behind another ambulance that was parked outside. Sydney walked in and saw the floor completely covered with stretcher cases. Two young women nurses on duty told him that they were overcrowded as it was, so they could not take his patients; besides, another ambulance was still waiting to hand over four wounded. Sidney realized that he was in a queue.

He went back outside to explain the situation to the driver and they decided that they would wait. They slept in the cab of the ambulance, until sometime next morning the nurse woke them up and told Sydney they now had room for his wounded men. Presumably a number of casualties in the clearing station had died in the night. So he and the driver carried the men into the church, wished the nurses good luck, then drove back along the crowded roads to their unit – or rather to where they believed it had moved. They arrived, but found nothing there. There was no sign of 144 Field Ambulance Unit, nor of anybody who knew where it was. The driver was adamant that he had returned to the location that he had been given previously.

There was only one thing to do. They drove back to the casualty clearing station to see if they could get any more information from there. Heading back, they met two more ambulances going in the opposite direction. They had 5th Division plates on the mudguards, the same division as the 144th, so they flagged them down and asked if they had any idea where 144 Field Ambulance was.

'No,' the other ambulance crews said. But 145 Ambulance Unit had gone to La Panne on the coast, just along from the Belgian border; a large hospital had been set up there. Sydney and the driver thought that was the best place to head for –

they could surely get some directions to their unit from the RAMC staff there.

With a shifting of gears and whining from the transmission, they headed north.

18

LES CLARKE ON THE EASTERN FLANK

25–30 May

We left Les Clarke, rifleman and former despatch rider, and his 6th Battalion Durham Light Infantry at the small village of Don on the canal line east of La Bassée. The battalion had retired there after German tanks outside Arras and severe shelling at Petit Vimy had cut the battalion in half. So few men were left alive, in fact, that the battalion was reorganized into just three companies, the HQ Company and 1 and 2 Companies.

During this halt while men were shifted around into their new units, some tea and breakfast were dished out. There was no peace, however. A large formation of bombers passed overhead on their way to bomb Wavrin just to the north-east. Twenty minutes later the cold morning air resonated with the rumble of the explosions.

Most of that day was spent digging in, as well as

distributing weapons and the dwindling supply of ammunition, sharing it out equally amongst the three companies.

There was no complaint about digging foxholes and putting up some earthworks. Nowhere was safe from enemy shelling or dive-bombing. Later in the day another wave of bombers appeared, this time heading not for Wavrin but for Don itself, a harmless rural village. The Stukas attacked, the bombs fell, and Les could hardly remember a day when he hadn't crouched in a trench, gauging how close the next bomb or shell would fall. The battalion stayed where they were that night, some of the men sleeping in barns or the village hall; billets anywhere else were hard to find. The next morning there were more reminders that everything was falling to pieces. Sid heard that rations were to be cut by fifty per cent. This instruction, which had come all the way from divisional HQ, caused a laugh. The fifty per cent to which they were still entitled would be very welcome, if they ever saw it.

It was harder to make jokes about the throngs of French troops that were passing through their lines, heading up the main road of the village, some in transport, many on foot, disorganized and clearly without any leadership. They were subdued, almost sullen, and Les noticed that there were many troops from North Africa, trudging, their heads down, without rifles or backpacks. It looked like a beaten army.

There was a brigade meeting that afternoon, and shortly afterwards a rumour swept the ranks of the battalion that they were to go back south to take part in a counter-attack. Four French divisions would also be involved. If the French Army could find four divisions to take on the Germans, thought Les, why were all these troops heading the other way?

Warning orders to be ready to move did arrive from the brigade, and with them came a further rumour that the battalion was to take part in an opposed river crossing: 'In other words, you would be paddling across a canal with Jerry taking pot-shots at you while you did it. Or, more likely, hammering you with tanks and machine guns.' The whole idea seemed madness to Les, who had never practised a river crossing. They had no boats – they had never even seen one before. That a battalion that had suffered so many casualties could reorganize itself and be thrown into a counter-attack seemed frightening. The men started to feel that too much was being expected of them.

A counter-attack was indeed being considered at divisional HQ and higher up the chain of command. Further west, the German 7th Division was crossing the canal at Givenchy, so holding the southern edge of the BEF enclave seemed vital. The General HQ knew how badly knocked about the battalions of the 5th and 50th Divisions had been. The new offensive to the south could make sense only with the support of the French First Army, which had promised to send three divisions and a cavalry corps into the fray. The war diary for the 151st Brigade records that these French units did not show up.

But there was another, more pressing reason for calling off the counter-attack. The eastern flank of the long British pocket had been defended by the Belgian Army to the north and by British units from I Corps along the old Franco-Belgian frontier line. This eastern flank was coming under a new attack from German Army Group B. They had pushed back the Belgian Army and a gap was growing between the junction of the Belgian and British forces. At this point in the line the German forces outnumbered the BEF by two to one. Gort understood what was happening. The British Army was facing a pincer movement from German Army Group A in the west and Army Group B in the east. If it succeeded, they would be cut off from Dunkirk and encircled. A whole British army would be captured. Gort had no reserves left. He knew it was unlikely that the counter-attack to the south would take place if the British didn't take part. But if the eastern flank broke, then the southern counter-attack would be cut off at the rear anyway.

Gort abandoned the counter-attack. Instead, the 5th and 50th Divisions were ordered to move north-east, to hold a line along the Ypres Canal. By the time that these orders filtered down to the divisions, the brigade and Les's 6th Battalion, the Germans were already putting 'vigorous harassing' artillery fire on the roads in and out of Lille, Armentières and Ypres.

In the 6th Battalion at Don, Les had spent another night under some heavy shelling from German artillery, which was now approaching from the south. At first light they started moving out on foot to concentrate at the next village, Herrin, and there was a rumour that the counter-attack was on. Lorries had assembled throughout the night and the battalion climbed on board. To Les's relief they were not heading south, but they moved out of Herrin and word went round that their destination was Armentières. The song 'Mademoiselle from Armentières' was on everybody's lips, but the journey was slow and desultory. Refugees and convoys of French troops made the roads impassable. The French Army paid absolutely no regard to the movements of any other forces, overtaking everything whenever they could, blocking roads with complete indifference. As the battalion's transports got mired deeper and deeper in the chaos there were angry arguments and slanging matches between some of the British officers and French drivers, who seemed to have no officers in charge of them at all.

After three hours they had travelled barely ten miles and then they stopped at a farm in a village to the west of Armentières. There they stayed for the afternoon and the night, getting almost no sleep, standing to at half an hour's notice to move out – to where, they had no idea. As they mounted up, Les learned that their destination was Ypres – or Wipers as everyone called it. It had an ominous sound. Ypres had been the site of a bloody battle in the First World War, at which the Germans had first used poison gas and thousands of men had been killed. It was a name that was part of everybody's folk memory.

But the trucks ground on, then came once more to a standstill, apparently because of further confusion about where they were meant to be going. Orders from the French Command, which were now relayed by the provost company on the road, were that the battalion should be on the move not to Ypres but to a town called Strazeele, which was now on the western front and was coming under attack. The distance between Ypres and Strazeele was barely fifteen miles. This was the width of the corridor that the BEF was trying to hold open so that all the units could fall back to Dunkirk.

The convoy of trucks remained stationary. In broad daylight, with no anti-aircraft cover of any sort, it really was a sitting duck for any German aircraft that were looking for targets of opportunity. It was insane, and everybody, from the CO to the cooks, was becoming increasingly agitated about

The JU 87 Stuka dive-bomber was a fearsome weapon, against which the British troops had no defence. Used in close co-operation with the German army, their attacks often preceded an assault by infantry and tanks.

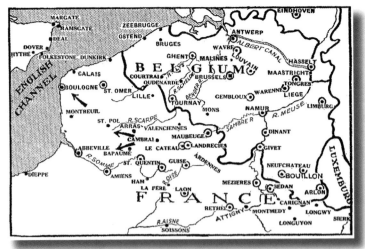

This map (**left**), published in the *Daily Mirror*, helped Stanley Chappell and his mates work out a route to Dunkirk after they were shelled out of the Mont des Cats. There was no safety on the beaches: shelling and bombing attacks killed many. Sheltering in the dunes provided some protection against the blast and shrapnel but the men on the beaches were forced to scatter (**below**).

The Royal Engineers built two jetties from army lorries. Men walked over them to reach boats that were unable to get close to the shore. Sydney Whiteside used one and never even got his feet wet.

Many ships were hit by bombs and sank. These men (**right**) are being hauled aboard a second vessel after their first rescue craft became a victim of an air raid. All sorts of small craft were pressed into service to get men from the beaches. This lifeboat (**below**) takes on some wounded, while others walk further into the sea up to their chests.

Many men were killed on the beaches or drowned in the sea. One veteran's lasting memory is of the sight of dead bodies washed up by the tide (**above**).

Two German ME 110 fighter-bombers fly over the devastation of Dunkirk (**below**). At the height of the evacuation it's estimated that there was an air raid every ten minutes.

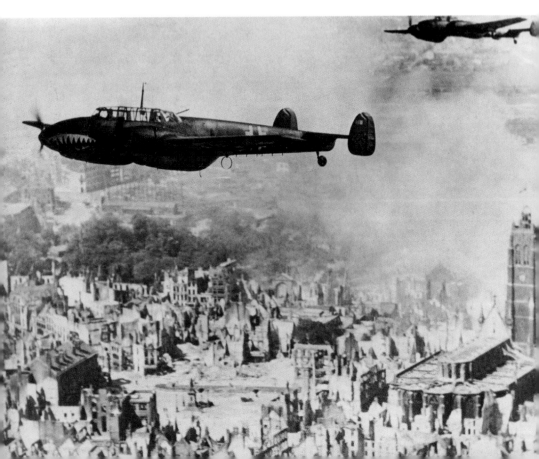

Signal

Signal, the German Armed Forces magazine, celebrates the German victory. A section of soldiers march along the beach, with the stranded wreck of a destroyer beyond them.

Aux portes de l'Angleterre L'infanterie allemande sur la plage de Dunkerque

Thousands of prisoners were rounded up and the French Army was broken. In a matter of weeks Germany controlled the European coast from the North Cape in Norway to Brest on the Atlantic.

Returning from France, exhausted men collapsed into a profound sleep (**above**), free, for the first time in weeks, from the fear of death or capture. Many of the men who were taken off the beaches had lost their kit, and their uniforms were soaked in oily seawater. The strain of their recent experiences shows clearly on the faces of these two men (**right**).

It was a long time since most of the men had seen any food or had a hot drink, and thousands of sandwiches and buckets of tea were laid on at the docks and railway sidings to feed the rescued army (**below**).

A troop train of men from Dunkirk is welcomed as it goes under a bridge. While the photo (**above**) is probably posed, the rescue of the BEF was an enormous relief to the country, and despite the gravity of the situation, it was viewed as a triumph.

The architect of the naval operation was Admiral Ramsay (**right**, in duffel coat). His career was thought to be over before Dunkirk but, instead, he continued in service to take charge of the seaborne planning for D-Day. He died in an air crash in France a few weeks after the landings.

Jack Haskett got out of France via Boulogne after meeting a German tank column. He later fought his way up through Italy to the Dolomites.

Les Clarke with his dog, Amos. Les fought several rearguard actions but left the army and joined the RAF as a gunner, where he went on to fight the Japanese in the Pacific.

Sid Lewis escaped a massacre, returned to France at D-Day and witnessed the German surrender to Field Marshall Montgomery.

Stanley Chappell, in the Royal Horse Artillery, was again evacuated from Greece, but went on to fight Rommel in North Africa, and saw the Afrika Corps surrender en masse.

their vulnerability. Les thought that this was just another step in the descent into chaos. They waited, irresolute, for two hours while the battalion staff tried to resolve the conflicting orders. Then came the grim news that the Germans had broken through at Strazeele, so the convoy started up and proceeded on its way to Vlamertinghe, a mile to the west of Ypres. It was 2.30 in the afternoon, and it had taken them four hours to travel twelve miles. Another meal of iron-ration biscuits and tinned fish awaited them. They were based at the local chateau and Les thought what a superb location it was, with pleasant grounds and fish ponds. It was a remarkably peaceful situation – such a contrast from cramped billets in town halls, or in bivouacs, or the jolting back of a 15cwt lorry. 'We all thought, "Wouldn't it be nice to stay here for a bit?" What did we know?'

The battalion's task was to relieve a regiment of French dragoons and set up defences along the Yser Canal, which ran north from Ypres. The company commanders went forward to look at the French defences, but Les had been in Vlamertinghe for barely an hour when the chateau was targeted by dive-bombers, and after the attack was over shells started whistling overhead, blasting the grounds and buildings. The enemy always seemed to know where they were.

That evening the men moved up gradually to replace the French troops in their trenches. The handover was accompanied by bursts of machine-gun fire across the canal, from both sides, with the occasional sudden naked exposure, or so it felt, from parachute flares dropped by the German reconnaissance aircraft that seemed to be permanently overhead. All movement ceased when one of these flares slowly descended, spreading an unnatural cold light over the area and casting deep black shadows. By the time the manoeuvre was finished it was 1.30 in the morning and impossible to see much in the dark. What Les did notice was that the trenches were poorly maintained and not deep enough. He thought it was a mark of poor morale, and poor leadership.

The day opened, and sniping became a constant danger, inhibiting the work that many felt needed doing on the lines of trenches. There were a large number of civilians on the road running along the opposite bank of the canal. Les was ordered to open fire to clear them off the road, because, he was told, the battalion HQ had intelligence that they weren't refugees but German soldiers in civilian clothes. Stories about Germans masquerading as refugees, or even as British soldiers, were now widespread amongst the troops. But opening fire revealed their positions and shortly afterwards mortars and shells started landing in the battalion area. The enemy clearly had a good idea where they were located because the fire was quite accurate, particularly close to the canal, and the barrage was endured for an hour and a half. Finally the British observation posts succeeded in locating the positions of the German gun batteries and the returning fire that zoomed overhead was a slight comfort. It may not have made much difference, but according to Les it always made him feel better if he thought that the enemy was not getting off scot free.

Rumours spread like flames in a cornfield that they were due to head out shortly. The troops on their right, the Northumberland Fusiliers, appeared to be pulling back and word went round that the army was pulling out from Dunkirk. Morale was very poor. Les was ordered to help with the destruction of the 2in and 3in mortars, which was apparently part of the process of getting rid of equipment prior to leaving for the coast. They were collected together and dropped down a well in the chateau grounds. It seemed a bit foolhardy, given that they were in the middle of a battle. It didn't do anything to help Les's spirits.

Life in general was now very physically uncomfortable. The German salvoes had not ceased; rather, they had noticeably increased in tempo. Despite a message from the battalion HQ that rations were on their way to the line, Les saw none. In addition, it was raining and there was thunder and lightning to add to the mix. The rain made vehicle movement difficult, causing the lanes and tracks to turn to quagmires. The slit trenches flooded and mud stuck everywhere, to boots, battle-dress and rifles. Even during the rain the fire from German mortars and artillery kept increasing. Their infantry had been advancing as well; small groups were seen very close to the opposite canal bank and machine guns had been infiltrated up to give them covering fire. Eventually they would make a bid to cross the canal.

Another French unit had withdrawn earlier in the day, leaving a gap between 2 Company and the town of Boesinghe. The battalion was so diminished in numbers that it was impossible to extend their line, and a machine-gun platoon had been put in to cover the gap. The situation was very fragile – the enemy had moved closer and was able to direct yet more sniper and machine-gun fire at the battalion's positions. At around six in the evening an intense barrage of shells began and a platoon of 1 Company gave way and retreated under the heavy fire. Then half an hour later German armoured vehicles, with bridging pontoons loaded on top, ground their way across the fields to the towpath.

Engineers who had sheltered behind the hulls of the tanks then went to work, manoeuvring the pontoons into the water.

The enemy shelling had cut many of the field telephone cables, so runners were darting to and fro between the platoon HQs and the battalion. The machine-gunners who were covering the gap at the northern end of the line were urgently needed to help repulse the enemy attempts to gain a bridgehead, but this would leave a gap in the line completely undefended.

The battalion HQ asked for an artillery barrage to be directed at the German troops on the opposite bank, and both companies were told to withdraw to create a safe distance from their own falling shells. After the salvo was finished, no one wanted to move forward again. German shells were still falling and the air was lethal with machine-gun fire from the opposite bank. Officers tried to urge the men to move, but while Lieutenant Caldwell of 2 Company was on his feet trying to lead his men forward, he was hit by shrapnel and collapsed in a heap. It didn't encourage anyone to follow him.

Les recalls that it was one of the worst situations he had ever been in. The German barrage was so intense that it was certain death to try to go back to their old positions. He felt trapped. The thunderstorms had flooded the drainage ditches behind them, so that they would have to wade through water up to their necks to move back any further. The artillery barrage from the British side had scuppered the enemy's bridging attempt, but their shelling was still so severe that it was obvious they were going to have another go. The barrage continued into the night, and a move to get some more men from the 8th Durham Light Infantry to their left to bolster the 6th's line ended in failure; the barrage of shells was too heavy.

At about two that morning, Les received a warning that they would withdraw at four. There were only a few foot-bridges over the ditches in the rear of the canal and men would be posted at them to guide platoons across. The withdrawal was to be completed in darkness, and quietly. Les thought that the Germans would never hear them anyway. Jerry was sending over salvoes every half an hour, as regular as clockwork. When his time came he was extremely relieved to get out of his slit trench and cross the drainage ditch, which had turned into a swollen, fast-flowing watercourse.

He walked through the battalion HQ position and went down a road for a mile or so before climbing into the back of a 15cwt lorry, one of a line waiting for the battalion. Then they slowly moved out to another wood near another village. Word had got round that they were to pull back to Dunkirk and once there get on board ship back to England. They had some breakfast, sheltering under the cover of the woods. It was hardtack biscuits with a mess tin of hot stew – Maconochies, which came in giant tins. It was impossible to tell what sort of meat was in it – not that there was very much – but it was welcome. Les hadn't eaten for over a day and hadn't had anything hot for several. They stayed where they were for most of the day, while reconnaissance planes circled overhead. No movement was to be attempted before dark. During the course of the day the sound of shelling grew closer: the Germans were still advancing.

That evening an instruction went round that all surplus kit, including signals equipment, was to be destroyed. Les didn't have much. As their transport arrived, shells started landing closer and nobody delayed climbing aboard the trucks. As they moved off, shells landed in the wood. Once more they were leaving in the nick of time with the enemy snapping at their heels.

Les looked out from the back of the lorry at fields filled with clusters of wrecked guns and transports, many of them burning, like some ghastly satanic scene. They passed through small villages and towns. White sheets hung out of every window and white flags flew over farms and village halls alike. Belgium had surrendered. It was just over two weeks since they had been welcomed with food and wine and cheering crowds. Now the houses were dark and shuttered, the streets deserted.

Just after midnight the lorries stopped. Ordered out, they were told to start digging in again, along the banks of another canal. So much for Dunkirk.

To questions about evacuation, Les was told that they were to hold the perimeter around the port. This canal was to be the south-eastern defensive line. They were going to be the bloody rearguard again. Les felt bitter. The battalion didn't have that many men left to lose. Maybe that had been the calculation.

By that morning, 30 May, they had dug slit trenches and firing positions along a line of the Furnes Canal, a narrow watercourse that would not stop very much. As they retreated, the canals that had been selected for defensive positions had been growing narrower and narrower, until now this one. It was hardly wider than the flooded drainage ditch that ran alongside the Lys Canal.

The Germans really had been hot on their heels. By 9.15, just minutes after the last sapper had walked off a small bridge on their right and the charges had exploded, mortar and machine-gun fire started landing on their line at the left. On the other side of the canal was the village of Bulscamp, its cottages clustered around a church whose spire was visible for several miles across the flat countryside. The Germans would have put observers in there straight away, thought Les; it was the best vantage point for miles. Sure enough, shells started landing very close to the canal and after ten minutes they were hitting the access roads to the bridge. Les started digging deeper, but the water table in the low-lying polder was not very deep and water started to seep into the floor of the slit trench around his boots.

The latest rumour was that they would have to hold the line here for up to five days to ensure that the evacuation at Dunkirk went ahead. 'Then what about us?' thought Les.

19

THE NAVY'S HERE

26–29 May

Throughout the two weeks after the start of the German attack, talks between the French and British governments about the conduct of the war continued, even as the situation worsened. As the Germans advanced further and further into French territory, the discussions took on an air of complete fantasy. It seemed to one man, Major General Sir Edward Spears – a First World War veteran who was now an MP and Winston Churchill's personal emissary to the French government – that the leading French politicians and generals were in a trance. On 26 May Spears met another veteran of the First World War, the French Marshal Philippe Pétain, now a venerated war hero and elder statesman. He told Spears that he considered the situation catastrophic. He further revealed that in the past two weeks sixteen French generals had been relieved of their command. Yet Churchill and the War Cabinet still proposed ways of continuing the war, reiterating to their French allies that the British would continue to do so whatever happened. General Gort, however, had no illusions about the gravity of the situation that the BEF found itself in. It was because of his original message on the 19th that the question of evacuation was being discussed.

Now, just one week later, the situation was far worse. The Official History gives a succinct description of the plight of the BEF. Two German army groups were squeezing the British, Belgian and French Northern Army in a pocket stretched out along a front of 128 miles. Some of the front was secured by French troops and some of it was held jointly, but the British area of sole responsibility was itself 97 miles long. Gort knew that he was not going to get any more reinforcements and that his troops' resources of ammunition, food and other supplies were very short. The major depots in the west were now cut off. The Belgian Army, which was fighting German Army Group B, was under enormous pressure and Gort had sent two divisions to support it, but he had received a message from the Belgian High Command that morning telling him that the Belgian Army was withdrawing under heavy attack, leaving a gap between the Belgian and British lines. If the Germans succeeded in breaking through here then they would be able to drive a wedge between the BEF and the coast. There would be nowhere to retreat to, and no evacuation.

The BEF was greatly outnumbered. The two divisions trying to fill the gap left by the Belgian Army were already below strength and were facing three divisions of Army Group B. In the west, Gort had one regular division, the 2nd, and three Territorial divisions, the 48th, the 44th and the 46th. The 48th

– Sid Lewis's division – had seen a great deal of fighting and was now composed of only two brigades, not three; the 44th Division was in a similar state. The 46th was another of the divisions that had been sent out for further training, like Jack Haskett's, and was undermanned. There were, in addition, some mechanized cavalry and the 1st Light Armoured Reconnaissance Brigade – but it was altogether a tired and rather motley force that had to confront the spearhead of Rundstedt's Army Group A. This totalled five armoured divisions and four motorized infantry divisions, which were moving north-east up the French coast. There were other German divisions in the rear acting as a reserve. Boulogne was in German hands, as was Calais, and German armour was stretched in a line from Gravelines on the coast in an arc that extended south-east past La Bassée to meet up with Army Group B advancing from the east.

The stage was set for the realization of Rundstedt's overall objective: to annihilate 'the continental sword of the English and then to attack England by air and sea'. Rundstedt, however, believed that this annihilation was not necessarily the task of Army Group A. There were still major battles ahead in the plan to sweep through France and defeat the rest of the French Army. Many of his Panzer regiments had suffered losses due to wear and tear and enemy action; they needed time for repairs to bring them back up to strength. He had five armies extended over a huge area, with widely separated fronts; there was also the possibility of some French attacks from the south, against which it was prudent to guard. Army Group B could grind on from the north and wipe out the British, while the Luftwaffe would ensure that they could not escape from the coast.

Rundstedt, in fact, had ordered a halt to any further advance late on 23 May. The order would not be rescinded until the 27th. Lord Gort was unaware of this; however, it did not affect the vulnerability of his forces one iota. The survival of the British Expeditionary Force was now in the balance. Gort's view, which he expressed to the secretary of state for war in a telegram, was 'that the greater part of the force and its equipment will inevitably be lost'. It was a grim prediction for the start of an unprecedented operation.

On the very first day of Operation Dynamo the difficulties of carrying it out became apparent. Admiral Ramsay had already seen destroyers lost in the evacuations of Boulogne and Calais. They were in short supply and were needed for the rest of the navy's responsibilities around the UK. Also, a much larger number of troops would need to come out of the harbour at Dunkirk, and Ramsay had expected that most of the lifting would be done by merchant ships, cross-Channel ferries and coasters.

One of the first of these ships to make the journey to Dunkirk was a ferry from the Isle of Man, *Mona's Queen*. The normal route from Dover to Dunkirk would be a distance of thirty-nine nautical miles. The ship would head south-east from Dover to a lightship off Calais, then the ship would steer east along the coast to Dunkirk. German artillery, however, was in place on the cliffs above Calais and *Mona's Queen* was straddled by two salvoes of shellfire from shore batteries as she turned by the Calais buoy marking the passage. The ship was pierced by shrapnel. Then two Junkers bombers attacked her and a stick of five bombs exploded alongside, about 150 feet away. She steamed on, but her crew and captain – all civilians – were shaken up by their close call at the hands of the enemy. The captain assembled the crew to tell them that Dunkirk was on fire and asked them if they would volunteer to go on. They did and took off several hundred men.

Many other ships also succeeded in getting through and taking off casualties and soldiers, most of whom were in support roles not immediately needed in the front line. But the approach into Dunkirk harbour was hampered by the wrecks of ships that had already been sunk in the previous day's air raids. These raids were continuing – one estimate was that there was a raid every ten minutes – and they were bad enough effectively to close the port. One ship, *Maid of Orléans*, carrying water for the garrison, as well as men from the Royal Army Service Corps and Signals Corps to help organize the port facilities, arrived when the harbour was being bombed and had to return to Dover.

By the end of the first day 27,936 men had been picked up from the harbour at Dunkirk, but the difficulties could only get worse. Any ship going by the quickest route would be the target of shells from the shore batteries at Calais, and then the crew would also come under the hammer of the Luftwaffe's air attacks. Approaching Dunkirk itself was like sailing into a cauldron of fire.

To the west of the great basin, the large oil-tank farm blazed menacingly. Warehouses along the wharves and docks burned vigorously and the huge cranes that ran on rails along the docksides lay toppled over and smashed. Behind the port, the town of Dunkirk had also been set on fire and the thick smoke from the various conflagrations billowed over everything. The smoke at least occasionally hampered the pilots dive-bombing the town and port facilities.

That night the Admiralty told Ramsay that Dynamo had to be speeded up, and that the aim was to lift forty-five thousand troops within two days, before the evacuation had to be abandoned due to enemy action. Ramsay knew that he would have to increase the number of ships available to meet this target. Small boats had been asked to register with the Admiralty a week earlier and the owners of these were now to be contacted.

On land, the army tried to organize the port and the beaches. The British perimeter was divided into three areas, one for each corps, with a collecting area located outside the perimeter. The corps were allocated their own section of the beach for evacuation. Ammunition and food stores were set up in the three areas, and casualty clearing stations were established at La Panne and Rosendaël. All transport, apart from artillery ambulances and headquarters vehicles, was to be abandoned outside the line of the canals that were going to make up the perimeter.

On 27 May ships were turning back because of the shellfire from Calais and the first casualties occurred. A motor vessel, *Sequacity*, was holed by shellfire and also bombed. She sank. *Mona's Isle* had embarked 1,420 troops at Dunkirk on that Monday morning, then on the return journey was straddled by shells and bombed. She did not sink, but twenty-three men were killed and sixty wounded. Other routes had to be found. Two seemed possible. The longer – 87 miles – ran to a point off Ostend and came in through the east. Another, shorter, route cut across a bank of shallow water and came to the French coast between Gravelines and Dunkirk. Neither route had been cleared of mines and they had other disadvantages.

They required ships to navigate a channel around the Goodwin Sands, and because they took longer it meant that there was a much greater chance that they would come under air attack. More ships would be needed to maintain the rate of evacuation.

Late in the afternoon of the same day, the 27th, Captain W. G. Tennant had arrived at Dunkirk in HMS *Wolfhound* to take up a post as the senior naval officer ashore. When he saw the state of the port he sent a signal saying that all available vessels should be sent to the beaches east of Dunkirk and that 'Evacuation tomorrow night is problematical.'

Ramsay had received a signal from Gort's GHQ saying that the position of the BEF was precarious, so he sent an anti-aircraft cruiser – *Calcutta* – nine destroyers, four mine-sweepers, seventeen drifters and two transports to work off the beaches between La Panne and Dunkirk. The problem with the beaches, however, was that the personnel ships could not approach closer than a mile or so, depending on the state of the tide, and nor were small lifeboats or naval cutters and whalers suitable for getting close to the men on the shallow sands of the beach. The progress of evacuation was slowing.

Captain Tennant then thought that ships might be able to berth at the eastern breakwater to the port. Normally ships did not berth there; it was merely a breakwater for the dock basin, but it was almost a mile in length and troops using it would avoid the burning dockyards. He signalled a ship to tie up there and it did so without any problem. From now on men could be picked up from the harbour as well as the beaches. On the 27th the number of men actually embarked fell dramatically, with only 7,669 troops landing in England.

If it was possible to use both the mole and the beaches, then more ships were needed, quickly.

Overnight, Captain Tennant had organized squads of men to help the boats tie up and appointed a pier master. He signalled that the ships should utilize the mole, and Ramsay took a gamble and sent his destroyers in. Six of them docked on the morning of the 28th. Furthermore, Admiral Ramsay mobilized other destroyers, from the North Sea and East Coast ports, and another eleven warships arrived to take part in the evacuation. Their presence provided a massive boost to the rate of embarkation. HMS *Codrington*, formerly based at Harwich, berthed at the mole in Dunkirk and took on seven hundred men, reversed away from the mole, returned to Dover and then, travelling at twenty-two knots, returned to pick up another nine hundred men. The other destroyers carried similar loads. These warships were fast and agile, their crews skilful and determined. On the same day more of the small boats had arrived and started to lift men from the beaches to carry them out to waiting ships, or to go back to Dover.

By the end of the 28th, the second full day of Operation Dynamo, 17,804 men had been brought back to England. After the hesitation of the previous day, the evacuation was now, it seemed, once more in full swing. The next day, the 29th, was to see a huge reversal.

The ships now running a shuttle service between the harbour at Dunkirk and Dover were attacked by German U-boats and, with increasing vigour, by the Luftwaffe. At midnight, as the day started, two destroyers were heading for Dover when one of them, HMS *Wakeful*, was hit by a torpedo. She broke in two and sank. Apart from a handful of the crew who were on deck at the time, all those on board drowned. The second destroyer, *Grafton*, stopped to search for survivors and she too was hit. In the darkness and confusion another vessel, the drifter *Comfort*, was mistaken for a German torpedo boat and the now sinking *Grafton* fired on her. So too did a minesweeper that had also come to search for survivors. The crew, and the rescued survivors of *Wakeful* on board *Comfort*, were killed by the gunfire and she was rammed by the minesweeper. *Grafton* remained afloat for most of the men on board to get off, but thirty-five army officers were killed by the two torpedoes that hit her. Another destroyer, HMS *Montrose*, was badly damaged by shellfire and had to be towed to Dover.

Mona's Queen, from the Isle of Man, one of the first ships to take part in the operation, hit a mine half a mile from Dunkirk and sank within two minutes. *Clan MacAlister*, the largest cargo ship to take part in the evacuation, arrived off the beach and lowered some army landing craft. As they brought the first load of men back to the ship she was bombed and set on fire; after a second bombing attack she was abandoned. Then, at four o'clock in the afternoon, an air raid on the port took a savage toll of ships and men. A big paddle-steamer, *Fenella*, was hit by a bomb. Some of the troops on board were killed, but the bomb passed through the hull and most of those on board were able to disembark back on to the jetty before she sank. A destroyer, HMS *Grenade*, was hit by a bomb and caught fire, but her crew was able to get her out of the entrance to the harbour before she sank. Very few men survived.

Two trawlers were sunk. HMS *Crested Eagle*, after taking on board survivors of *Fenella*, moved away from the mole and was then struck by a bomb. She caught fire, and the crew grounded her on the beach to avoid blocking access to the port. The ship burned out, again with heavy loss of life. Other ships off the beach were also hit. The paddle-steamer *Gracie Fields* sank during her tow back to Dover. A paddle-minesweeper, *Waverly*, was hit and sank, with many of the crew drowning, along with three or four hundred troops. Two Southern Railway ships were also bombed and sank in shallow water.

By seven o'clock on the evening of the 29th Admiral Ramsay was told that Dunkirk harbour was blocked by damaged ships and that only the beaches could be used for evacuation. The message was wrong, but meant that many units of the BEF, trying to make their way to the coast, were diverted away from Dunkirk.

But despite the growing casualties among men and ships, the evacuation continued and another 47,310 troops were landed back in home ports. Meanwhile, thousands more were struggling to reach the perimeter of the Dunkirk beachhead.

While the Royal Navy was moving into concerted action and the Luftwaffe was focusing its strength against the ships sailing to and from Dunkirk, the German Army was also advancing. On the eastern flank General Bock's Army Group B was pressing against the Belgian and British forces, as well as against the French First Army along the Scheldt. The advance of Bock's forces had been far less spectacular than the dynamic thrust of Rundstedt's Army Group A. The reasons were simple. Bock's Army Group B had no armoured units. All of his Panzer divisions had been assigned to Rundstedt and his remaining infantry was overwhelmingly reliant on horse-drawn transport. Inevitably, their forward progress was slow. In addition, the Allies were entrenched in the prepared defensive lines along the French border and the German infantry struggled to dislodge them. The Germans were making some progress, though. On 24 May they had been able to break the Belgian defences along the River Lys, and by midday on the 26th the Belgian Army was pushed back northwards and a gap at Ypres between the British and Belgian lines was widening.

In the west, Army Group A was pushing forward, sweeping past the strongpoints that Gort had set up in Wormhout, Hazebrouck and Béthune, but taking heavy casualties in the process and finding it hard going. Rommel had been held up at the La Bassée Canal, and the last-ditch stand at Mont des Cats showed that the soldiers of Army Group A were having to fight hard for every mile.

But events moved fast on the 26th. As the Belgian Army fell back, the Germans were heading towards Ostend. Although the gap between the British and Belgian forces was widening, Bock did nothing to exploit it. Lord Gort saw the danger and made plans to withdraw to the network of canals that surrounded Dunkirk, linking the towns of Nieuport, Furnes, Bergues and Dunkirk itself. Then on the 27th, the Belgian government, influenced by the knowledge that the British had started to evacuate, sent a delegation to General Bock to seek terms. They were going to capitulate. With the Belgian Army laying down their arms, the gap between Ypres and the coast at Nieuport was wide open, as was the line along the coast to Dunkirk itself. Bock sent two divisions to seize the gap, but they were not fast enough. Gort ordered the armoured cars of the 12th Lancers to cover the gap between the edge of the British 50th Division and the coast, and they managed to stop the Germans at Nieuport. Their limited strength was boosted later that day with a force made up of engineers, men from various artillery and anti-aircraft units and French soldiers from their 60th Division. These men held the enemy at bay until they could be relieved by the 12th Brigade from the 4th Division on the night of the 29th.

On the western side of the small pocket around Dunkirk, General Guderian made a tour of his armoured units. The leading tanks of the 1st Panzer Division were just eight miles away from the harbour of Dunkirk, but they were faced with open, flooded terrain crisscrossed by drainage ditches and canals. Guderian had already had some experience of sending his tanks against determinedly defended strongpoints on waterways and in blocked and barricaded streets. He decided that 'Further tank attacks would involve useless sacrifice of our best troops.'

Throughout the next two days troops of Army Group A and B moved up towards the perimeter of Dunkirk. There was little coordination between them. Paralysis and in-decision accompanied various plans to move against the defenders. On the 30th all operations against the perimeter were placed under the control of Army Group B. The Panzer units started to move away to regroup for the onslaught against the rest of the French Army in the south. One more attempt was made to cross the canal at Furnes, but it was beaten back.

The Germans were shortly to realize their dream of capturing the whole of France, even to the Atlantic coast, but they had not wiped out the British Army.

Behind the perimeter, with the unlucky rearguard holding the line, thousands of men gathered on the beaches, hoping that somehow, in some way, they would climb on board a boat and get away to England and safety.

20

THE SAPPER ON THE BEACH

28 May–1 June

R eg Beeston in the 224 Field Company Royal Engineers was detached with his unit from the 48th Division around 26 May. The division was sent to the western flank and ended up fighting at Wormhout and Hazebrouck, but Reg and his mates went north. He thinks they arrived at Dunkirk a day or so later, around the 28th, but cannot be sure. Since the fighting on the Tournai Canal, his days had merged seamlessly into an endless succession of demolition, retreat and seeking shelter from air attacks. The field company had effectively been organized in a completely ad hoc fashion for weeks and the war diary of his unit ceases abruptly on 12 May. They were sufficiently trained to fit in with any division and would get on with any job that obviously needed carrying out. It was likely that engineers had been directed to Dunkirk to prepare the port for evacuating large numbers of men, but German air raids had superseded that decision.

Reg's first sight of the huge plumes of smoke pouring into the sky above Dunkirk was frightening and ominous. A few months later the Blitz on London and other cities in Britain would make sights like that commonplace, but for Reg, and almost everybody else who saw them for the first time, this giant evidence of a burning town was like an intimation of Armageddon. Reg, like most of his comrades, was depressed and angry at what, to him, had seemed nothing but retreat. Dunkirk in flames sapped his spirits even further.

They had disposed of most of their equipment, but they drove into the town over the rubble and were directed east to the beaches. There the sight that met Reg's eyes depressed him even more. He realized that there were thousands of soldiers on the beach. They were queuing up to the water's edge, with thousands more waiting in the dunes inland. It was a sight that was at first impossible to understand.

Reg is not a man to dwell on things, and moreover the Royal Engineers had a job to do. However bad the situation, something could be done to improve it and doing that thing kept despair at bay. Among the engineers' equipment were collapsible boats intended to be used in river assaults. Each company had three of these as part of its standard equipment and there were several companies of field engineers along the fifteen miles of shallow beach that stretched from Nieuport to Dunkirk. The boats could carry eight men, or ten at a pinch, with two engineers rowing. Their shallow draught meant that they were able to get closer to the beach than the navy's sea boats or the lifeboats and naval cutters that were currently being pressed into service. Using the collapsible boats would help to speed up the rate at which men were transferred from the beaches to the ships standing off in the bay. So Reg and his mates assembled their boats and started their ferry service. Reg was amazed to see their commanding officer, Colonel Tony Gardiner. He had found a horse from somewhere and he was riding up and down the beach, chivvying the soldiers into orderly queues for the rowing boats.

Reg and his mate Chuck Casborne worked on one boat. They could, depending on the state of the tide, make six trips a day, sometimes rowing out to sea for almost two miles to reach a larger ship to unload their passengers. 'We got maybe sixty out a day. With the other boats in the company, that was 180 men a day. But there were a lot of other boats doing it as well.'

During the persistent air raids, everyone took shelter in the dunes and the queues of men disappeared as if by magic. Reg realized that the soft sand of the dunes absorbed the blast and the shrapnel from the bombs. But the raiding Stukas, and the occasional German fighters, also flew along the beaches firing their machine guns at the crouching soldiers and there were always dead and wounded after the attacks. Reg had got used to the dive-bombing. 'After a week or so of lying face down as the bombs whistled down, you didn't feel the fear that you did the first few times. It was still very stressful, though, and the stress came out in other ways.'

By 30 May there was pressure to get more men off the beaches and the Royal Engineers came up with a solution that would allow larger craft to keep working at low tide. They organized the construction of a temporary jetty at La Panne where the General Staff had set up their headquarters and which was an assembly point for embarkation. At low tide the engineers drove or towed lorries and cars out on to the foreshore as far as they could, lining them up nose to tail. With ladders and planks lashed to the tops of the vehicles, soldiers could walk further out to sea on them, and when the tide rose they were able to climb straight into some of the larger boats. It speeded up loading a great deal. Later that day another similar jetty was built at Bray Dunes, a small seaside resort further down the coast, closer to Dunkirk, where another collection point for the troops had been set up.

But this inspired piece of engineering didn't mean that Reg and his mates could stop their own efforts. The troops that were lifted from the beach were replaced by others – the task seemed endless. Reg and Chuck rowed for three days and some of the night, to and fro. The days of rowing merged into each other and it became an almost robotic activity. They were existing on very short rations and by the third night they were utterly burned out. They went back into the dunes for several hundred yards to sleep. The high dunes protected them from the winds, and they cut off the sounds of thousands of men, the orders and curses and the noise of battle. They slept for hours, waking the next morning. It was late, judging by the sun.

Walking down to the beach, Reg was astounded to see that it was almost empty and there were no ships in the bay. Now he started to be alarmed about whether he was going to get back to England. During his trips out to the vessels in the bay he had occasionally thought about when it was going to be his time to climb aboard a ship and head for home, and he was sure that 224 Field Company would be collected together and all taken off en masse. But now they were nowhere to be seen. Reg and Chuck ran down to the beach. The tide was going out, and it went out fast. They rushed to the shoreline and splashed out on to one of the jetties. To their relief, they saw a paddle-steamer. They waved and waved and it started to come into the shore; it was able to approach quite close. They climbed down into the water and waded out, the water getting deeper and deeper, until they could reach a line thrown over the side of the paddle-steamer.

As they climbed on board, Reg experienced an enormous wave of relief as the fears and stress of the last two weeks fell from his shoulders. He realized how much anxiety had been bottling up inside him and how exhausting it had been. But instead of heading out to sea, the paddle-steamer pulled away from the beach and went to the mole at Dunkirk to take on some wounded men. Shells and bombs were hitting the harbour, and Reg spent another fraught few hours before the paddle-steamer – which Reg thinks was *Tynwald* – thrashed away from the jetty.

The danger was still not over. Twice German aircraft flew over the ship, their bombs dropping close enough to send showers of water over the decks. Despite becoming super-ficially inured to the random and deadly dive-bombing attacks on the retreat from Belgium, Reg found that being on the exposed decks of a boat that was the only target for miles was horribly frightening. The paddle-steamer escaped serious damage from the bombing, but the explosions were near enough to send shrapnel flying and injure some of the men on the decks. One man close to Reg lost both his hands as a result of a nearby blast. He had been a pianist in civilian life.

Tynwald continued on its way, however, finally docking at Harwich. Reg walked off the boat on to the dockside. He had never felt so exhausted in all his life.

21

SYDNEY WHITESIDE AT LA PANNE

29 May–1 June

Sydney Whiteside and the driver of his ambulance managed to find their way to La Panne without any more incident and once in the small seaside town they reported to the CO of 145 Field Ambulance Company. Nobody at La Panne had any idea where Sydney's unit was, and they didn't care. There was a casualty clearing station at La Panne and business was brisk. Wounded were brought in from the beaches, the result of the continual air raids and machine-gunning by enemy aircraft, and there was some desperate fighting going on around the perimeter of the Dunkirk enclave, particularly in the north close to the Belgian border. Sydney was ordered to stay and help.

La Panne was peaceful most of the time that he was there. There were no air attacks or shelling, but the Germans had cut the water supply to Dunkirk and the surrounding areas, so the only clean water came from water tanks on trailers that had been shipped in on transports which were then loaded up with men to take back to Dover or Ramsgate. Most of this water went to the wounded, but there was enough for the staff to have three cups of tea a day – better than most of the troops were getting at the time.

La Panne was the town closest to the Belgian border and the Germans were slowly pushing into the perimeter. The British HQ would have to be evacuated, and so too would the wounded. In the evening of 29 May patients were loaded on to a fleet of twenty ambulances to be driven to Dunkirk and shipped out. Sydney went in one of the vehicles. They waited until dark before setting out – a convoy would be immediately pounced on by the Stukas, who cared nothing for ambulances or giant red crosses painted on tarpaulins. It was not a long journey, but there were no maps and they couldn't use any of the ambulances' lights.

By now the situation had deteriorated so much that there was no one to organize guides, nor any of the signs that were a normal part of a unit's route planning. The sea was visible to their right, and Sydney thought that if they kept it in sight they would get to Dunkirk and eventually reach the mole. He had never been there. They had been directed straight to La Panne, so all they had seen of Dunkirk when they arrived was the smoke from the fires. The road they were on forked, however, and the leading ambulance went left. Soon Sydney's ambulance was driving through a built-up area, rocking and swaying across rubble that spread across the road from the bombed ruins of small terraced houses on either side. They came to a small square where several of the houses were burning, and a Royal Engineer stopped them and told them that there was a large fire ahead and the way was blocked.

They took another side road, eventually coming to a wide street where two rows of abandoned army lorries left a narrow lane between them. They began driving down it, but a convoy of French vehicles started coming the other way. The leading French car drove up to the first ambulance and stopped, then the next vehicles followed it until the road ahead was totally blocked. The drivers of the French vehicles stopped their engines then walked away. They seemed wholly indifferent to what would happen, or what the drivers of the ambulances would do. More British army lorries had driven up behind the ambulances and the convoy of wounded was completely blocked in.

It appeared that nothing was going to be done until the morning, so Sydney fell asleep in the cab. When he woke it was daylight and he could see that the road ahead was still blocked by a long file of vehicles. They had all been abandoned. There was no one in attendance or anywhere near them. It was daytime and Sydney thought it a good idea to get the wounded under cover.

Across a field there was a water tower and a flat building that looked as though it could accommodate the stretcher cases, so Sydney walked over to it. The door was locked, but Sydney had a revolver that he had taken off a dead officer in the casualty station, just in case, and he thought that he could shoot the lock off. Standing a little way away, he fired at the lock, but it didn't burst open as he had seen happen in the cinema. The door stayed obdurately locked. Six bullets didn't make any difference. One of the drivers, meanwhile, had noticed that a window was unlocked. He climbed through it, found a key inside the building and opened it up. The wounded were then given some shelter for the day, and eventually they were placed on the back of some 30cwt lorries that were found for them and driven off to the port. Sydney walked back the few miles to the dressing station at La Panne. It had taken around thirty-six hours to move eighty wounded men ten miles to a hospital ship.

By 31 May all of the casualties from the casualty clearing station at La Panne had been evacuated and the medical facilities and the General Headquarters were about to be closed down. They were now in range of the German artillery that had reached Nieuport and the perimeter around the beaches was rapidly shrinking. Sydney fell in with 145 Field Ambulance Unit and the rest of the medical team, marching along the top of the beach towards Dunkirk. He was surprised to see that the beach was deserted, apart from a few men in the beach parties and a few units waiting to be told where to go. The day before he had seen it packed with thousands of men, in long queues that snaked their way across the beach. It was one of the most unnerving sights that he had seen. Thousands of men, waiting, and ships and boats in the water, many wrecked or burning. It was impossible to imagine that they would escape. Now they had gone. He marched on with his companions for about two miles until some German aircraft came over, then they scattered and took cover; but the enemy planes were heading for other targets further along the beach and they were left alone. They resumed their march until they got to Bray Dunes and one of the vehicle jetties that had been built out to sea.

Sydney and the rest of the men in his party – they totalled about sixty altogether – walked out along the planks, old doors and ladders that had been laid out on the roofs of the vehicles. The makeshift jetty was very shaky in some parts. When they got to the end of the line of vehicles, where the sea came almost up to the roof of the lorries, they climbed into a navy cutter and were ferried out to a destroyer. The ship had scrambling nets hanging down the side of the grey, rust-streaked hull, and Sydney was surprised how easy it was to get on board. He hadn't even got his feet wet.

He made his way into the ship and sat down in the crew's mess area with his back to a bulkhead. Looking at his watch, he saw that it was nine o'clock. A little while later he looked at it again. It said 5.20. He was completely taken aback and started wondering if something had happened to his watch or if he had misread the time, when he realized that he had dropped straight into a deep sleep, driven by utter exhaustion and nervous tension, and that it must now be 5.20 the next morning.

The destroyer wasn't moving, so Sydney assumed that the ship had already docked somewhere in England and that he would soon be able to get off. He put on his webbing and his backpack, then climbed back up the companionway to the forward deck. But when he got to the gangway it was blocked by soldiers packed closely together. He could see above the heads of those nearest to him that the whole of the deck was crowded with men.

'Where are we?' he asked.

The nearest chap looked at him. 'Dunkirk.'

Then it sank in to Sydney's confused mind that the destroyer had merely travelled along the coast to take on board hundreds of extra men. Sydney had no chance to say anything more, because in front of him came an immensely bright flash and a very loud explosion, immediately followed by another. The two were separated by less than a second. Sydney had never been so close to a bomb before. Two men in front of him fell suddenly to the deck; they had taken the full force of the bomb blast and also caught the shrapnel. They had sheltered Sydney, who was apparently unharmed, though he now believes that he was seriously affected by the blast.

The two men closest to him were not dead, just badly hurt with several shrapnel wounds that were pumping out blood. He knelt down and did what he could to put dressings on their injuries and make them comfortable. In his own mind this did not take him very long, and when he had finished treating the two men he went forward to help with the other casualties. He saw that someone was lying half out of a hatchway and went to do what he could for him, but when he got there he found that there were just two legs lying on the deck. There was no sign of the rest of the body. He could see no one else lying on the deck. Instead, there was a macabre pile of dead men laid neatly along the side, reaching to a height of about four feet. The bodies had been placed tidily on top of each other, and he could see that it had been done with care because the corpses were laid alternately head to toe, presumably to stop them toppling over. None of the dead men seemed to be badly injured, except for a trickle of fresh blood coming from some of them. Sydney could not imagine how this pile had been built in the little time it had taken him to dress the wounds of two men, but he thinks now that he must have been suffering a form of waking black-out. He went around the ship and saw two groups of soldiers who had dressed their own wounds. He helped one or two of them and when he returned to the fore deck he saw that the pile of bodies had gone. A petty officer was talking to a sergeant and Sydney asked what had happened to the dead. 'Oh, we've tidied them up,' said the sailor.

Sydney then asked where all the rest of the men were and was told that they had left the ship because it had been holed by the bombs and was probably sinking. The sailor seemed to Sydney to be remarkably calm when he said this, and then he ambled off. The destroyer was stationary at the very end of the mole, which stretched back to the harbour and was nearly a mile long. It didn't seem that there was any way for Sydney to get off.

He decided to stay on board, and the destroyer was eventually towed out to sea. He was worried about what to do if the ship did sink, but he found a lifejacket and kept it near him, then he went back to sleep, extremely puzzled, but also reassured by the lack of urgency or alarm on the part of the destroyer's crew.

Sydney was woken up once during the trip and was asked, very politely, to go to the stern to join the rest of the crew, because the captain wanted to try to get the hole in the bow above the water line. When he got to the stern he found another twenty or so soldiers, who had been working in the bows with the crew of the destroyer trying to plug the hole, with only partial success. But their efforts did pay off because the ship, although damaged and flooded, was towed slowly back to the UK and finally docked at Margate.

Sydney climbed up the gangway. When he reached dry land, the sense of relief at being back on English soil once more was almost overwhelming. He felt close to tears and could hardly maintain his composure. He was home, and safe. It was unbelievable.

22

LARRY UREN IS RESCUED

29 May–1 June

Larry Uren from the 1/7th Battalion Queen's Royal Regiment stood on a French roadside jammed with vehicles and refugees and had no idea where he was. The men of the battalion had been ordered to make their own way to Dunkirk. He knew vaguely that it was north, but had no map or compass. Three or four other lads from B Company were near him in a similar situation. They decided that they had had enough of walking in the past few days and attempted to flag down some lorries that were trying to force their way up the road; the drivers seemed happy to let them climb aboard. There were men from other units, but they seemed to know as little as Larry or his mates.

They had been making slow progress for several hours when the lorries ground to a halt – apparently there were some Jerries blocking the road ahead and they would have to turn back. Larry and his mates climbed out. Several of them were concerned about driving into a trap and wanted to make their own way, avoiding the roads and travelling cross-country, so they set out. They were not the only ones. Hundreds of others were choosing the same way to get to the coast. They walked for several hours – across fields of wheat, through farmyards, sometimes walking along lanes, always trying to head north. Larry was extremely tired and hungry, but dared not rest. He was sure that the enemy was close behind him. He was probably suffering from exhaustion and battle fatigue, as was almost everyone heading for the beaches now.

Time became elastic, but Larry's journey to Dunkirk was marked by one incident. He and his mates decided to walk for a while along a road, where they quickly became part of a large group of refugees and French soldiers. A flight of German Stukas flew over and dive-bombed the long line of civilians on the road. Larry tried to bury himself in the ditch by the side of the road as the bombs exploded. When the raid was over the dead and wounded lay everywhere. 'It was extremely vivid, because the bombs rained down and people were blown to smithereens. We were bomb-happy at that point after the raid. There was an abandoned lorry up the road and we went up to it; we wanted to get away. In the back were big crates of chocolate bars and whisky. It must have been a NAAFI lorry. I took a load of chocolate and two bottles of whisky. Then I said I'd drive it. We got going. A French soldier was sitting next to me and he was shaking after the raid. It was terrible. I gave him a bottle of whisky and he drank it down like it was water. I said, 'You might as well keep the bottle.'

They drove for a couple of miles, then as they came down

a hill Larry saw a bridge over a river. As he approached a sapper sprang out on to the road waving a red flag. 'I thought "I'm not stopping," and I put my foot down. He leaped out of the way and we shot over the bridge. The road was a T-junction on the other side and we came off the road, and at the same time the bridge went up. I thought there would be hell to pay. But they said we should leave the lorry as all transport was being stopped outside Dunkirk.'

They walked on, and as darkness fell they looked for somewhere to sleep. 'But I couldn't sleep. I slept for maybe two hours, then woke up, I was that anxious about being surprised by Jerry. I wanted to keep moving. I was feeling very low. We were exhausted, we were almost living rough and had been for a few days, really, but we also were feeling that we had lost our pride. That had started a while ago. We did not like to think that we had been beaten, that we were retreating.'

They eventually reached Dunkirk the next afternoon. As they got closer the enormous pillars of smoke provided a good landmark to aim for. They were also now part of a huge mass of soldiers heading for the town. Larry walked to the jetty through roads blocked with rubble and burned-out vehicles. At one point he was collared by a naval officer and told to help unload a ship that had brought some mobile water tanks and other equipment. But before very much could be taken off the ship some Stukas appeared out of the smoke and dropped their bombs on the western side of the port, near the oil-tank farm, and also on the mole. There was fire everywhere and Larry thought that he would be burned to death. He scrambled back off the mole. Unloading was stopped, and when the air raid was over Larry was told to walk along the beach towards the sand dunes and a small resort called Bray Dunes; he would be taken on to a ship from there. When he got there he collapsed in the sand and slept for eight hours. When he awoke there were thousands of men on the beach and another air raid was under way. 'I was on my own now, with no idea what to do. I saw hordes of men queuing to be taken on to small boats, but I wasn't with my unit. Some men were – they were more organized.' He stayed on the beach for two days. The air raids went on constantly and Larry found them frightening. All he had to eat was the chocolate he had in his pockets, and he was becoming completely demoralized. 'I didn't think that I would get home again. I thought I was finished and was bound to get captured.'

Then, on the third day, he went down to the water's edge. 'I was lucky – a rowing boat beached near me and I got on it. We rowed out to a destroyer.' Larry clambered up the netting and got on board. The ship was already fully loaded. 'I was on the deck with hundreds of others. This matelot came along with a big baker's tray of mugs of cocoa. Then a Stuka came down and we were hit! The cocoa went up in the air. I hadn't had a drink for three days!' There was pandemonium on the deck – hundreds of men were wounded and the ship was badly damaged. She started listing heavily and the captain gave the order to abandon ship. By now the deck was so close to the water that Larry just stepped into the sea. Around him were hundreds of men, some swimming, some drowning, dragged down by their uniforms. Men were dying next to him. It was a horrible sight. He had got this far but death seemed everywhere.

'I could swim, but you wouldn't get very far with your boots and greatcoat on, as many of the lads had. I was lucky.'

A Thames barge that had quickly motored to the rescue threw out some ropes and Larry was able to grab one and haul himself aboard. The barge crew took on as many soldiers as they could, then they set out for England, the soldiers, Larry among them, packed like sardines on the deck. He was soaking wet, shivering from cold, fear and despair, but the barge chugged on and wasn't attacked on the journey. They landed at Dover, where finally he was given a mug of tea and a sandwich. It was the first food he had had for days. It was almost overwhelming. Larry could not really believe he had got back. All he wanted to do was go home.

23

STANLEY CHAPPELL ADRIFT

29 May–2 June

Stanley Chappell was in the back of a 30cwt lorry, fleeing from the German assault on the Mont des Cats, where the last two guns of L/N battery and the 44th Division had fought a deadly rearguard action to hold open the corridor to Dunkirk. He thought they had got clean away, but their road was blocked by an enormous crowd of refugees, retreating soldiers and vehicles. Then Stanley heard an approaching aircraft and his blood froze. His companions hammered on the roof of the cab and the driver veered off to the side of the road. They all leaped from the lorry and sprinted into the nearby fields and ditches, diving to the ground, hugging it for safety. A Messerschmitt fighter hurtled above them, machine guns and cannons firing, bullets zinging off metal, thudding into the road close to Stanley, and he pressed his head into the earth as it roared overhead. He heard the engine fade away, then tensed again as the noise returned and the plane went over once more, so low that the rush of air and the racket of the engine were like an express train thundering above him.

He stayed, embedded in the soil, until the sound of the aircraft had finally faded into the distance. Now he could hear the crackling of flames and the screams and sobs of wounded people. Rising to his feet, he saw that the road was littered with dead people, dead horses, dead dogs, even some dead chickens whose bodies had spilled out of a wire cage amongst a pile of bedding and furniture. To his surprise, their lorry was untouched. The driver started the engine again and drove forward, easing their way past a burning car and a lorry that had been driven into a ditch, the driver hanging out of the door with half his body blown away. Stan felt his stomach heave.

They were now extremely nervous and leaped out of the vehicle at any hint of another attack. There were several false alarms, the aircraft passing above them on their way to other targets, but soon there was a repeat of the first attack. This time their lorry was smashed, the cab ripped open and oily water running out from under the engine. People were becoming hysterical, with some of the civilians clearly totally unhinged. Stan too felt a sense of desperation; he could feel that an air of panic was developing. The engine of a French army lorry started up and moved forward, the driver shifting up through the gears. As it went past them, Stan and his mate Bert ran and jumped on to the back. Just as the lorry speeded up, a French soldier ran along behind and grabbed hold of the tailgate, but the lorry was going too fast for him to get a foothold. Stan tried to shout at the driver, while others smacked the rear window of the cab, but the driver put his foot down and the lorry leaped ahead, people scrambling aside to avoid being run down. The driver was desperate to get away and nothing would make him stop. The French soldier was dragged along the road for several hundred yards until he let go, and Stan saw him tumble along the road until he finally came to rest in a heap. They drove on for another mile, then the road was again completely blocked by damaged vehicles. They would have to walk, and Stan was very keen to do so. He felt that it would be safer; he would be much less of a target on foot and the panic of the French driver had completely unnerved him. They had a map torn from the *Daily Mirror* that showed Dunkirk on the coast. It would have to do.

He and Bert walked in the warm sunshine for a mile or so, listening to the birds, when they heard horses behind them. A troop of French cavalry was trotting down the road. As they drew level Stan gestured to them that he would like a ride. The troop came to a halt and one of the cavalrymen gave the reins of two riderless horses to Stan and Bert, so they both climbed on to the mounts' backs and followed the troop as they spurred their horses on.

Stan rode like this for several miles. Once more on horse-back, his thoughts turned to his first days in the Royal Horse Artillery, when he had ridden over the Downs on a misty morning, cantered through villages, straight-backed, his boots gleaming, the young girls waving. They were days of innocence, it seemed to him, days that had gone for good.

The troop was eating up the miles, Bert too enjoying the ride, but it didn't last. The cavalry was not making its way to Dunkirk, but instead turned west, so Stan and Bert dismounted and once again they were on foot. But they had managed to leave behind the dreadful congestion of the shot-up convoys, and the traffic was much lighter.

Passing a farmhouse, Bert spotted a motorbike lying in the yard. They went in to look it over and it seemed in good condition. The farm was deserted, so Stan set the bike upright then tried to kickstart the engine. It wheezed slightly, then barked into life. They both sat astride it, Stan let in the clutch and it pulled away. The bike had plenty of power, but Stan took it easy, threading their way past abandoned lorries and the debris of retreating armies and fleeing civilians.

They rode along until the sound of explosions reached them. Stan slowed and went forward cautiously. Ahead of them was a crossroads and German artillery was sending shell after shell into it. Several army trucks had stopped in front of them, but Stan could see that the shells had hit one or two further up and there were bodies lying in the road. He knew that it was random harassing fire and that the battery firing the shells probably couldn't see it, or know what the results of their fire had been. Nevertheless, to try to drive over the crossroads seemed suicidal. Stanley checked the motor-cycle's tank – there wasn't much fuel left. That decided it.

He and Bert took to their feet again and decided that they would try to cut across country. They felt they wouldn't get lost: overhead were streams of aircraft heading in the same direction and it seemed safe to assume that they were making for Dunkirk and the British troops assembling there. If they went in that direction, they would be sure to get to the coast. Walking over the fields, cutting through the hedgerows and narrow lanes took them away from the road and they found a more tranquil atmosphere. Stanley, however, realized that he was very nervous. Sitting under the shade of a hawthorn tree for a rest he noticed that he couldn't relax. He was anxious and wanted to keep on the move.

As they got closer to Dunkirk they could see the thick columns of black smoke rising to the sky. Large numbers of aircraft patiently circled above the town before starting their dive. It looked to Stanley that there was anything up to fifty in a great swarm. They were aghast. It was impossible to imagine how anything could survive under that onslaught. Stan wondered whether getting to Dunkirk was the wisest thing to do, but they had no other plan. Did he really want to be taken prisoner? It was a dreadful prospect, not to see home again, his parents and his sisters.

So he and Bert continued walking and finally came to a road that, it seemed, would take them directly to Dunkirk. It was clearly visible ahead. The country had become flat and as they walked further down the road the fields on either side were covered in water. Entering the outskirts of Dunkirk was like walking through a smashed-up ghost town. Buildings had been reduced to rubble, the wreckage of vehicles lay everywhere, the streets were full of broken glass and debris, and the air was thick with smoke and the smell of burning oil and wood.

It was approaching dusk, and walking down to the sea front Stanley saw what he thought were rows and rows of corpses. It was a chilling sight. He thought these must be the casualties of the bombing they had witnessed earlier. They had walked into a town of the dead. But suddenly one of the bodies stirred and asked him if he knew the time. They were not dead – just hundreds of men lying under blankets or greatcoats trying to sleep. Stan and Bert passed on and found a space on the beach where they too lay down. Exhausted, they slept.

When Stan woke next morning the sun was shining and the sea was a flat calm, but it was like a pleasant day in hell. The sullen red fires at the port poured black smoke into the sky and the beach was filled with thousands of men who sat or stood aimlessly; the crowds spread back into the dunes and the wreckage of boats stretched all along the coast. Here and there the bodies of drowned men had been left by the tide, or they drifted face down in the shallow water, their sodden greatcoats swirling around them.

Stanley walked along the promenade looking for food and water, but there was nothing. The army had ceased to function. He suddenly realized what had happened. Here he was, without a regiment, without a weapon, his gun destroyed, all his kit, his personal possessions gone – and the same had happened to the thousands of men on the beach with him. They were not soldiers any more, just ordinary men who wanted to get home.

Fighting was still going on, however; the sounds of artillery could be heard in the distance. Presumably some rearguard action was being fought, the enemy still being held off. And out to sea ships were appearing, destroyers and minesweepers by the look of it, heading to the harbour. All was not lost. Stan walked along with Bert and they found a tin of corned beef, which they opened and ate. The idea of going to the mole seemed foolish in the light of the bombing that they had seen the previous day, so they walked along the beach to where men were already forming up in huge lines and small boats were rowing into the shore. Some men had kept their rifles, although what they would do with them Stan hardly knew, and some units were still intact. It was the sergeants, the NCOs, who were most obviously keeping order.

The two men walked for a mile, but could find no trace of their regiment, so they thought they had better get in line and joined a queue of men who were waiting patiently, shuffling slowly closer to the water's edge. Stan saw only one break in discipline, when a large lifeboat beached and there was a mad scramble, but the naval rating in charge ordered the men back and they obeyed. It might have been because he was waving a revolver. But he saw no real panic or collapse of self-discipline. There were two air raids during the day on his part of the beach and men rushed back to the dunes for some shelter as the bombs started exploding. When the planes had gone, they went back once more to the beach.

Stan waited all day, but by nightfall he thought that the crowd of men waiting for rescue had barely diminished. Bert had wandered off to see if he could find some water; he never returned. The next morning was Friday, 31 May, and Stan queued again, but there seemed to be fewer boats than the day before and for the first time he thought that he might not make it home. He was swept by a wave of despair so strong that it was only the presence of hundreds of other men around that stopped him from falling to his knees.

It didn't last. He wasn't the type to give in. Anyway, men were still fighting a few miles away and at the age of nineteen he was too young to lose hope. He noticed that the lifeboats and cutters that were coming close into the shore to take men out to the boats in the bay were struggling to avoid the pieces of wreckage that littered the beach. There were planks, boxes, tyres, ropes and jagged pieces of metal stretching out for about four hundred yards. Stan thought that if he could get out beyond the shallows, then there was a good chance of being picked up by one of the ships that were waiting out there. He wasn't that good a swimmer, but he could surely build a raft out of the debris that was lying about?

He walked along the beach and saw a face he recognized. Standing on the edge of the dunes, looking glumly out to sea, was Ken Morrell from his own troop. He rushed towards him, to find out if he had seen Bert or anybody else from the regiment. He hadn't, but then Stanley explained his idea about building a raft to get out to the ships that they could see waiting in deeper water. Ken's face lit up at the plan. He was only too happy to help.

They pulled some spars and planks from the sand and tied them together with lengths of rope, then they lashed this rough wooden square to some petrol tins for buoyancy. It was like something out of *Robinson Crusoe*. After several hours they had a wooden platform ringed with petrol tins. But when they tried to lift it to carry it into the sea it was too heavy! They couldn't even drag it along. They struggled with it for half an hour, then gave up. What a wasted effort! Stan felt that he was behaving like a lunatic; perhaps some side effect of shell-shock had taken hold of him.

Then he spotted, about two hundred yards away against the sea wall, an abandoned Bren-gun carrier. Perhaps that could be used to push their raft? But would it work? The chances were that it had been disabled. Stanley climbed in and, to his joy, it started up! He drove it down to the beach and they decided they would tow the raft into the sea. They secured it with some rope, Stanley drove the carrier into the water until it started coming over the sides – and then the engine gave out. But the raft was floating. They took off their clothes, piled them in a heap on the raft, then walked it away from the beach until the sea came up to their chests. Now they climbed aboard and, with a piece of wood each for an oar, they tried to propel themselves out to sea. It was hard work, but they made some progress, getting further and further away from the beach. As they did so, the wind grew stronger and the waves bigger. Soon the planks and petrol cans began to work loose. Stan and Ken climbed into the sea and pushed the raft, but it was pointless. The ropes parted and the planks and spars drifted apart. They were left swimming, watching their clothes drift away on the swell.

As Stanley clung on to a piece of wood, he couldn't see very far past the waves. He had lost sight of any ships. He couldn't see Ken either. He was going to have to swim back to the beach or drown. A mixture of thick oil and petrol floated on the surface of the water, making his eyes sting. It was cold and he was starting to shiver. He was alone. He felt very frightened.

Then he heard a shout and a lifeboat broached sideways on to him. It had appeared from nowhere. Hands reached down, hauling him over the side, and he rolled over and lay in the bottom. He was covered in thick oil from the sea. A minute later Ken Morrell joined him in the bottom of the boat and they both lay there shivering, but within a few minutes the lifeboat crew had opened up the throttle and they were bumping along the side of a passenger ship. Stanley was helped up a narrow gangway and given a cup of cocoa and a greatcoat. Collapsing on the deck by a ventilator, he downed the sweet cocoa in one gulp. But he was quickly roused up again to help haul in the lifeboat. A young naval lieutenant urged them on, saying, 'Get a move on – we have to be out of here before there's another raid.' Nobody needed any more encouragement. Within ten minutes the boat was gathering way. Stanley lay down again and went to sleep. It was the first time in twenty days that he could let others worry about his safety.

The next thing that he can remember is walking from the quay at Margate, still wearing nothing but an army greatcoat, being given a mug of tea and a packet of sandwiches. He had made it.

24

LES CLARKE IN THE REARGUARD

30 May–2 June

The numbers of men evacuated from the port of Dunkirk and the beaches at Bray Dunes and La Panne increased every day of Operation Dynamo. On 30 May 53,823 were taken off, almost 30,000 of these from the beaches. On 31 May a wind picked up and blew in towards the shore, making it harder for the exhausted crews of the small boats to approach the harbour without broaching to. Lord Gort and General Brooke had been evacuated, as had 68,014 men the same day, 45,000 of them from the harbour. But there were still men on the front line, defending the perimeter.

Les Clarke and the 6th Battalion Durham Light Infantry were at the Bergues–Furnes Canal near to Bulscamp, which had just been overrun by the Germans. Les found himself digging in again at four o'clock in the morning of the 30th. Many of the battalion's trenching tools had been thrown away, as had the mortars. Les had thrown his 2in mortar base plate down a well in the grounds of a chateau some days ago – though it seemed like weeks.

A few hours later the trenches were reorganized to provide greater depth, but they needed more men to do the digging work and they also needed some barbed wire for a better barrier. They were promised both, though Les didn't believe anything that he was told any more. However, some Royal Engineers did arrive, who provided some extra muscle and trenching tools, but they waited in vain for the promised coils of wire. The engineers themselves were in no better shape than Les and his mates. Rations were scarce and they were all as exhausted as each other.

That night there was a lull in the firing, though nobody slept. Despite the depth of Les's fatigue, his nerves were too tightly strung for him to sleep even for ten minutes. At six o'clock that morning heavy shelling started once more, the artillery fire landing mostly on the left, where the 9th Battalion Durham Light Infantry were dug in. The shelling continued throughout the morning, pounding away, keeping everybody down and confined to their slit trench. At midday Les heard the explosions of some very large shells immediately to his right; short salvoes, but with a sound and an effect that suggested the shells were far bigger than those of the field artillery and mortars they had experienced so far. The shells seemed to come from their rear and a runner was sent back to the battalion, questioning whether they were being shelled by their own naval guns.

Sadly, they weren't. The gunfire was coming from German heavy artillery to the north-east in Belgium. The enemy had advanced to the Belgian border, although for the moment they were being held on the fortified line by some French troops. Soon even the port of Dunkirk would be within range. Shortly after this fusillade from the big guns, the Germans chose to launch an assault across the canal line on Les's left, pushing against the 9th Durham Light Infantry. Les was low on ammunition, as was everyone else. The men of the 9th were pushed back and a sergeant sprinted along the line of trenches behind the 6th telling the men to pull back before they were surrounded. It was out into the open, moving back with bullets from snipers and machine guns zipping past. The terrain was open and flat – a death trap. The only advantage was that it gave no cover to the Germans either. They had to move more than half a mile to the reserve positions that had been held up 'til now by the 8th Durham Light Infantry. Some didn't make it, falling to the ground dead or wounded. The next line, called the Ringslot Canal, was in fact little more than a ditch. More trenches were dug along the side of the road that ran alongside it. Some Bren guns had also been brought forward from Dunkirk and these were given out to the two companies that were all that was left of the 6th. They were now permanently under fire. The German artillery got their range within minutes and shells started pounding the battalion HQ.

Les didn't think that they had much of a future. The gunfire from the Germans, now just a few hundred yards away, never seemed to let up. There were non-stop explosions from shellfire and mortars, sniping and machine-gun fire from close range. The combined headquarters of the two Durham Light Infantry battalions and the Northumberland Fusiliers, set up in a chateau to the rear, was on fire. A runner who had got through reported that the transport was ablaze; all that remained was a little Austin 7 and one 30cwt truck. So if they were going to go anywhere, they were going to walk – although the last Les had heard, the intention was to keep them here for as long as it took for the evacuation to be completed. That is, less some of the rearguard . . .

Behind Les lay Dunkirk itself, the target of most of the enemy bombers that flew overhead. He could see towers of black smoke rising into the sky from the town. It was too far away to see the flames, but the fires must have been huge because even at this distance he could see the red light flickering on the underside of the thick billows of smoke. God knows what the port had been reduced to. There was a rumour that thirty thousand Royal Marines had landed at Dunkirk to keep the port open. Les had no idea whether this was true or just some story told to keep their spirits up, but he felt that it was highly unlikely that he would get away.

As the shelling continued, there was another loud blast from the area of the chateau and a great ball of fire rose in the air. An ammunition dump had been hit. The explosions continued as bullets detonated in the heat. Now some strange sense of calmness had overtaken Les. He had stopped thinking much about anything beyond the next few minutes, and certainly had given up thinking about reaching home again.

Towards the end of the day a sergeant came along the line with news that they were to pull out later that night. This galvanized Les: at last there was a way out. No sooner had he begun to feel slightly more optimistic, however, than mortar shells started hitting the road next to the ditch. They were to stay in position until the 9th and the Royal Northumberland Fusiliers had pulled out. They really were the rearguard. But it was unlikely that the Germans would launch an attack at night. They might have enough time, and the cover of darkness, to get away.

An hour later Les climbed out of the trench and the men lined up quietly, then crossed the fields to their rear, reaching a road where they marched west. Behind them the chateau was still burning and ammunition continued to explode spontaneously in the fires that consumed the transport and the trees surrounding them.

Shortly the battalion came to a line of railway trucks on a siding behind the sand dunes and they started digging in underneath them. They were on the beach. There was nowhere to go except into the sea or along the dunes to Dunkirk.

At daybreak there was shelling from the south-west, two salvoes every half an hour. One salvo just missed the end rail truck under which they were sheltering; another hit a French ammunition lorry on the road and it exploded. Les had some biscuits and a bit of corned beef, but there was no water. Their orders were to remain where they were, because there was the possibility that they would have to turn and face the enemy again. Once more the two companies were stood to, weapons and ammunition distributed.

Les could see the wrecks of two merchant ships, their funnels and masts rising above the tide, oddly angled. Thousands of soldiers were gathered along the beach, some in groups waiting, others in streams that moved along the beach heading to the town. Still the thick smoke poured upwards into the sky. He heard the sounds of battle, machine guns and explosions all around. Les thought it was absurd that they should have to face the enemy again. It could only be a final hopeless gesture; they were exhausted and weakened, incapable of putting up much of a fight against an enemy that seemed to have limitless reserves of both men and ammunition. For the first time in the last two weeks Les saw some British aircraft, as an enormous aerial fight took place above the beach. There seemed to be as many as fifty fighters on the British side, and as many, if not more, enemy bombers.

Les and two of his mates were now part of around sixty men from the battalion who were digging shallow pits in the dunes as some protection against the bombs and the shelling. As the enemy had advanced from the east, the beaches were now in range of their artillery. The battalion had moved its HQ to the west of Bray Dunes to the little hamlet of Zuydcoote, and here they found they were being shelled from the south-west as well.

Desperate for something to drink, Les and three mates decided to go in search of some food and water. They crouched low and ran into the roads of the little seaside town. It seemed deserted until they came to a small warehouse that looked undamaged. The wide wooden doors were padlocked, but Les's mate got out his bayonet, quickly levered off the hasp and they pushed the doors open and walked in. They had found Aladdin's cave. It was a food store. There were tins of jam, tins of meat pâté, bottled fruit, bars of chocolate and tins and tins of cigarettes – yard upon yard of shelves carrying everything that they had been missing for days. Les started helping himself to the food; there were even some fresh apples and pears that he tucked in to. Then one of his mates came up with a stone jar that he had found. He took the cork out and had a swig. It was rum! They knocked it back, and Les immediately felt tipsy. It didn't have to be strong, the condition they were in. After a few more swigs he could barely stand straight. He stuffed his pockets with chocolates and tins of pâté, shoved a tin of cigarettes in his blouse and they walked out. He knew that he was drunk. They made their way back to the battalion.

They stayed as low as they could, sharing what rations they had with their mates, the liberated luxuries from the warehouse keeping them going. The next morning he and the rest of the battalion were ordered to go down to the foreshore and move along to the embarkation point in Dunkirk where they would be able to get on a ship.

Les could see that that wasn't the end of the story. The bombing, which had started early in the morning, was really picking up. There was constant machine-gunning of the shore areas by dive-bombers and fighters. Men who still had their rifles would lie flat and try to fire back. It was useless, but any effort at retaliation felt better than just lying there and having to take it. At least the soft sand of the dunes helped reduce the effect of the blast from shells and bombs.

The Stukas were not only pounding the port of Dunkirk and the ships edging in to lift off the thousands lined up there; they were also attacking the boats that were moored off the beach which Les was marching along, struggling through the sand. He had lost contact with the 6th Durham Light Infantry now. Some of his mates were a few yards away, but he seemed to be in a group of men from the Northumberland Fusiliers, and there were also some French soldiers who were trying to get to the port.

He kept marching, sand in his boots, the sea breeze whipping it into his face and neck. A sergeant shouted out, 'Come on, lads – look lively! The navy won't wait for ever.' It spurred no one into moving any faster. Les plodded on through the dunes, past a small village where the houses along the front had all been reduced to rubble, and eventually he reached the edge of Dunkirk. Thousands of men were now slowly shuffling along in front of him; some naval ratings and NCOs were urging them to move along and not to push. Wounded men on stretchers were carried past; to Les, most of them looked in a very bad way.

The crowded line of men led on to the mole, where the gaping holes caused by shells and bombs had been bridged with planks. There was nowhere to go when the Stukas re-appeared. They wheeled over, and anti-aircraft guns on the other side of the harbour started firing, every gun on the ships blasting away, from Vickers machine guns to the larger calibre guns in the turrets of the destroyers. Amidst this cacophony the sailors on board urged men down the gang-ways and planks leading on to the deck. Some men just jumped on to the deck, risking a broken leg or worse. Les felt someone pushing him in the back – it was some of his mates from the battalion – and he realized that he was pushing as well. A Stuka flew above them, like some giant malevolent bird of prey, and Les felt that moment of panic at being com-pletely exposed. The plane was not aiming at him, however. It shrieked down, releasing its bomb, which plunged into a ship further along the mole. The explosion sent shrapnel and burning fuel oil flying through the air and Les experienced a sudden pain against the left side of his face and in his shoulder. He felt the heat from the blast, as if someone had opened the door of the furnace in the foundry where he used to work. He was being jostled on board a boat in front of him, the mass of men threatening to overwhelm the small pleasure craft. It started tilting dangerously, a gap opening between the side of the boat and the mole. The crew were rushing along the deck shouting to the men to get back as the boat tilted crazily. Les collapsed in a heap with a score of men around him and water started to pour over the deck. 'We're sinking,' shouted someone as the crew began laying into them. 'A big Cockney bastard,' according to Les, yelled at him, 'Get off the boat before we f****** capsize!'

Les's mate Jed Stone, a former docker from Liverpool, shouted to him to jump before the boat turned over, but Les couldn't swim. Jed grabbed him by the shoulder and pushed him overboard, then jumped in after him. Floundering in the stinking oily water, Les felt the collar of his tunic held tight around his throat and he was pulled backwards until his feet could touch some stone steps, then he was hauled out. He stood there, soaking wet and covered in black oil, with the side of his face burning and a sharp pain in his shoulder.

They climbed up the steps to the harbour wall again and lay there. Les couldn't stop shivering – he would have paid a high price for that jug of rum from the warehouse now. He and his mate sat on the breakwater, a scene of utter chaos in front of them. Black smoke was swirling over the harbour; everywhere men were struggling in the water, some shouting for help; another Stuka was screaming down; and the ship that had already been hit was on fire, its decks crowded with men, some of whom were already leaping overboard. The captain and crew had unmoored the ship and a destroyer, its guns blazing into the air, was trying to tow it away from the mole.

Then the ship seemed to shudder and the smoke and debris from another direct hit shot into the air. More men jumped or were blown into the water, and none of the men on deck was standing now. Still the destroyer towed the ship away, and Les realized that the captain wanted to get her clear of the mole before she sank and blocked the harbour.

Les and many of the men who had struggled back through the sea stood or sat wrapped in their soaking greatcoats. He waited for hours, struggling to keep warm, before another boat docked at the mole as darkness fell. Once more he shuffled forward. This time, however, he climbed aboard without any incident and the ship docked at Ramsgate harbour a few hours later, at six in the morning. There were so many vessels ahead of them, with thousands of men struggling to get up the gangways on to dry land, that Les's ship was held off outside the harbour for another two hours before it could touch the jetty and the tired – and in Les's case wet – and wounded men could get off.

Les climbed an iron-rung ladder up the side of the harbour wall and there he was met by young Guards cadets, who were handing out cigarettes – packets of five Woodbines each – and some volunteers from the Women's Royal Volunteer Service and the Salvation Army were dishing out mugs of tea and a wad. It was the first cup of tea Les had seen for a long time – but he didn't get his cigarettes, his tea or his sandwich; instead he was grabbed by two women from the Red Cross. They had immediately spotted the side of his face, which had been badly burned by the bomb blast when he was on the mole. He was pulled out of the queue of hungry soldiers and taken to a makeshift ambulance, converted from a delivery van, which drove him to Ramsgate Hospital. There his burns and the wounds from the shrapnel in his shoulder were dressed, and he was kept in bed for a week. He didn't complain. He slept a lot.

When he was discharged from the ward Les was given £3, a new uniform that didn't fit and was told to take seven days' leave, then report to the Duke of Wellington Barracks in Halifax, West Yorkshire. So he went home to Bishop Auckland, where for the first time he was able to visit his mother's grave. He stayed with his aunt, and while he was there Les answered the door to a telegram boy who had ridden up on his red pushbike. The telegram was addressed to his aunt and it informed her that Les was regrettably missing, presumed killed.

25

SID LEWIS FINDS A WAY HOME

29 May–2 June

After handing over the wounded men from Wormhout to the casualty clearing station, Sid Lewis and the driver of the lorry decided to get on to Dunkirk. They had lost touch with their battalion and Sid's company. Nobody knew where they had moved to. It seemed certain that the enemy was close on their heels, and after the fighting at Wormhout Sid couldn't imagine that there was anything left that was going to stand in their way. They had chosen a narrow side road that led not directly to Dunkirk but went via the village of Wylder, but after a while they were stopped by a military provost post and told that their vehicle must be abandoned.

Sid started walking. It was getting dark, but although he was tired and hungry he did not feel like stopping. There were hundreds of men on the road and in the fields, all heading in the same direction. He had little idea of where he was going; he had decided just to follow the crowd. Occasionally they would hear the noise of aircraft and an agitated wave would sweep through the crowd of men; and if the noise appeared to be coming closer then there would be a rush for the shelter of ditches and hedgerows. After several hours, however, the fields on either side of the road became flat and low-lying, semi-flooded and crisscrossed by wide ditches. Apart from these there was no shelter. Sid felt extremely vulnerable along this road, but there was little that he or anyone else could do about it. Eventually the road crossed the Belgian border again and Sid wondered if this was the wisest thing to do, but the few military police and occasional officers along the route indicated that they were still on the right path.

Sid lay down to sleep at last by the side of the road, but only for a couple of hours. He awoke and got going again before it was light. Like most of the men, he knew that the Germans were snapping at their heels. He was ignorant of the wider picture, where the fighting was or where the enemy was; all that he knew was that for days he had been marching. In the last two weeks the war had been nothing like the fighting in the Saar. There were no fixed lines, no listening patrols, but hard assaults by the enemy from the air, with tanks and from every direction. Nobody was going to stand and fight now.

He walked on, still with his helmet, his rifle slung over his shoulder, his pack and blanket roll. There was no panic and still some solidarity. Men he didn't know would still offer a cigarette or share some meagre rations. But they all had one overriding aim. They wanted to get to the beach or to Dunkirk.

Sid could see a huge cloud of smoke to his left, which he assumed was Dunkirk, and streams of aircraft moving overhead. The sound of shelling, the noise of big guns, came from all directions, drifting on the wind but not that far away. There were officers in the road now, asking men what unit they were from, where they were heading, and the crowds seemed more organized. Sid still had his stretcher-bearer's pack with him, and the sergeant at the checkpoint looked at him and pointed: 'La Panne.'

So he walked on and after another few miles he reached the small seaside town. Here there were all the signs of the General HQ that had been set up, along with another casualty clearing station. There were plenty of ambulances and transport, and there were some rations and tea available, but little else. He could find no trace of his 2nd Battalion Royal Warwickshire Regiment. He went to the casualty clearing station and was drafted in as a stretcher-bearer. Casualties were coming in, and occasionally some would be moved out in fleets of ambulances, taken along the road to Dunkirk for evacuation. Thousands of men thronged the beach and the crowds seemed to stretch all along the coast to Dunkirk, marked out by the huge columns of smoke that never seemed to get any smaller. They were a permanent fixture, like the sea or the dunes.

To the west was the small seaside village of Bray Dunes, where yet more men gathered. There were ships in the distance, warships, tugs, the occasional paddle-steamer, and smaller boats moving in and out taking men from the beaches. Men were forming lines out across the beach towards the water, where little boats could ferry a dozen or so at a time out to the waiting ships. There were also the wrecks of ships, four or five big ones and lots of smaller ones closer inshore. Things were moving slowly, and it looked as though people would never get off.

Sid stayed at La Panne for several days, working with the medical staff of the clearing station, but he was not part of their establishment and he hadn't succeeded in finding anyone from his battalion or regiment. He would go to the casualty clearing station, work there and receive some rations, but he had slipped through the net and was not on the roll of any of the units in La Panne. The truth was that Sid was in a state of shock, partly dissociated from the world around him. The evacuation of La Panne took him by surprise.

He awoke one night in the abandoned house where he slept to find the town empty. The beach was deserted as well. He was completely disorientated because it was about four in the morning. Scrambling up, he rushed down to the water's edge. The tide was in, but it was still too shallow for any ships to come closer. He saw a flickering signal light from one of the ships – Morse code, but too fast for Sid to read it.

Suddenly he felt afraid that he was going to be stranded and taken prisoner. Agitated, he walked up and down the beach until it was fully daylight. He could see nothing on the horizon, but all at once he decided to walk out to sea. He strode forward, going further and further out, until the water was above his waist, then up to his chest. He threw away his rifle – unslung it, took the bolt out and threw that away, then threw the rifle in the other direction. Next he took his great-coat off, because it was sodden and weighing him down. He was beginning to get so cold that he thought of going back, but he was sure that soon a boat would see him. Why he had waded out into the sea he didn't know, because he couldn't swim. But he was no longer acting rationally. He stayed there, getting colder and colder, until he saw a rowing boat. Sid did nothing, but it headed towards him. The man in it was shouting, but as he got nearer Sid realized he couldn't understand him. The rowing boat drew close and the rower grabbed Sid, helping him struggle into the boat. The rower started talking and Sid recognized that he was Belgian. The man turned the boat and rowed out, with Sid shivering in the stern, shaking with the cold. They went out further and a destroyer came into view. The Belgian rowed up to the side and helped Sid climb up the scrambling nets, then a couple of sailors hauled him up the last few feet. He was pulled on to the steel deck of the warship and helped below. A blanket was thrown round him and a mug of cocoa was thrust into his hands. It had a large shot of rum in it and it burned down Sid's throat, but it was an extremely good sensation. For the first time in many weeks, he started to feel warm and safe.

Although Sid can't remember very much of the days that he spent in La Panne, or what else happened on the destroyer, he can still remember that he was rescued by the crew of HMS *Harvester*. The Belgian rower was, and remains, a mystery.

So six men had found their way to the beaches at Dunkirk and from there been carried by sailors – either working seamen or men of the Royal Navy – back to safety in the United Kingdom. The last day that ships of Operation Dynamo took men from the mole at Dunkirk was Monday, 3 June. In all, 338,226 men were rescued from the small perimeter around the last positions held by the British Expeditionary Force. Their experiences could not have been that much different from those of the men whose stories we have been following. The vast majority were young, with no experience of warfare and only elementary-school education. Some, like Stanley

Chappell, had been professional soldiers, while others had been raw recruits. Whatever their level of training, they took a pride in their uniform and had no doubts about why they were fighting. In a few short weeks they had experienced the total horror of war – towns and villages smashed, women and children blown apart, whole countries and governments on the verge of collapse. Their friends and comrades had been killed or grievously wounded in front of their eyes, and they themselves had brought tragedy to unarmed civilians. They had seen their own army reduced to chaos and experienced unrelieved fear for their own lives. Yet they had survived, in some shape or other, and got back home.

Very few believed that there had been any sort of victory. No one that I have spoken to is proud of what happened to the British Expeditionary Force. Their survival, however, was a success. The fact that these seven men are still alive to tell the story of how they and nearly four hundred thousand others got away is proof of that. Hitler, the German Army, Generals Rundstedt and Rommel had sought to smash the British Army in France and cut off Britain from her empire. They failed.

Epilogue

AFTER DUNKIRK

The events of May 1940 must stand out as some of the most dramatic in world history. The fortunes of three great powers had been utterly transformed.

Holland, Luxembourg and Belgium had been invaded and rapidly overwhelmed by the German Blitzkrieg. Germany now controlled the coastline of Europe from the Arctic Circle in Norway to the Atlantic coast of France. With a fascist government in Spain, and Italy soon to enter the war on its side, Germany – brought to its knees by war a generation earlier – now controlled or influenced the whole of the continent.

France, which had been victorious against Germany in the First World War, had suffered a catastrophe. Its huge army of two million men had proved to be poorly led and organized, falling back in disarray while the French government collapsed in factional infighting. The great nation that had itself dominated Europe under Napoleon was occupied by German troops and would shortly sign an armistice.

Britain was completely isolated, without allies in Europe

and unable to use the Royal Navy to mount an effective blockade against Germany. Over 330,000 men were lifted from the beachhead at Dunkirk, but these returned to Britain without arms or equipment. Their artillery, their transport, ammunition and fuel was left destroyed or abandoned in France. The German Army and Luftwaffe were now camped just on the other side of the English Channel, and in the Mediterranean Italy was shortly to declare war against the United Kingdom. The situation for Britain could not have appeared more serious. Opinion around the world, and amongst a few members of the British government too, was that sooner rather than later Britain would have to follow the French example and sue for peace.

The three weeks since 10 May had also proved tumultuous for the proud men of the British Expeditionary Force. They had seen their world turned over and their army embark on a morale-sapping series of retreats. Young men without any experience of warfare had been confronted by a deadly combination of armoured columns, modern artillery and air power for which they had been totally unprepared. The British Army had been let down by the armies of its allies, but the ordinary soldier didn't blame them. What they constantly complained of was lack of communication, lack of planning and inferior equipment. These perceived weaknesses, and the permanent withdrawal in the face of superior forces, contributed to a sense of hopelessness and defeat. However, for the most part this rapidly changed once they had landed back in England.

Bombardier Stanley Chappell, who had been so despondent at the constant withdrawal, felt his spirits buoyed up by being back in the UK. Disembarking, he got on a train that carried him to a camp in Devon. There he did nothing for several days. The weather was fine, Stanley got kitted out with a new uniform, was paid and went to the local pub every night. Various stragglers took several days to return to the regiment, but once all the men had been accounted for Stanley was given seventy-two hours' leave.

The country was now threatened by invasion, and on his return the 2nd Royal Horse Artillery was sent to Kent. Armed only with rifles and Bren guns, they were ready to fight a German invasion as an infantry unit. Even without their 25-pounder guns and their transporters, Stanley and the rest of the regiment quickly regained their discipline and their morale.

Jack Haskett, who had been captured, then managed to get to Boulogne and avoid the perils of Dunkirk, was also reunited with his regiment, and they were based in various locations around Kent and the Isle of Sheppey guarding against a German invasion.

Those men whose units were attached to the 48th Division ended up stationed in Devon and Cornwall. Sapper Reg Beeston, hauled on board the paddle-steamer *Tynwald*, arrived at Harwich where he got on a train for Chepstow. He spent the next few weeks working in the fields of the West Country farms, haymaking. It was a glorious summer and Reg could not think of a pleasanter way to recuperate. It was hard work, but enjoyable, deeply satisfying. When it came to an end his 224 Field Company was given the task of laying mines around the beaches of Cornwall – a task that was not at all relaxing. The most unpleasant time of all was when they were sent into Plymouth in the aftermath of a huge air raid to defuse unexploded aerial mines and bombs.

Sid Lewis went to Kingstown Barracks in Herefordshire, then also went as part of the Home Defences to a barracks in Plymouth. He was there during the series of air raids, helping with the recovery of the dead and the wounded. Deeply disturbed by that, the 2nd Warwickshires went to other parts of the country, mainly in the south of England, and Sid was in Croydon when that town was also hit by a devastating air raid.

Sydney Whiteside, from the 244 Field Ambulance Unit, spent the night after he disembarked at Margate in a large transport hangar in Catterick, where five hundred men bedded down on mats laid on the floor, then he went on leave. He spent the time during the Battle of Britain in Devon and Cornwall, then applied for a commission in the Ordnance Corps, where he eventually became an ammunition control officer.

Larry Uren had gone to Reading, then on to Salisbury by train, after he landed. At the depot there he was given a travel warrant home. His uniform was still creased and stained by sea water from when he had to abandon ship and he was a bedraggled sight, but his mother soon cleaned and pressed it. He stayed at home for another week before returning to Salisbury. As soon as he arrived he was ordered to help put up canvas tents for a huge military camp on Salisbury Plain, and it took another week before the sergeant in the orderly room pointed out to Larry that his 1/7th Battalion was now based in Knutsford in Cheshire. Another train took him there, where he was warmly greeted by Captain Dickenson, in whose company he had spent so many weeks in France. He was kitted out with a new uniform, then given a travel warrant and granted two weeks' leave, so he went back to his village once more, where the local constable could not understand why Larry was always at home.

Rifleman Les Clarke of the 6th Durham Light Infantry was discharged from hospital and given seven days' disembarkation leave. A few months after he returned to his battalion he was in trouble. Les was on parade when a junior lieutenant asked if there were any 'Dunkirk runners' present. Les had heard the phrase before. The evacuation from the beaches had been hailed in the press as a great success, almost a miracle; others, however – mainly in the army, men who, as Les remarked, 'hadn't been there' – saw it as a shameful defeat. Les had always had a problem with officers who looked down on him and he was incensed by such a remark from a very young and very inexperienced lieutenant. He stepped forward and gave him a punch to the jaw that knocked him flat. He was put on a charge. Striking a senior officer was a serious offence, but the CO's sympathy was with Les. He received the very lenient punishment of seven days confined to barracks.

But Les had had enough of the army. Shortly after he hit the lieutenant his sergeant major asked if there were any volunteers who wanted to join the 'pouffes'. Les at first thought he had said the 'Buffs', a nickname for the Royal East Kent Regiment. The sergeant major then said that their sergeant would kiss them goodnight, they would be given white sheets to sleep in and as much Brylcreem as they could use. The word 'Brylcreem' made it clear to Les that the sergeant major was talking about the RAF, who were known as Brylcreem boys. Before the war it would have been unthinkable for someone as poorly educated as Les to volunteer for the RAF. But now he was trained, and they needed men. He felt that it was time he had a bit more glamour in his life, so he volunteered and started training as an air gunner.

The months that followed the final evacuation of France were dominated by the aerial combat of the Battle of Britain, but as the threat of invasion faded and the Luftwaffe started the night-time bombing of London and other cities, men who had been picked up from the beach or out of the sea were getting ready to embark once more.

Stanley Chappell and his Royal Horse Artillery had finally been equipped with new 25-pounder guns and in November 1940 they were in Liverpool in full kit, climbing up the gangway of the SS *Scythia*, a 20,000-ton liner converted into a troop ship. As she slowly pulled away from the dockside the air raid warning started howling. Stanley was glad to be getting away. The next morning, he saw that they were in a convoy of twenty ships heading out of the Irish Sea. His journey took him via Freetown in Sierra Leone, Cape Town and Durban to Port Said and Egypt.

Stanley moved forward with the regiment in time to see the defeat of the Italian Army at Benghazi. Driving along in the quad, to his amazement he met the first of an enormous column of prisoners of war, the leaders of the 150,000 who had surrendered. But his stay in Cyrenaica was brief. In early March he was living in a tent outside Alexandria, before embarking and sailing to Greece. Then the Greek campaign became for Stanley a repeat of the fighting in Flanders – a period of battle, then a discreet withdrawal. Once again he was told that he had to destroy his gun. As he pulled the lanyard and the barrel of the 25-pounder split apart, he realized that it was almost a year since he had done the same thing in France. Then at night he embarked on to a landing craft. He was lucky, because he was taken directly to Alexandria, not Crete, which was evacuated a month later and where the navy suffered many casualties.

'I owe a great deal to the Royal Navy, and so do a lot of other soldiers. Being saved by them twice within the space of twelve months seems a shocking coincidence. But a lot of us from Dunkirk were in Greece as well. I remember thinking "I hope there's not a third time."'

Back in Egypt, the battery was re-equipped yet again and became part of the Eighth Army under General Montgomery. After advancing against Rommel's Afrika Korp to El Agheila, Stanley caught malaria and was invalided back to Cairo, but recovered in time to rejoin his battery at El Alamein, staying with them as they fought all the way until the Germans surrendered on 12 May 1943. It was three years almost to the day since he had been alerted in the small town of Lannoy in France that the Germans had invaded Belgium and Holland. It had been a long war, and was to be even longer. Two years later Stanley was in Antwerp celebrating the final capitulation of Germany and the death of Hitler.

It was a long war for everybody who was in the BEF in Flanders, and none of them imagined that the brief and bloody taste of war that they had experienced at La Bassée or Arras or Wormhout would be merely that. It was instead an introduction to five more years of equally bloody and shocking battles in places that they had never even heard of.

Larry Uren's 1/7th Battalion Queen's Royal Regiment was brought up to strength and became the 131st Infantry Brigade, and in 1942 he also was shipped to North Africa. He landed and took part in the battle of Alam Halfa in

August–September 1942, and then he was at El Alamein. As the massive artillery barrage started at the beginning of the advance and the German artillery replied, he lay there, surrounded by the most unbelievable noise, with shells landing all around him, wondering who would come out alive. Larry, whose first experience of a dive-bombing Stuka had petrified him, charged forward at the German lines when the time came. 'Something takes hold of you. You are no longer human.' As he reached the enemy positions, a German soldier charged at him. Larry saw him out of the corner of his eye, moved, and the enemy bayonet cut through his inner arm. He was sent back to a field dressing station, but discharged himself and returned to the battalion in time to take part in the invasion of Italy, where he stormed the beaches at Salerno.

The Queen's battalions returned to the UK in 1944 and Larry landed in Normandy on 8 June. A week later, his battalion suffered very heavy casualties at the battle of Villers-Bocage, fighting against a Panzer battalion in an effort to bypass the town of Caen. Eight officers and 120 men were lost in the battle. Larry survived, continuing to advance across Europe, and he ended the war in Copenhagen. He was wounded five times altogether.

Reg Beeston stayed in the Sappers, but early in 1943 he decided to volunteer for parachute training. The extra money was interesting, but it was the scent of danger and adventure that really motivated him. He thinks he was lucky to avoid Arnhem, but in 1945 he was flying over Norway in a Lancaster bomber as one of three engineers that would parachute on to an airfield near Oslo to remove the mines and booby traps put there by the occupying German forces. The

Norwegian Resistance had got there first, however, and his plane was able to land normally. They were the first British soldiers to land in Norway. Once there, Reg and his two companions travelled to Narvik, then moved north, accepting the surrender of German troops and dealing with the detritus of war. Eventually he reached the giant German battleship *Tirpitz* that lay capsized in the Tromsø fjord with three thousand dead bodies inside the hull. It was a sombre site. Reg then prepared to go to the Pacific, but the Japanese surrender stopped that. Instead he was sent to Palestine, where the war between Zionist Jews and Arabs was getting under way. He was demobbed in 1946 and then, still looking for adventure, went to Basra in the employ of the Iraqi Petroleum Company.

Jack Haskett rejoined his unit when they got back to the UK, then volunteered to be trained as a signaller. Following his course he was drafted into the Royal Artillery, who then sent him on a Catering Corps course. From then on he was the cook for his unit. In 1942 he travelled to Iraq and was stationed in Basra, then went to Transjordan and Tunisia. From there he took part in the invasion of Italy, landing at Anzio, moving all the way up Italy to Rome. After that his unit went to Venice and he finished the war in the mountains near the Yugoslav border.

Sid Lewis had never recovered from his experiences at Dunkirk and his behaviour became increasingly erratic. The two severe air raids in Plymouth and Croydon, where a large number of the men in his unit were killed, did not help. He couldn't sleep and became increasingly nervous, often having nightmares – not about being shelled or bombed, but about the time when he was surrounded by German soldiers in the forward listening post in the Saar.

Eventually Sid realized that he couldn't carry on any longer and went to see a medical officer, who recommended that he should transfer out of the Royal Warwickshire Regiment to the Pioneer Corps, which had recently been formed and was looking for recruits. Sid took his advice. The Pioneers' medical officer who examined Sid, however, realized that he was suffering from battle fatigue and sent him to a treatment centre in Prestatyn in Wales. It was a large country house with a number of patients and Sid stayed there for six weeks. He can't remember much about the treatment beyond the fact that he did very little but sleep. It did the trick, however, and he went back to the Pioneer Corps, with whom he landed in Normandy shortly after D-Day in a unit that built temporary roadways from the beach, then moved forward to lay down prefabricated airstrips for Typhoon ground-attack aircraft. This didn't end the horrors of war for Sid, however. He was at the relief of the Fallingbostel prisoner-of-war camp and saw the results of the typhoid epidemic in the Belsen concentration camp. Sid's battle with Germany ended at Lüneburg Heath when he was a guard at the ceremony in which Field Marshal Montgomery took the surrender of the German Army. Despite the victory in Europe, however, Sid, like Reg Beeston, was then sent to Palestine. He finally left the army after the Suez Crisis of 1956.

The young men left alive who fought at Dunkirk are now all in their nineties. What they experienced in the three weeks from the start of the German offensive in Europe to the last ship pulling away from the Dunkirk mole is unimaginable to most people in Britain today. Yet for most of them Dunkirk was just a brief introduction to a long war that lasted for another five years, in which the experiences of Dunkirk were to be repeated two or three times. Most people alive today wonder whether they would be able to show the courage and fortitude required to get through those long years of war.

Yet all those Dunkirk veterans that I spoke to for this book say that they were lucky. They were lucky because they knew so many people who did not survive the war, and they remember their comrades who were in the line of fire, killed by a bullet or a shell, or who could not quite reach the rope thrown to them and whose sodden greatcoat and boots pulled them to the bottom.

Dunkirk and the retreat from Belgium was not something that any of them would care to repeat, but many of them say that they would not have missed their wartime experiences for the world. With the threat of death came a greater sense of being alive. The fear has gone now, but they remember the comradeship and the knowledge that they could survive the worst that fate could throw at them. The journey from Dunkirk to Alamein, Italy and the Normandy beaches was long and hard, and only those that made it know how tough it was.

BIBLIOGRAPHY

Aitken, Leslie, *Massacre on the Road to Dunkirk*, Patrick Stephens, London, 1977.

Divine, David, *The Nine Days of Dunkirk*, Faber and Faber, London, 1959.

Ellis, Major L. F., *The War in France and Flanders 1939–1940*, HMSO, London, 1953.

Fraser, David, *Knight's Cross: a Life of Field Marshall Erwin Rommel*, HarperCollins, London, 1993.

Liddell-Hart, B. H., *The Rommel Papers*, Da Capo Press, New York, 1982.

Montgomery, Bernard Law, Viscount Montgomery of Alamein, *The Memoirs of Field Marshal the Viscount Montgomery of Alamein K.G.*, Collins, London, 1958.

Sebag-Montefiore, Hugh, *Dunkirk: Fight to the Last Man*, Viking, London, 2006.

Spears, Major General Sir Edward, *Prelude to Dunkirk, July 1939–May 1940*, William Heinemann, London, 1954.

Thompson, Major General Julian, *Dunkirk: Retreat to Victory*, Sidgwick & Jackson, London, 2008.

Unpublished

Chappell, Stanley, *The Whole Wide World*.

Documents

National Archives War Diaries:
WO33/1670   Despatches of the Operations of the BEF
WO33/2724   Despatches of the BEF (Maps)
WO167/218   3 Division G Branch War Diary
WO167/275   44th Division G Branch War Diary
WO167/300   50th Division G Branch War Diary
WO167/380   25th Infantry Brigade War Diary
WO167/389   131st Infantry Brigade War Diary
WO167/463   2nd Regiment Royal Horse Artillery
WO167/729   6th Battalion Durham Light Infantry
WO167/811   1st/7th Queen's Royal Regiment
WO167/839   2nd Battalion Royal Warwickshire Regiment
WO167/978   224 Field Regiment Royal Engineers
WO177/725   144 Field Ambulance

PICTURE ACKNOWLEDGEMENTS

Credits read clockwise from top left. Every effort has been made to trace copyright holders and those left uncredited are invited to get in touch with the publishers.

Section one
Modern portraits: © Rod Shone; old photos courtesy of their subjects.

Gamelin and Gort: *Picture Post*, 30 September 1939; English soldiers at the Fort de Sainghain, Belgium, 1939: Getty Images; Hitler at his headquarters in the Ardennes, May–June, 1940: Getty Images; General von Rundstedt, *c.* 1940: Getty Images; Rommel in northern France, May–June 1940: Bundesarchiv Bild 146-1998-043-20A; German soldiers march into Warsaw, 1939: Getty Images.

Soldiers with kitbags, 1939: courtesy Larry Uren; 2nd Regiment Royal Horse Artillery, La Bassée, December 1939: Imperial War Museum/O 2141; 2nd Battalion Warwickshire Regiment, Rumegies, 22 January 1940: Imperial War Museum/ F 2212; transportation by train of Matilda Mk 1 tanks, Cherbourg, 28 September 1939: Imperial War Museum/

O 576; disembarkation, Cherbourg, 29 September 1939: Imperial War Museum/O 70.

German army crossing border, 10–11 May 1940: © ullstein-bild/TopFoto.co.uk; Heinkel shot down near Tournai, 12 May 1940: Imperial War Museum/F 4416; German army crossing the Meuse, 13–14 May 1940: © ullsteinbild/TopFoto.co.uk; British forces pass Belgian refugees, 12 May 1940: Imperial War Museum/F 4410.

Pontoon bridge over La Bassée Canal, 27 May 1940: Imperial War Museum/RML 147.

Section two

Map, *Daily Mirror*, 27 May 1940: mirrorpix; emergency pontoon, La Panne, 5 June 1940: © ullsteinbild/TopFoto.co.uk; survivors from *Bourrasque* picked up by *Branlebas*, May 1940: © 1999 Topham Picturepoint/TopFoto.co.uk; allied soldiers on the beach, Dunkirk, June 1940: © ullsteinbild/TopFoto.co.uk.

Body of British soldier on the beach, Dunkirk, 4 June 1940: Imperial War Museum/COL 291; cover, *Signal* magazine, 1 July 1940: © TopFoto/TopFoto.co.uk; French prisoners, May–June 1940: Bundesarchiv Bild 1011-383-0302-10A; German plane flies over Dunkirk, 4 June 1940: © ullsteinbild/TopFoto.co.uk.

Troops aboard a train, May–June 1940: Getty Images; returning British soldiers, May–June 1940: Time & Life Pictures/Getty Images; train carrying returning troops, 26–29 May 1940: Imperial War Museum/H 1695; Admiral Sir Bertram Ramsey: © Bettmann/CORBIS; soldiers arriving home, 31 May 1940: Imperial War Museum/H 1632.

All: © Rod Shone.

INDEX

ABOUT THE AUTHOR

Mike Rossiter is the author of a number of bestselling books on military history – *Ark Royal*, *Sink the* Belgrano, *Target Basra*, *I Sank the* Bismarck (which he co-authored with John Moffat), *Bomber Flight Berlin* and *We Fought at Arnhem*.